The Selfless Leader

THE SELFLESS LEADER

A Compass for Collective Leadership

Stephen Brookes

First published 2016 by
PALGRAVE

Palgrave in the UK is an imprint of Macmillan Publishers Limited, registered in England, company number 785998, of 4 Crinan Street, London, N1 9XW.

Palgrave Macmillan in the US is a division of St Martin's Press LLC, 175 Fifth Avenue, New York, NY 10010.

Palgrave is a global imprint of the above companies and is represented throughout the world.

Palgrave® and Macmillan® are registered trademarks in the United States, the United Kingdom, Europe and other countries.

ISBN 978–1–137–35789–2

This book is printed on paper suitable for recycling and made from fully managed and sustained forest sources. Logging, pulping and manufacturing processes are expected to conform to the environmental regulations of the country of origin.

A catalogue record for this book is available from the British Library.

Library of Congress Cataloging-in-Publication Data

Names: Brookes, Stephen, 1955–
Title: The selfless leader : a compass for collective leadership / Stephen Brookes.
Description: New York : Palgrave Macmillan, 2015. | Includes index.
Identifiers: LCCN 2015032810 | ISBN 9781137357892 (paperback)
Subjects: LCSH: Leadership. | Management. | BISAC: BUSINESS & ECONOMICS / Management. | BUSINESS & ECONOMICS / Leadership. | BUSINESS & ECONOMICS / General.
Classification: LCC HD57.7 .B7624 2015 | DDC 658.4/092—dc23
LC record available at http://lccn.loc.gov/2015032810

Printed in China

DEDICATION

I dedicate this book to two wonderful ladies who have had a profound impact on my life, my thoughts, and my actions.

First, I dedicate this book in loving memory of my mother **Patricia Francis Kathleen** (known to all as Pat) for giving me my zest for life, my insatiable quest for knowledge, and the desire to fulfil all that is good.

Second, I dedicate this book to my wife, **Kate Moss**, the most selfless person I have ever known and who has the uncanny knack of understanding me better than I understand myself!

Finally, I also wish to dedicate the book to my father, **Reginald Harold**. My mother sadly passed well before her time, just as she had fulfilled her ambition of becoming one of the most traditional nurses that one could hope for! My father, who sadly passed away peacefully just before I completed the manuscript, would have been proud that it has been published.

Table of Contents

List of Figures	viii
List of Tables	x
Preface	xi
Acknowledgements	xiii
Prologue	xiv

Part I: The Changing Context of Leadership — **1**

1   Exploring Thousands of Years of Leadership in Seventeen and a Half Pages — 3
2   Rediscovering the Lost Values of Leadership — 21
3   Understanding Knowledge, Realism, and Research and Its Impact on the Practice of Leaders — 39
4   Understanding the Language and Reality of Leadership — 51
5   From Vision to Delivery — 67

Part II: Leading in a Complex World — **79**

6   Exploring Contexts and Mechanisms as Whole Systems — 81
7   Understanding the Challenges of Leadership — 101
8   Collective Vision — 109
9   Being Outcome-Focused — 123
10   The Importance of Multi-Level Leadership — 135
11   Partnership Working — 145
12   Action Oriented — 159
13   Systems and Structures — 175
14   Skills and Behaviours — 189

Part III: Making a Difference — **201**

15   The Practice and Professionalization of Leadership — 203
16   Leading through 360° Intelligent Networks, Knowledge, and Skills (LINKS360®) — 215

Epilogue — 243
References — 247
Index — 261

List of Figures

2.1 Public value framework   33
2.2 Elements of public value   35
4.1 External contexts of public leadership   55
4.2 Values to vision and core purpose   58
4.3 Values to vision questions   60
5.1 Collective leadership framework: Internal and external contexts   69
5.2 From values to vision, with everything in-between   70
5.3 Four Ps representing the mechanisms of collective leadership   73
5.4 Completed collective leadership framework with desired outcomes   76
6.1 Triangular energy events   88
6.2 Basic rules of the 12 degrees of freedom   89
6.3 Metatron's cube   93
6.4 Tetrahedron within Metatron's cube   94
6.5 Metatron cube and collective leadership   95
6.6 Hypercube representing internal and external contexts   95
6.7 Icosahedron   96
6.8 Compass 360 framework and icosahedron   97
7.1 Leadership Values Tree   105
7.2 The dynamic process of negotiated order   107
8.1 Underlying theory of collective leadership   110
11.1 Trust cycle   148
12.1 Integrated problem-solving and decision-making model   165
12.2 Seven principles for leading adaptive work   171
13.1 Leadership, management, and governance cycle   179
13.2 Tetrahedron of governance   181
13.3 Knowledge-based approaches filtered by 'social sciences' and 'leadership'   184
14.1 Commitment to leadership goals/independence from leader   193
14.2 Consent and dissent/constructive and destructive   193
14.3 Impact through capability, capacity and competence   196
15.1 Academic journal articles that include professionalizing practice   205
15.2 Professionalizing to professionalization   207
15.3 CPD, reflexivity and feedback   209
15.4 Tetrahedron of evidence-based activity   210
15.5 An applied leadership challenge   212
16.1 Metropolitan local authority analysis (all cohorts)   218
16.2 Summary of statistical correlations (community safety partnership
      and local authority)   224
16.3 Hotspot map (community safety partnership and local authority)   225
16.4 Collective leadership perceptions in tackling health inequalities   226

16.5 Transform leadership inventory 229
16.6 Transformational leadership behaviours (local authority and private
        sector organization) 230
16.7 Transform leadership behaviours (community safety partnership) 231
16.8 Transformational leadership behaviour (trust) 236

List of Tables

4.1   Values to vision   60
5.1   Leadership contexts, behaviours and values   68
12.1 Characteristics of 'wicked problems'   163
13.1 Academic articles focused on knowledge   183
16.1 Correlation for collective leadership values
        (collective vision and outcome focus)   220
16.2 Community safety partnership and local authority descriptive statistics   221
16.3 Statistical associations (collective vision and outcome focus),
        community safety partnership and local authority   223
16.4 Transformational leadership behaviour similarities
        (community safety partnership and local authority)   233
16.5 Association between developing a collective vision
        and the setting of clear goals   235
16.6 Collective vision and trust   237
16.7 Outcome and action focus associated with openness and transparency   238
16.8 Multi-level leadership and openness and transparency   238
16.9 Public value outcomes and openness and transparency   239
16.10 Public value outcomes and maintaining momentum   240

Preface

As I outline in the Prologue, this book has been a long time in its making. It has been quite a challenge, not least in targeting the book to its relevant audiences. It takes a particular stance in placing the work within the area of a textbook as well as a practical guide for accomplished, developing, or aspiring leaders, and also draws up on realist research and academic literature. In this sense, I would prefer to describe it as a 'prac-ademic' text aimed at both the practitioner and academic audiences.

I have intentionally taken a very personal style. I have practised leadership for over 30 years. In the last ten years, I have supplemented this with teaching, executive education, and applied research. I also offer my humble treatise for a new theoretical perspective on twenty-first century leadership. There has been a clear focus on individual leadership over the last 2000 years. It is only recently that the notion of collective leadership is emerging as a prominent approach to the *ship* of leadership. I argue throughout the book that collective leadership is both shared and distributed and, just as important, should be motivated by the notion of leading in the public interest rather than individual self-interests.

I am grateful to many colleagues and friends, too many to mention, for the support in both challenging and building on my thoughts and practice of leadership. I hope that I rise to the challenge that I set myself at the outset in writing about leadership from a new perspective. A second aim is to bridge the gap between theory and its application in practice. Knowledge is useless without effective application. Gaps that this book aims to bridge include the oft-neglected link between the development of leaders within the context of shared values and a collective vision. A further gap is the lack of focus on outcomes that are in the public interest and where leadership takes place at many levels both within and across diverse organizations and enterprises. Leading in the public interest is not just for public leaders; it is equally important for leaders in the for-profit sector to balance the public interest with corporate priorities through partnership. Leaders need to be adaptive to their operating environment and actions should be focused on evidence-based problem-solving and decision-making, properly supported by the right systems and structures. Finally, the development of skills and behaviours should be as much part of the collective leadership role as any other. Skills and behaviours influenced by a true sense of the shared values from all of those who are either involved in or affected by collective leaders are likely to be more effective.

As a final point, I want to draw reference to the importance of the human impact on the motivation of leaders. First and foremost, selfish motivations often mask words espoused as selfless aims. Second, unless systems are naturally occurring phenomena, humans will have created them, and, as we know, humans are both fallible and innately selfish. Third, everything that we do in our lives involves relationships, and egos (both individual and organizational) are often the nemesis of leading people with a purpose. The purpose must be the right one, and, in paraphrasing Aristotle: Leadership is about 'doing the right things, for the right reasons, in the right places, by and for the right people'.

Acknowledgements

I am grateful to many colleagues and friends, too many to mention, for the support in both challenging and building on my thoughts and practice of leadership. I would also like to thank Carol Bailey, freelance indexer at CBindexing for compiling the index.

Prologue

THEM OR US? LEADING THROUGH INTELLIGENT NETWORKS

St Paul saw the light on the road to Damascus. I saw it on the westbound carriageway of the M62. (Pease, 2001:7)

THE UNSELFISH GENE?

The Damascus moment referred to by my long-time friend and colleague Ken Pease was the moment he made an interesting link between the increase in vehicle crime and poor crime-prevention measures. I had mine as I walked past a well-known university bookseller in Manchester. After many years of practising and studying leadership, I had been musing over the problem of individual versus collective leadership approaches. The 30th anniversary edition of Richard Dawkins's *The Selfish Gene* was on display. It occurred to me that perhaps we are innately selfish? If the answer to this is 'yes', then it may impact in two ways. First, it will make it harder for leaders from different backgrounds and roles to agree on shared aims, and second, it is likely to emphasize individual motivations over and above collaborative aims. This is an important conceptual point. Is altruism a realistic aim for leaders? The *Oxford English Dictionary* defines altruism as 'Disinterested or selfless concern for the well-being of others, esp. as a principle of action' (OED, 2012). Sober and Wilson suggest that 'action', as well as 'motive', represent two sides of the same altruistic coin. However, they also say that identifying whether a person is altruistic presents a problem.

People who never help others are seldom considered altruists. On the other hand, when people do help others, we want to know why before we call them altruists (Sober and Wilson, 1998:17).

If I ask myself, 'Do I want this book on leadership to be as successful as any of the other 100,000 plus books published in the past?' The honest answer, of course, must be 'Yes'. Dawkins and his eminent predecessors have provided the foundation for this answer in arguing that we are innately selfish given our natural need for survival; however, as he argues in his latest edition, we can 'teach' people to be more altruistic. This is followed by a further question: can we develop a collaborative rather than a selfish gene in the long run? Several deep-rooted and controversial values are then brought into play. Some originate from thousands of years of history. This includes the creationist versus the evolutionist perspectives of life. Other more basic examples include those of a local community activist or office team leader trying to defend a position based on his or her own self-interests, (often called 'NIMBYism' or the 'WIFM' factor[1]). These predominantly biological accounts of selfish genes do not present the full picture. Some have argued that our 'cultures' have evolved alongside our genes and have exponentially increased the ability to transfer knowledge from mind-to-mind (Pagel, 2012). This is tantamount to suggesting a 'fast-track' in human evolution. The presence, or absence, of either a selfish or an unselfish gene is the first stage of the story. The second stage, I suggest, is about conditioning through culture. As we know, culture change takes time, often spanning generations, but this is a mere speck in time compared to the 60,000 years or so of human evolution since the *Homo sapiens* inhabited our planet and began to develop, among other things, 7000 different languages to assist in communication and thus, collaboration (Pagel, ibid). Stage three of the story will suggest that collaborative behaviour can be taught and – if we try hard enough – the culture may change over time and create a leadership paradigm that favours collaboration rather than control. Who knows, perhaps our offspring over even more generations to come may just develop the unselfish gene, influenced by this cultural environment. I will leave the biologists and the psychologists to further consider this argument and will confine my story to that of creating the conditions that may enable selfless leaders to emerge and practise collective leadership based on shared values, rather than individual leadership based on self-interest.

My starting point is strikingly simple. There is an increasing recognition that all (individual) leaders are necessarily flawed. As Grint argues, 'they are not the embodiments of perfection that we would like them to be' (Grint, 2005:1). Part of this, for sure, is likely to be due to incompetence or inability, but it can equally be because we are innately selfish. Our genetic disposition will predispose us towards this default behaviour. As our culture has developed, intelligent action and motives have shown the benefits of collaborative rather than competitive behaviours. Over time, this has become deep-rooted within our culture with an increasing predisposition towards shared values. But this is far from universal. Although some argue that selfish behaviour is in the minority (Benkler, 2011), this only happens automatically if the context is right. Context is thus all-important in considering leadership.

Taking a somewhat provocative approach, this book will suggest that the crises of leadership (so often identified in recent scandals) are more to do with the selfish and egotistic motivations of individual leaders rather than the selfless and collective motivations focused on shared values. I will draw on a number of case studies to illustrate this. After all, it has been suggested that 'Psychopaths are four times more common among senior executives' (James 2013, reviewed in Browning, 2013:27). In supporting a shift towards collective leadership, the book will argue that this approach has more potential to translate shared values towards relevant and appropriate leadership behaviours. This in turn is more likely to lead to increased trust, confidence, and legitimacy. In advancing this argument, I will also explore whether

---

[1]'Not In My Back Yard' or 'What's In it For Me'.

there has been a false distinction between 'public leadership' and 'non-public' (or commercially based) leadership. Perhaps we should all aspire towards a model of New Public Leadership, the key purpose of which is to 'lead in the public interest'. This would apply whether you are a CEO in the banking industry or the Chief Officer of a public service organization (PSO). Principles of selfless leadership underpin this purpose.

The key challenge is for senior leaders to create the conditions (the context) in which selfless behaviour is encouraged and rewarded, rather than setting the diktat from 'above' and then putting in place control measures to ensure that 'their' objectives are met, regardless as to how they are achieved in some of the more extreme cases of selfish leadership. A further organizational impact to arise from a selfless approach to leadership is to move away from the 'not-invented-here' syndrome (resulting in a lack of knowledge transfer) to one of 'borrowing with pride'[2] (in which we shamelessly take other people's good ideas and transfer them to our own setting). The important bit, of course, is to credit that other person or organization with having developed this good practice, rather than steal it, amend it, or plagiarize it, and then present it as our own! Surely, this doesn't happen often?

There are three critical challenges that this book seeks to explore.

The first challenge is to know ourselves. Our own individual experiences in life and our professional and work life shape our values. We ignore these at our peril. Leaders are part of their own leadership narrative and journey.

The second challenge is to work towards achieving consensus and 'do unto others as we would wish to be done to us'. This is not easy. No leadership can sensibly take place without resort to relationships. As Schluter and Lee (Schluter and Lee, 2009:81) argue, 'A key question to address is the balance between individual and group reward.' Can a selfish leader support such? He or she can only do so if there is an equal effort to understand 'significant others'.

A third challenge is to work collectively to achieve the aims and objectives in support of the shared values through appropriate behaviour. A leader who is able to accept that he or she does not have all the answers is a much stronger leader than the leader who is unable to do this. It is the role of the leader to ask the intelligent question and create the conditions to enable 'collective others' to consider solutions.

The overall aim is demystifying the complexity of leadership and to move away from its prime focus on the individual and more towards the collective, but building on the past rather than replacing it. Speaking back in 1958, Herbert Simon (featured in Chapter 2) was comparing advances made in operational research with the absence of progress in relation to managerial activity. These were described as 'ill structured problems' (Simon and Newell, 1958:4). Leadership could be such a problem. Simon is credited as the first to formally use the term heuristic problem-solving, which is one of those lost values of leadership that this book tries to rekindle while ensuring the integrity of the problems tackled.

---

[2]I first came across this term while working for Her Majesty's Inspectorate of Constabulary. It was used by the (then) HM Inspector, Mr. John Stevens (now Lord Stevens) in describing how crime initiatives should be 'borrowed with pride'.

Problem-solving features strongly within the concept of intelligent leadership. The development and use of knowledge and skills is equally important. This will benefit from problem-solving approaches. Knowledge, intelligently analysed, shared, and used can be a valuable tipping point in successful leadership. One commonly distinguishing factor between knowledge and skill is that knowledge is what is contained in the head and skill is that which is done by the hand. It is more complex than this, but it works well as an early distinction. I argue that it distinguishes between leadership (knowledge and wisdom) and management (skills and experience).

Einstein once argued:

> Science can only be created by those who are thoroughly imbued with the aspiration toward truth and understanding. (Einstein, 1954:43)

KNOWING THYSELF

> The first step is to understand oneself before you can understand other people. Know thyself. And knowing himself, he may learn to use advances of knowledge to benefit, rather than destroy, the human species. (Simon and Newell 1958:8)

Individual reflection is an important precondition for organizational or network reflection. DeRue and Ashford argue, 'You learn how to go forward by looking backward' (DeRue and Ashford, 2010:26).

I regret that I had not practised reflection more during my own leadership career. I had a promising start. In 1984, I was a uniformed sergeant in a provincial police force and had just returned from a weeklong tour of duty during the miners' strike in the North of England. In seeking promotion to Inspector, the Assistant Chief Constable asked me in my interview, 'What is good leadership?' Unprepared, I pondered this. I responded that leadership cannot be defined. Good leadership can be assessed by the results of a team when members do what the leader/s want them to do because *we all* want to do it. I distinguished 'we' from 'them'. I was promoted to Inspector within months. Often reflecting on that question and response, I remain as passionate about it today as I did in 1984. This influenced the first part of this prologue's title: 'us or them'. Inclination to reflect should be automatic, not prompted by self-fulfilment!

This book has been in the making for a long time. Using experience as a leader in a range of different contexts, I will describe why and how this influences my realist approach to research. To develop leaders through a realist approach has similar promise. I have often said that I would dearly love to write a book entitled *Them*; wherever I went or with whom I ever spoke about leadership challenges, the retort would be, 'It's *them*!' – those along the corridor, those upstairs (the 'bosses'), those in our partner organizations, and, when speaking to the bosses, those either at Whitehall (for the public sector) or the shareholders (in the private sector) or even the great public! However, it is more about encouraging an approach that focuses on *us* rather than *them* and understanding the importance of collective responsibilities.

For so long – in both my practice and (more recently) research and teaching of leadership – I have been 'banging on' about a three-lettered word that gets in the way of effective leadership: ego. I also extend this to organizational egos, often associated with competing values as a result of 'the underlying relationships that reside in organizations' (Cameron, 2006:7; Cameron and Quinn, 2011).

The study and practice of leadership is one of the oldest, and most difficult, concepts to grasp. It could be a strong contender for the title of the world's oldest profession! It affects us all. Everyone has been a leader at some time in life, often without recognizing it! It is also cross-disciplinary, relying on history, psychology, and literature as well as many others and not just management science (Simon, 1957). It is an 'ology' based on many 'ologies'!

Given its long antecedents, is it thus possible to suggest a formidable change in the way that we think about leadership? Why is this necessary? Describing the holy grail of leadership may satisfy my self-interest. This is not my aim. I do want to encourage a new way of thinking about leadership. This includes offering new frames of reference to aid understanding. Understanding the past is just as important as understanding the future (Handy, 1999).

DO UNTO OTHERS

Do to others, as you would have them do to you. (Luke 6.31)

Difficult leadership challenges exist. Many of these relate to the importance of values. A number of scandals have put the issue of leadership 'on trial'. This includes the recent economic crisis. Never before have we been in a position where the individual nature of senior leaders has overshadowed and destroyed collective values. We can look to Enron and world.com and the more recent banking crisis that has led the so-called developed world into recession where 'constructive dissent', as described by Grint (2005), appears to have been ignored by senior leaders in preference to 'destructive consent'. Under the ambit of 'new public management', the last 20 to 30 years have seen an encouragement of private sector management techniques being applied to the public sector. There is a strong base of literature that is critical of this approach in skewing leadership towards what can be counted rather than what counts (Brookes and Grint, 2010). The interaction between the economic climate and public services, for example, is clear, and with significant cuts being made to public services, perhaps it is not just about transformational leadership change but rather revolutionary leadership change.

As Jim Collins expressed (Collins, 2001), we need to 'confront the brutal facts of the reality'. We need to confront the dark side to leadership. It has been argued, 'Sometimes the dark side of leadership eclipses the bright side to the detriment of both the leader and the organization' (Conger, 1990:44). The root of crisis is often about degeneration of values. For example, Hopper and Hopper suggest that the original puritan values of the 'great engine companies' in early American history gave way to greed, with leaders focused more on individual interests than the greater good (Hopper et al., 2007).

OF ONE HEART AND MIND: SHARED VALUES

> All the believers were one in heart and mind. No one claimed that any of their possessions was their own, but they shared everything they had. (Acts 4:32 (New International Version))

A brief synopsis of 1000+ years of leadership thoughts will provide a background to the argument that we need to rediscover the lost values of leadership in an increasingly global and complex business and public service operating environment. Even given these long antecedents, I agree with Yukl that 'extensive research on leadership behaviour has yielded many different behaviour taxonomies and a lack of clear results about effective behaviours' (Yukl, 2012:66). The collective leadership framework places behaviours as a high-level outcome of shared values. I will suggest that part of the problem is that the focus of traditional leadership theories has been more about the individual than the collective. If most (individual) leaders are indeed fundamentally flawed in some vital respects, is this because they are driven by intrinsic values and motivation? If so, the role of collective leadership is to mitigate those flaws by focusing on shared values. Based on a review of literature and my experience and research over many more years than I care to remember, a range of case studies will be explored against a framework for leadership through 360° intelligent networks, knowledge, and skills assisted by a moral and value-laden leadership compass.

Ron Heifetz said of leadership that it involves passion and moral values; the adaptive leadership challenge is to tackle these values if we are to influence suitable behaviour (Heifetz, 1994). Shared values are critical.

The Research Approach and Leadership Frameworks

The research underpinning this book commenced in 1997 and has continued through to the present day. Although it was initially developed in the public sector, the emerging frames of reference and supporting inventories were applied across a number of organizations (including the private sector) in support of executive education programmes. It was applied at different levels of leadership but with an overriding focus on the strengths and weaknesses of collective leadership. These frames of reference and inventories form the basis of the book, supported by the empirical evidence.

In considering research approaches, as with leadership itself, history is replete with both theory and debate. Although the purpose of the book is not to outline in detail the philosophical approaches and methods of research, it is important to briefly state my approach in this regard. In epistemological terms, I am conscious of the seminal work of Thomas Kuhn, who disagreed with those philosophers who believed that philosophy was basically about justification and question, as opposed to discovery (Radder, 1997). Although strongly criticized by others, Kuhn's work has been considered influential beyond the philosophy of science, not only in the history of science but also in areas such as the social sciences and humanities. The work of Kuhn indicates that science never grows through accumulation; rather it changes through revolution (Hands, 2001) and 'revolution' is a form of innovation.

The history of leadership literature often follows the accumulation route, although one should never lose sight of the past. In suggesting that we take account of what 'went before', I look to the opportunities of 'revolution' through a new way of thinking about leadership from the singular to the plural. I would not go as far as claiming this as a new paradigm of leadership. This is a bold claim to make. I prefer a position where 'each evolutionary period creates its own revolution'.

The term evolution is used to describe prolonged periods of growth where no major upheaval occurs in organization practices. The term revolution is used to describe those periods of substantial turmoil in organization life (Greiner, 1994:1–2).

This does not mean to imply that I am in agreement with Kuhn's position that the progress of science is revolutionary rather than linear, based on his view that old theories cannot be compatible with new ones. In contrast, I have also considered the Lakatosian heuristic Methodology of Scientific Research Proposals (MSRP), which argues that scientific progress can only be realized by looking at the successes and failures of a sequence of theories with general core assumptions (Lakatos, 1978). It may thus be a combination of revolution but based on looking at the best and the worst of the past and then trying to predict the future. This comes back to the importance of reflection but at a much wider level, beyond the individual. Research, as with the practice of leadership, exists at multiple levels.

Kuhn's contention that we should focus on discovery is an important one. It aligns with the notion of heuristics, a process or method for attempting the solution of a problem.

In keeping with the aim of 'discovery', a realistic evaluation approach has been adopted throughout. As Pawson and Tilley argue:

> Most evaluation studies seem to be one-off affairs. They neither look back and build on previous findings, nor look forward to future evaluations. (Pawson and Tilley, 1997:115)

The realistic evaluation approach thus seeks to create a realist template to show how the goal of creating cumulative bodies of evaluation research – which hitherto has been elusive – can be attained. For this reason, my research projects also followed a case study approach (Yin, 2009) using multiple methods and multiple case studies. The benefits of this approach are pervasive, not least of which is the view of Cook et al. (1992, quoted in Pawson and Tilley 1997:115) who suggest that:

> The immense diversity of social life ... and the great welter of factors underlying any social phenomenon make it difficult, if not impossible, to derive conclusive knowledge from any single study, no matter how well designed or intelligently analysed.

No single uniform answer to a given question is sufficient. Cook et al. (ibid) prefer a family of answers, related by principles that emerge only through the course of much research. Time again features.

One benefit of using a realistic evaluation approach is that leaders and leadership adapt and change according to the attributes of the people involved in leading, those who 'follow', and internal dynamics. A second is that leadership activities produce complex patterns of outcome, with winners and losers, successes and failures. A third is that the external conditions for leaders and leadership are apt to vary and to change over time, and as Tilley (Tilley, 2010) argues, 'sometimes in chaotic and inherently unpredictable ways'. The realist is interested in identifying and testing configurations, rather than one-to-one causal relationships. The relatively simple framework relies upon the configuration of context, mechanisms, and outcomes (CMO configurations) (2010:634).

The word context stems from the Latin *contextus*, which comprises the two words *con* (together) and *texere* (to weave). It describes the circumstances that form the setting for an event (i.e. leadership) and helps understanding. In this sense, context is not something that is directly controllable but does have a clear impact on intentions. In organizational and leadership scenarios it is also sometimes referred to as the operating environment. This describes surroundings or conditions that have a clear impact on organizations.

Much of the leadership literature refers to the importance of context. A full understanding of the meaning of context is important in both developing and evaluating leadership as a collective endeavour. It is particularly important to take note of the provenance of the word context in terms of 'weaving together', a notion that the book refers to throughout in support of the interrelated nature of leadership and in understanding that the varying contexts are dynamic and interrelated. Context is now a global phenomenon embracing both national and international cultures. Hofstede describes culture as the 'collective programming of the mind which distinguishes the members of one human group from another' (Hofstede et al., 2010:6). Nakata suggests the need for a move beyond Hofstede, given the changing global conditions that have emerged (Nakota, 2009).

Realists are also interested in 'mechanisms'. The term mechanism is used in answer to 'how' questions. For the purposes of the underpinning research, leadership is considered as a form of intervention, which may affect the target behaviour. Mechanisms can often be invisible. For example, in relation to leadership, Tilley (2010) refers to 'inspiration'.

He argues:

> We cannot directly observe this inspiration, even if we may be able to observe the behaviours that may be activating the inspiration and the behaviours that are produced as a consequence of that inspiration! (Tilley, 2010:636)

This distinction between the 'unobserved' (i.e. inspiration) and the 'observed' (i.e. behaviours) has been increasingly important as my research and evaluation continued in the sense of the 'unobserved' (leadership values) and the 'observed' (leadership behaviours). The coupling of context and mechanism produces the third element of the configuration: the outcome. This is represented by public value as a high-level outcome of collective leadership. This suggests, quite rightly, that CMO configurations (context-mechanism-outcomes) are multi-level in much the same way as I argue that collective leadership is multi-level. This will be explored throughout the book.

Analyses and modelling of the data took place throughout the research. The development of frames of reference followed. Such frames can be useful in explaining a set of ideas, such as philosophical or religious principles or used as explanations or means of interpreting or assigning meanings. This is a useful way of explaining concepts. I adopt several frameworks nested within the overall framework of collective leadership. This influences the second part of this prologue's title: 'Leading through Intelligent Networks'.[3]

The main theme of **Part I** of the book is that of understanding the changing context of leadership. The first two chapters explore the historical context of leadership, the values that underpin leadership, and how those values seem to have been lost in time and space. The discussion will be supported by Rudyard Kipling's six honest serving men in an attempt to make sense of the vast array of leadership theories:

> I keep six honest serving-men (They taught me all I knew); Their names are <u>What</u> and <u>Why</u> and <u>When</u> and <u>How</u> and <u>Where</u> and <u>Who</u>. (Kipling, 1907)

Chapter 3 explores the role of knowledge and research and its application to practice by focusing on the realistic evaluation approach in the development of a collective leadership framework. Chapter 4 then considers the language of leadership and the differences between frameworks and model in relation to both research and practice. It introduces the 20P collective leadership framework and with Chapter 5, unpicks each element in terms of its provenance and meaning based on the three-fold elements of realistic evaluation: context, mechanisms, and outcomes.

The theme of **Part II** concerns the practice of leadership in an increasingly complex world. In Chapter 6, we explore the challenges presented to leaders, not least of which are the increasing global nature of leadership and the importance of whole systems approaches, based on geometric and mathematical foundations. In Chapter 7, the discussion turns to the contextual challenges facing leaders in the 'real' (as opposed to the 'theoretical') world of leadership. Chapters 8 to 14 define and develop the concept of collective leadership, supported by a collective leadership inventory (CLI).

Collective leadership asks the intelligent questions and encourages collective others within networks to consider the solutions. It favours leading-in-the-round rather than leading-through-the-line. Immediate crises may need leadership from-the-front. I prefer the term 'networks' to 'organization' given the former's pluralistic and heterarchical characteristics as opposed to the latter's more singular and hierarchical nature. In an interesting anthropological study of complex societies, hierarchies were described as 'elements, which on the basis of certain factors are subordinate to others and may be ranked'. The authors made an important point:

> Hierarchy – inasmuch as it is often a reductionist metaphor for order – has disproportionately influenced theory building in both social and natural scientific contexts. (Crumley, 1995:2)

---

[3]LINKS[360]® is a registered trade mark owned and licensed by Compass Leadership Limited and supports the frameworks and inventories outlined in this prologue.

Although related to anthropological studies, this work has resonance with leadership structure within which personal agency operates. Crumley argues that the conflation of hierarchy with order 'makes it difficult to imagine, much less recognise and study, patterns of relations that are complex but not hierarchical'. This resonates with Cameron and Quinn (2006:8), who suggest a need to 'understand the simple structure that underlies all organizing activities'. Understanding these structures, they argue, help 'to create new and more effective patterns of organizing'.

Conversely, a heterarchy may be defined as 'the relation of elements to one another when they are unranked or when they possess the potential for being ranked in a number of different ways' (Crumley, 1995:3). This argument aligns to my focus on leading through 360° intelligent networks and is explored throughout these 7 chapters.

Part III will describe how collective leadership can make a difference to leadership outcomes. Chapter 15 provides an insight on the links between the practice and professionalization of leadership. It introduces the concept of action learning but builds on this through its focus on serving the public interest as its outcome.

Practice and theory go together. As Kurt Lewin once said, 'There is nothing so practical as a good theory.'

If one does not inform the other, a complete cycle of leadership development cannot take place. Invariably, these two ideas occupy attention in separate ways and, often, separate direction. The chapter brings together the practice and pedagogy of leadership. 'Practice' defines the 'actual application or use of an idea, belief, or method, as opposed to theories relating to it' whereas pedagogy represents a method or practice of teaching. In this book I consider the concept as a form of 'original thinking applied' and describe how the practical challenges can be used as a reflective means of developing leadership throughout a network of organizations. As many commentators argue, a simple definition of pedagogy – as with the concept of leadership itself – is difficult to identify. An interesting description of pedagogy is one that describes it as being 'about service, an educative journey, and interrelationships and to a certain extent rhetoric and persuasion' (Mcshane, 2007). The intelligent alignment of practice and pedagogy holds promise in encouraging the form of intelligent leadership that can act as the 'tipping point' between purpose and vision and practice and public value results. Action learning is a means of bringing purpose to practice through experiential learning. The application of collective leadership is explored in detail in Chapter 16, reinforcing the nature of collective leadership and through research based on the 20P framework and the Collective Leadership Inventory (CLI). The chapter also introduces the Transform Leadership Inventory (TLI) which, together with the CLI, formed a collective 360° leadership assessment and development approach through the research in a number of different organizations.

The arguments of the book are drawn together in a brief epilogue. An overall summary will be given describing why a new way of thinking about leadership can be encouraged in the future, while building on the past. This can be achieved by leading through 360° intelligent networks, knowledge, and skills.

Collective leadership is more likely to have an impact through clear, constructive, and consistent communication than the iteration of individual messages that are so often misinterpreted or ignored. The book will outline how the development of collective leadership can be aligned to organizational and cross-organizational cultural visions and aims through the application of applied leadership challenges. This follows an action learning approach which aligns shared and distributed leadership to the cascaded goals and objectives in a way that secures mutual benefit for the individual, teams, organizations, and, potentially, entire communities. A key theme throughout this book is that 'leadership both begins and ends with people'. So, if we are innately selfish, how do we resolve this difficulty? Let us begin that journey!

Part I

The Changing Context of Leadership

1 Exploring Thousands of Years of Leadership in Seventeen and a Half Pages[1]

IN THE BEGINNING ...

A good question to ask as we begin our journey is 'where do we start?' In the sense of my quest not to lose sight of our past, it must be at the beginning of course! However, in taking the liberty of slightly reversing this, for the purposes of this chapter, we want to keep in mind our endgame, that is, 'where do we want to get to?' In the opening pages I used a distinction between 'management' and 'leadership' and rather simply described this as representing the difference between the hand (skill) and the head (knowledge) but within the context of the heart (doing what is right). One of the key skills of a leader is in balancing the head and the heart in encouraging the hand. One of the key challenges for leadership in the modern world is that there has been too much management and not enough leadership. Many commentators have addressed this distinction. This ranges from those who said that 'management is doing things right whereas leadership is doing the right things' (Bennis and Nanus, 1985) to Grint, who equates management with command and leadership in tackling wicked problems (Grint, 2008a). The difference, I suggest, is in the inclusion of the heart in asking yet another question: 'Are we doing the right things for the right reasons?' It may thus be evident that another key skill of a leader is to ask the intelligent questions. We can indeed look back in history in understanding the ethical and moral grounding for leadership in setting the right context for the right questions.

Leadership predates the emergence of humankind, for example in relation to animal origins and pecking orders, seen most significantly with the dominance

---

[1]With acknowledgement to my friend and mentor, Nick Tilley, who introduced me to the notion of understanding evaluation in 17 and a half pages (Pawson and Tilley, 1997).

effects in primates (Bass and Stogdill, 1990:4). However, I want to begin my hitch-hiker's guide to leadership by first 'meeting' some of whom I describe as the Old World Leaders (OWLs[2]), which includes (but does not necessarily begin with) the Greek Philosophers. The old world is generally taken to mean the world, as it was then known, to the inhabitants of Europe, North Africa, and the Near East before the discovery of the new world in the Americas, Australasia, and South Africa. Unsurprisingly, I will then compare what I call the New World Leaders (NWLs). The 'new' and 'old' world distinctions are perhaps best known in describing 'wines of the world'. Rather partial to a glass of new world wine myself, this does not necessarily mean that I ignore old-world wines, as I quite like to partake in the odd sip of Rioja or good Burgundy! As with the study of leadership, the distinction between old-world wines and those of the new are grounded in differing philosophical schools of thought, with the old world focused on tradition and the new world more willing to follow experimentation; although, in today's more global environment, there is now a much greater tendency to move beyond these boundaries in winemaking. At the end of this chapter, I will briefly refer to what I finally call Global World Leaders (GWLs), not necessarily global in the sense of global empires but, rather, global in the sense of a greater openness to learning.

PUTTING NEW WINE IN OLD BOTTLES?

As with many of our old proverbs, they originate from spiritual scripts. This includes my sub-heading:

> Neither do men put new wine into old bottles: else the bottles break, and the wine runneth out and the bottles perish; but they put new wine into new bottles, and both are preserved. (Matthew, ix, 17)

It is thus not the 'content' that is important (whether it be 'old' or 'new' wines) but rather its preservation. One of the main themes of this book is that leadership (as with wine) is context specific. To illustrate: Glass bottles today are far more resilient, and recycling is actively encouraged. During biblical times (in the old world), 'bottles' were made from the skin of goats. Once new wine was poured in, the skin would stretch and perish.

What one drinks (or how one leads) is then a matter of choice (but, preferably, not at the same time!). What we need to do, then, as with wine, is to preserve both the old and new ideas and consider these within differing contexts. If one eats fish, then the tendency is to drink a white wine; if one eats red meat then, often, it will be accompanied by red wine. If one chooses to lead in a particular situation, then, often, tried-and-tested means of a leadership style will be adopted; in another situation, a different style may accompany the practice of leadership. However, in both cases, this is not mutually exclusive. Although I do not eat fish, I very occasionally drink white wine, but generally chilled and usually when (very infrequently) relaxing in the sun!

---

[2]The acronym with the species of the 'wise old bird' – the owl – is not necessarily coincidental.

This is my first description of the context of leadership (with many more to follow!). In the 'old world', new forms of leadership would be likely to 'stretch' the capability and capacity of our OWLs. In a global world, this is much easier for our GWLs who lead in a postmodern, post-industrial, and more chaotic world. Our NWLs were faced with the onslaught of the challenges of the Enlightenment and the Renaissance, followed by modernity and industrialization. Time is thus one of the main currencies of leadership.

As I described in the introduction to this book, our story at the beginning should not ignore the role of nature and evolution. As with all living creatures, we have innate characteristics as opposed to learned characteristics, much of which is learned from nature. But this does not take account of changing contexts. As Finney argues:

> The silverback in you – wisdom as already-learned experience – may not be able to make the crossing to the new life. So you must generate new capacities to survive in the ecosystem in which you find yourself. Sad to say, you must learn all over again. (Finley, 2000)

FROM THE SILVERBACK TO THE OWLS

As with our primal ancestors, many of our OWLs decided on a course of action within the context of their time, including a sense of the possibilities open to them. Some of their failures were just as spectacular as more contemporary examples (Cotterell et al., 2006). However, as our ancient philosophers point out, human *reason* distinguishes us from our primal origins.

Leadership is thus as old as earth has been inhabited, irrespective of primal or human beginnings. We can first determine accounts of ancient leadership from as early as Egyptian pharaohs. For example, Ramesses II in 1274 BC displayed immense personal courage in thwarting an attack and was far more outnumbered than the apparent numbers involved in the vintage account of Henry V, whose merry band of brothers defeated a much larger French army at Agincourt. Courage is thus one of the earliest characteristics of our OWLs, but, as Cotterell et al. argue, a practical problem in comparing what I describe as the OWLs and our GWLs is the changing attitude to leadership, the dramatic shift from command and control to cooperation and joint effort.

First, let us meet Aristotle, a great old-world philosopher (himself informed by both Socrates and Plato). Aristotle inspires my seventeenth 'P' of collective leadership –which underpins all of the preceding sixteen: Phronetic leadership. What on earth is this, you may ask! To reassure you, this is the last time that I will actually use this term, other than in setting the conceptual framework for what I shall hitherto refer to as 'intelligent leadership'. However, in keeping with my second major quest of understanding the language of leadership (in the sense of its past), let us briefly consider Aristotle's contribution.

Aristotle, arguably one of the most eminent of Greek philosophers, distinguished the word phronesis from other forms of wisdom (such as episteme and techne), relating it more to practical wisdom rather than simply intellectual wisdom, but within the context of ethics. Although the term phronesis encompasses intellectual wisdom, it also highlights the importance of linking theory to practice. It can thus be equated with practical wisdom. In today's world, I view this as that of intelligent leadership: Not only acquiring relevant knowledge (episteme or epistemology) and reasoning (nous) but also applying this knowledge in practice (phronesis). It is about practical judgement shown by good leaders.[3] This is summed up well:

> Practical wisdom (phronesis) is the intellectual virtue concerned with doing. (Aristotle et al., 2009:xvi)

In outlining what Aristotle viewed as good ethics, it is as well to reflect upon this at the beginning of our journey to understand selfless leadership and keep this in mind as we explore the examples of selfish (or toxic) leadership. He identified a number of virtues, and we will explore the concept of virtues in more detail in the next chapter. Some of the virtues identified by Aristotle include:

- Happiness as a public good.
- Excellence of character or moral virtue.
- Moral virtue as conscious choice.
- Self-mastery.
- Friendship and partnership.

Aristotle also considered the impediments to virtue, describing three things that humans should avoid:

- Evils or vices are the opposites of virtues.
- Incontinence is the opposite of self-restraint. They are weaknesses in which people passively follow an urge rather than a deliberate choice.
- Being beast-like or brutish, which Aristotle describes as the opposite of something more than human, being heroic or god-like.

Aristotle is not the only classic author to have used the phrase 'brutish'. Although a classic, we still have to fast-forward by over 1600 years to the work of Thomas Hobbes, who described his world as 'too solitary, poor, nasty, brutish and short'.[4] Hobbes, who was writing at the time of the English civil war, was arguing in favour of a strong central authority to avoid what he saw as the evil and discord of civil war. Perhaps we could ask whether leadership has suffered from the same difficulties?

HAS LEADERSHIP BEEN TOO SOLITARY, POOR, NASTY, BRUTISH, AND SHORT?

One could be forgiven for thinking that my view on the history of leadership has taken a rather dystopian view in which everything that could be bad about leadership has been that bad or, conversely, that the future of leadership is utopian and collective leadership will solve all of society's wicked issues. Clearly this is not the

---

[3]Nicomachean Ethics, Aristotle 1144b in Book VI.
[4]'Chapter XIII: Of the Natural Condition of Mankind As Concerning Their Felicity and Misery', *Leviathan*.

case, and the balance is likely to be somewhere between the two. These questions do need to be asked, and, in particular, we need to look at both history and the current leadership context and to consider its dark side as well as its bright side.

Leadership theories began their journey focused on the innate qualities of an individual. This then evolved to a study of the behaviours adopted, the situations in which leadership takes place, and leadership that is specific to particular functions. These theories have their place but arguably they tend to ignore leadership's increasingly important dynamics within a changing context of uncertainty.

The 'individual' is the focus of most leadership studies; from earliest times, theories have focused on what it is that makes individuals good leaders. The theme of the book is that we need to 'think differently' about leadership. I argue that leadership is about collective activity by communities or groups of people. We do not need to 'throw the baby out with the bathwater'; leadership theories are cumulative. Thinking differently concerns an understanding of the complexity of leadership in the twenty-first century. Values play a key role in understanding these complexities. We need to make sense of the theories so that this thinking can be applied in practice.

The chapter will consider the problems of defining leadership within a historical and contemporary perspective and will act as a foundation for the remainder of the book. As Stogdill (1974:259) argues, 'there are almost as many definitions of leadership as there are persons who have attempted to define the subject'.

A publication by the Department for Further Education and Skills (DFES) observed that:

> On 9 August 2003 there were 12,963 books on leadership. If we were able to read at the rate of one per day this would equate to 35 years of reading, including weekends. By 28th February 2005 this had already increased to 47 years and 17,138 books. (DFES, 2007:58)

On 9th January 2009 a further search revealed that this had risen to almost 30,000, over double the original number, and a basic search on Amazon in 2014 revealed just fewer than 100,000 titles. Forget about reading them in your lifetime!

We start by exploring the definitional aspects of leadership over time, moving beyond the classics of our Greek forefathers; the origin of the words 'leading' and 'leadership' derive from the old German word 'lidan' (to go) and an old English word 'lithan' (to travel). In this sense, leadership could be defined as 'leading the way' through one's own action. The chapter and the book will suggest that leadership is about asking the intelligent questions through networks and building appropriate knowledge and skills. The best leaders ask the right questions and allow those with the knowledge to suggest the best answers. This has rarely featured in leadership theories.

SIX HONEST SERVING MEN

Who, what, and where, by what helpe, and by whose,
Why, how and when, doe many things disclose.
The Arte of Rhetorique (Wilson, 1560: 39[5])

---

[5]English rhetorician Thomas Wilson, who introduced the method in his discussion of the 'seven circumstances' of medieval rhetoric.

The analysis of the leadership literature will be supported by Rudyard Kipling's six honest serving men – which followed Wilson's *Arte of Rhetorique* (1560) – in an attempt to make sense of the vast array of leadership theories:

> I keep six honest serving-men
> (They taught me all I knew);
> Their names are <u>What</u> and <u>Why</u> and <u>When</u>
> and <u>How</u> and <u>Where</u> and <u>Who.</u>
> (Kipling, 1907)

First, the 'Who' Question

The individual leader is the main focus in the sense of 'the born leader' (great man theory) and their characteristics or traits. Historically, these early theories were about military and political leaders; followers were taken for granted. A relationship between the leader and follower was less important. This is changing, and leadership can be dispersed.

This approach is intuitively appealing and supported by much research. As the earlier discussion illustrated, the fascination with 'individuals' as leaders has a long history, as long as life itself. Although the ancient historical accounts have appeal in themselves, the first real attempt to study the characteristics of individual leadership was that of Thomas Carlyle (1795–1881) in his account of the 'Great Men[6] theory of leadership' (Carlyle, 1852). This early theoretical perspective is said to have viewed individual leaders 'as independent agents, able to manipulate the world at will' (Grint, 2005:1471). Carlyle studied leaders as widely diverse as William Shakespeare (the hero as poet), Oliver Cromwell, Napoleon, Dante, Samuel Johnson, Jean Jacques Rousseau, Robert Burns, John Knox, and Martin Luther through to the Prophet Muhammad. Grint undertook a similar task (Carroll et al., 2008) in examining (more recent, but, still historical) leaders, including Henry Ford, Horatio Nelson, Adolf Hitler, and Martin Luther King. However, Grint in his later work differed in his view, arguing that 'the context is not independent of human agency, and cannot be objectively assessed in a scientific form' (Grint, 2005:1471). In this sense, Grint was arguing that leaders socially construct the way in which leaders are viewed; in other words, they, themselves, construct their own sense of the reality, which defines the meaning that society then follows.

The focus on 'who' shifted in contemporary understanding in considering the traits that individual leaders (or potential leaders) possessed. Some have argued that this was a first attempt to characterize an effective leader (Bass et al., 2008; Stogdill, 1974). This may have been true in relation to the measurement of traits scientifically, but our OWLs were often attributed with what could only be described as traits. For example, in returning to the ancient pharaohs, the qualities of authoritative speech, perceptiveness, and a sense of justice were attributed to the Pharaoh in *The Instruction of Ptahhotep* which was written in 2300 BC (Bass et al., 2008:1).

---

[6]At this point in time, there was no effort to explore the role of women as 'great leaders'.

We can also move forward to the Renaissance – in considering the 'who' of leadership and a first glimpse of the 'dark side of leadership'; this period gave rise to Machiavelli's argument that:

There is nothing more difficult to take in hand, more perilous to conduct, or more uncertain in its success than to take the lead in the introduction of a new order of things. (Bass 2008:4)

Bass tells us that Machiavelli's *The Prince* (1640) was the ultimate pragmatist who believed that leaders needed steadiness, firmness, and concern for the maintenance of authority, power, and order in government. Quoting Kellerman (1987), it is argued that it is 'best if these objectives could be accomplished by gaining the esteem of the populace, but, if they could not, then craft, deceit, threat, treachery, and violence were required' (Kellerman, 1987). The Machiavellian phrase entered our language and is common parlance today, generally used in a derogatory way. It relates to a person who adopts Machiavellian principles in preference to morality, an intriguer or schemer. This is particularly important in relation to our concern with selfless (and selfish) leadership.

Interestingly, Machiavelli's *The Prince* is often portrayed as the first such treatise that set out advice on the requirements of a ruling leader. Yet, some 350 years earlier, a Sicilian Arab, Muhammad ibn Zafar al-Siqilli, wrote a handbook for a prince. An interesting account of this, and comparisons made with Machiavelli's Prince, identifies some similarities (such as the importance of advisors) but also significant differences. In particular, Machiavelli's Prince would 'heap' gifts on his advisor to 'assist' in aligning the advisor to the Prince's cause. Conversely, Muhammad ibn Zafar al-Siqilli advises his Just Prince:

The king who believes that the minds of princes are superior to those of counselors has fallen into great error. If he acquires the bad habit of contradicting a wise and faithful counselor – without manifest reason – it is certain that he will never prosper. (Kechichian et al., 2003)

Considering the question of 'who' are the leaders, it thus provides a good insight for inspiration and the selection of leaders, but it does little for the personal development of leaders and takes no account of context. Moreover, there is no agreed list of qualities. If there were, we can chuckle but will probably resonate with Grint's comment:

Only those who can walk on water need apply. (Grint, 2010:99)

In essence, Grint tells us, the trait approach says that 'the individual leader is critical but the context is not' (Grint, 2000:2). We would be wise to take note of the advice offered by Zimbardo in his discussion of the 'Lucifer' effect (Zimbardo, 2008) in avoiding what I shall refer to as 'The Dark Side of Leadership' in the next chapter. Zimbardo argues:

'most of us hide behind egocentric biases that generate the illusion that we are special. These self serving protective shields allow us to believe that each of us is above average on any test of self-integrity' ... and 'that we look to the stars through the thick lens of personal invulnerability when we should also look down to the slippery slope beneath our feet'. (ibid:5)

When faced with evil, people will distance themselves from this and attribute it to the 'other' person, based on 'evil' as an entity that can be explained by personal characteristics of individuals (what Zimbardo refers to as an essentialist perspective); the alternative is that we are all capable of evil, depending on circumstances (referred to as an incrementalist perspective). The first perspective pertains to the 'who' and the second, the 'what'. The traditional approach has been to identify inherent personal qualities that lead to the action: Genetic make-up, personality traits, character, free will, and other dispositions. Zimbardo tells us, 'Given violent behaviour, one searches for sadistic personality traits. Given heroic deeds, the search is on for genes that predispose towards altruism' (ibid:7).

Throughout my thirty plus years of experience I have witnessed many moments in which individual leaders have focused exclusively on their own traits without any reference at all to the context (which includes those who they 'lead') and, moreover, situations in which the view of leadership is socially constructed. A good example of this is in relation to the 'cloning' of the leader in the appointment of new leaders. I experienced this when being interviewed by a chief constable in relation to my assessment to progress further in the chief officer ranks of the police service. This was back in the mid-90s when – faced with a question on the response to the future of police leadership – I suggested that perhaps we should look to a regionalization of policing through the leadership of 'commissioners'. The chief constable replied: 'Well, what would you have me wear – a large hat with a plume on it?' My response was simply, 'Whatever floats your boat, Sir!' I had realized that I was unlikely to be successful, a hypothesis that turned out to be absolutely correct!

Second, the 'What' Question

Some theories then began to take account of *what* leaders do. These considered the links between task and employee, the leadership style of leaders, and forms of transactional leadership.

Although leadership theories have existed for many hundreds of years, their rapid development from the early ancient and classic theories started to increase exponentially. Space does not permit a detailed alignment of this argument, but it can be said that theories of leadership developed alongside the growing (and relatively new) approach to the study of organizational theories. We can, perhaps, look to the latter stages of the industrial revolution to see these beginnings. Social historians have well illustrated what can only be described as the continuing 'nasty, brutish and short lives' of those who worked at the 'coalface' of the 'modern' industrial world. The best visual depiction that I have seen of this was the film produced by (and featuring) Charlie Chaplin entitled 'Modern Times'.[7] Produced at the latter stages of the industrial modern world, once again, we can chuckle at its humour (for example,

---

[7]Distributed by United Artists (1930s–2003), release date: February 5, 1936.

as Charlie Chaplin is strapped to an automatic feeding machine that predictably goes wrong, under the proclamation 'feed your men whilst at work' in securing increased productivity). There is also a serious side. Irrespective of whether you agree with Chaplin's portrayal as a political agitator – allegedly subject to surveillance by the state[8] – the image of human resources as part of a machine, and the later image of Chaplin being carted off to an institute for the mentally disturbed by the proverbial 'doctor in a white coat', resonates with history's account of 'modern times' with a sense of hopelessness at a time of rapid change. In keeping with the increasingly developing fascination with 'all things scientific', this approach by organizations and its leaders was strongly influenced by Frederick Winslow Taylor's notion of 'scientific management', with its focus on improving efficiency and Fayol's principles of management (Fayol, 1930). Both were writing at the same time, although Fayol's thoughts took almost 40 years to have a real impact due to a lack of translation from his original work in French.

Attention gradually shifted from the 'nature' to 'nurture' debate. In relation to behaviours of people at work, John Watson offered an early indication of this (Watson, 1930). One quotation illustrates his thoughts well:

> Give me a dozen healthy infants, well-formed, and my own specified world to bring them up in and I'll guarantee to take any one at random and train him to become any type of specialist I might select – doctor, lawyer, artist, merchant-chief and, yes, even beggar-man and thief, regardless of his talents, penchants, tendencies, abilities, vocations, and race of his ancestors. (Watson, 1930:82)

Although this could be considered quite radical for its time, a final sentence that is often omitted in more contemporary accounts highlights this as aspiration, rather than empirical research where he draws attention to the lack of evidence in the history of studying human behaviour:

> I am going beyond my facts and I admit it, but so have the advocates of the contrary and they have been doing it for many thousands of years. (ibid)

Watson was arguing that psychology should focus on the behaviour of individuals rather than their consciousness. In a review of Watson's 1930 work, preceded by similar writing over the previous 20 years, Partridge provides a fascinating insight to Watson's response to the 'storm that appears to have been created' when he said that Watson 'seems to believe that the storm over behaviorism prevails because behaviorism has had a way of trading upon the "hoof of somebody's sacred cow": in other words because it requires the giving up of established mores' (Partridge, 1932:188). If this is not an indication of the power of ego, then what is! We can also see a further reference to our term 'brutish' when, in his earlier writings, Watson saw no dividing line between 'man' and 'brute' (Watson, 1913). It represented a theory of learning that relied upon the conditioning of behaviours through interaction with the environment. In keeping with the scientific approaches of the time,

---

[8]http://www.paperlessarchives.com/chaplin.html

it favoured the study of observable behaviours rather than internal states, because the latter, Watson argued, are too subjective.

The seminal 'Hawthorne Studies' marked a turning point in considering the role of human behaviour from both an organizational and leadership perspective. Based on a series of experiments in industrial history in the late 1920s and early 1930s, its original purpose was to study the effects of physical conditions on productivity. However, an unintended change (for the purposes of the research) in the working conditions (lighting, working hours, and refreshment breaks) was introduced (Mayo, 1933). The study highlighted the importance of the social context. Taking place at Western Electric's factory at Hawthorne, the study concluded that it was not the physical conditions that improved productivity but, rather, that concern was actually being applied to their working conditions. As the research continued it became apparent that informal employee groups (those that were not evident within the traditional organizational charts) were just as important as the formal groups. The importance of human relations began to emerge.

A further influential study, undertaken in the 1940s, concluded that leaders exhibit two types of behaviours in the achievement of goals: people-oriented (consideration) and task oriented (initiating structure). Known as the Ohio State University Leadership Study, a Leaders Behavior Description Questionnaire (LBDQ) was created and used, and these two factors (consideration and initiating structure) accounted for most for the differences in exhibited behaviours. The first factor concerns the extent to which a leader exhibits concern for the welfare of the members of the group, emphasizing interpersonal relationships, mutual trust, and friendship, whereas the second, initiating structure, focuses on how the leader defines group member roles, initiates action plans, and how the leader both organises and supervises the tasks (Bass and Stogdill, 1990).

Leadership styles also emerged as an important factor and remain influential today. Leadership styles represent different approaches undertaken by leaders in providing direction, steering action plans, and motivating people. In 1939, Kurt Lewin, a psychologist, set out to identify different styles of leadership and identified three major styles: Authoritarian (autocratic), participative (democratic), and delegative (laissez-faire) (Lewin et al., 1939). One of the most important contributions that Lewin made was to identify the importance of the situation as a whole in determining the behaviour that is exhibited, the point also raised later by Zimbardo. An authoritative style provides clear expectations of what needs to be done, but results in less creativity. It is best applied to situations where the leader is the most knowledgeable and time for group decision-making is limited. Participative leadership was seen to be the most effective, with an increase in creativity and motivation, but the participative leader still has the final say. Interestingly, delegative leadership resulted in less cooperation and productivity. It could apply in situations where the group members are highly knowledgeable, but leads to poorly defined roles and a lack of motivation.

A link between leadership styles and leadership behaviours was described in a two-dimensional leadership grid that aligned concern (for people and for the task) with the style of the leader (Blake and Mouton, 1964). Five styles emerged, ranging from 'impoverished' (low concern on both dimensions) through to 'team leader' (high concern on both dimensions). The three styles that further populate this range include 'authoritarian' (high concern for task/low concern for people), 'country club' (low concern for task/high concern for people), and the 'middle of the road' (midpoint on both dimensions), which the authors described as the 'politician'.

The final aspect of the 'what' question that I want to briefly describe is that of transactional leadership. A classic study is that of James MacGregor Burns, who studied the political, social, and psychological dimensions of leadership (Burns, 1978). He was one of the first to suggest that leadership is less to do with images of the good and great and its accompanying notions of power and domination, but is more to do with a process of aligning with the consciousness of those who are led. He was making a distinction between 'transactional' and 'transformational' leadership. In the first (and in keeping with the traditional thoughts of this time), leadership is about one person taking the initiative (for example, in political elections, as well as organizational settings). Burns argued that leadership is meaningless without its connection to common purposes and collective needs. We will return to the concept of transformational leadership briefly below but in more depth within the next chapter.

In conclusion, the 'what' is thus important but we should avoid thinking that there is a 'one-best-way' approach because it very much depends upon both the context and the situation. In relation to these behavioural approaches, Bass tells us (1990) that this approach to leadership enables distinctions to be made between different behaviours and in exploring the links between satisfaction and productivity, but its empirical support is weak and it is not possible to identify a universal leadership style. As other authors and I have discussed (and will discuss), the links between leadership styles and outcomes is much more complex than this. The biggest warning is one that Burns made in arguing that (within transactional leadership) there is often a bias towards self-interests (or what Bass describes as pseudo transformational leadership) (Bass and Steidlmeier, 1999) in which the leader purports to focus on the followers' interests but is actually focused on the leader's own interests. I will now continue and consider the 'when' question (situational) and the 'where' question (in terms of positional context) before moving on to the important 'how' and 'why' questions.

Third, the 'When?' Question

As leadership theories continued to develop, the importance of context emerged. There are two primary approaches to the early contextual theories, which are contingency theory and situational leadership theory. There has been a tendency to consider these two approaches as if they were one. While there are clearly some similarities, there are also some significant differences. I prefer to describe them as two sides of the same coin.

The context is defined by time, and thus time is part of the currency of leadership. 'When?' is a good question to ask. Task, relations, and the right contexts form the backdrop to these approaches. Both contingency theory and situational leadership put the individual at their hearts. However, contingency theory focuses on the effectiveness of the leader based on his or her individual leadership style and is dependent on the situations that the leader favours, whereas situational theory relies on the use of a leader's individual skills and ability to lead in a particular situation. A key difference, therefore, is that contingency theory focuses on the present situation whereas situational theory is determined by the attitude and behaviour of the leader. In this sense, the contingent leader is viewed as more inflexible than the situational leader. Both approaches also have different assumptions in relation to followers; contingency theory assumes that all followers will act the same based on the style of the leader, whereas situational leaders assume that followers will differ in their responses dependent upon their particular levels of competence, commitment, and maturity.

Contingency theory was influenced by the University of Ohio study (described earlier) and a later study undertaken by the University of Michigan (Cartwright, 1965; Tannenbaum and Schmidt, 1957), which considered leadership as an organizational, rather than personal, leadership style. The first, as we know, looked at the individual perspective based upon the alignment of consideration (of people) and initiating structure (task). The second study looked at the importance of group behaviours.

Fielder was the first to introduce the concept of contingency theory in the 1960s (Fielder, 1964). Similarly, the leader's task structure and leader–member relation motivations were prominent, but there was a third dimension, position power, and all three were mitigated by the preferred leadership style of the individual leader. This identifies the 'favourableness' of the situation. Certain styles will be effective in certain situations. Style is measured by what is called the Least Preferred Coworker (LPC) style.[9] People who are task structured (low LPC score) will be effective in very favourable or very unfavourable situations, whereas 'People who are relationship motivated (high LPC score) are effective in moderately favourable situations, that is, in situations in which there is some degree of certainty but things are neither completely under their control nor out of their control' (Northouse, 2009:115). Although somewhat controversial in terms of the validity of its measures, Northouse reminds us that it has 'made a substantial contribution to our understanding of leadership processes' (Northouse:126).

Situational leadership theory was also influenced by the Ohio and Michigan studies but also built on the work of Blake and Mouton in combining task and relationship behaviours (which they call directing and supporting) and extending this by describing four different types of leadership behaviour (Hersey and Blanchard, 1969); this includes 'telling' (high directive/low supportive), 'selling' (high directive, high supporting), 'participating' (low directive/high supportive), and 'delegating' (low directive/low supportive). In this sense, it is the role of the leader to both

---

[9]This scale asks leaders to recall a coworker (previously or currently) they work with least well and to characterize this individual with ratings on a series of 8-point bipolar adjectives (e.g., distant–cold). High LPC scores reflect more positive descriptions of the least preferred coworker, whereas low LPC scores evidence more negative perceptions. Fielder argued that an individual with a high LPC score is motivated to maintain harmonious interpersonal relationships, whereas an individual with a low LPC score is motivated to focus on task accomplishment (Northouse, 2009).

reflect upon and adapt his or her behaviour in accordance with each follower's level of competence, commitment, and maturity.

In both cases (contingency and situation), leaders recognize when the right situations occur in terms of tasks and relationships. However, in the case of situational theory, the maturity of leaders and followers is a controlling factor. Both approaches help to identify when to intervene with followers and provide insights about effective leadership in different situations and dyadic leadership relationships, and both have been influential in shaping approaches to flexible, adaptive behaviour (Yukl, 2009), particularly in relation to situational approaches. The approaches are intuitive and simple to understand and widely applied. However, there is not a huge empirical base in relation to the extent to which leadership development focuses on these aspects nor in relation to the study or observation of the processes by which leader behaviour influences follower behaviour.

Fourth, the 'Where?' Question

It is useful at this point to reflect on our last three sections before moving on to the last three. I have chosen to use Kipling's six honest serving men as my framework for understanding and comparing leadership approaches.

The question of 'who leaders are' is much rooted in history and narratives supported by a range of differing traits, whereas what leaders do is closely aligned to behaviours and leadership style. The question of '*where?*' often looks at the 'position' of the leader within the organization. This assumes a formal authority, whereas people without authority often lead. An increasing recognition of networks provides a foundation for more dispersed leadership.

The links between the 'who' of leadership and the 'where' have been closely associated throughout the history of leadership. At a time of crisis, followers often look to positional leaders and evaluate their behaviour 'based on whether they should be believed' (Allen, 2004:65). The role of positional leadership is thus critical to the reputation of the organization. Positional leadership is also associated with power, legitimacy, and authenticity. I will discuss the importance of authenticity in the next chapter, but suffice to say at this juncture that the authenticity of a leader will be determined by the leader's propensity for either selfless or selfish motivations.

Power, as we know all too well, can be misused. There is a wealth of literature on the concept of power, which I do not intend to repeat here. However, Lord Acton summed up the dangers well:[10]

Power tends to corrupt and absolute power corrupts absolutely. Great men are almost always bad men, even when they exercise influence and not authority: still more when you superadd the tendency or the certainty of corruption by authority. (Acton et al., 1907)

---

[10]Letter to Mandell Creighton (5 April 1887), published in *Historical Essays and Studies*, by John Emerich Edward Dalberg-Acton (1907), edited by John Neville Figgis and Reginald Vere Laurence, Appendix, p. 504.

Having power is the ability to influence outcomes and achieve goals, outside your realm of direct control, but not necessarily through your own efforts, whereas legitimacy (traditionally assigned to the legitimate descent of a ruler to rule) concerns the extent to which a leader's right to lead is accepted by the majority based on a principle, rule, or lawfulness. However, power without recourse or constructive debate can result in the sort of corruption that Lord Acton referred to. This is not just limited to the turn of the nineteenth and twentieth centuries but has also been evident in many of the 'leadership scandals' that have been exposed in our contemporary world, such as Enron, world.com and Mid Staffordshire Foundation Trust (three examples that I will refer to in support of what I will describe as the 'dark side of leadership').

It is often considered that it is the 'position' of the leader within the organization that gives the 'authority' of leadership (Grint, 2005). However, leadership can be either formal or informal, or undertaken 'with' or 'without' authority (Heifetz, 1994).

Fifth, the 'How?' Question

As we have reviewed, studies in relation to leadership have traditionally focused on the relationship between the leader and the follower. Contemporary leadership studies need a more empirical approach in looking at how leaders fulfil their roles. The book describes leadership as a shared and distributed process; intelligent leadership is the key to that process. Understanding leadership in this way is a relatively recent approach and, as Pearce and Conger describe it, our understanding 'of the dynamics and opportunities for shared leadership remains quite primitive' (Pearce and Conger, 2003:2). Heifetz (1994) argued that it is within the process of leadership that its effective evaluation can take place. Leading in a complex world requires both shared and distributed leadership, and intelligent leadership sits at the heart of this (Brookes, 2011). The two terms are often used interchangeably; however, my view is that the two terms are distinct. Shared leadership is described as:

> A dynamic, interactive influence process among individuals and groups for which the objective is to lead one another to the achievement of group or organizational goals or both. (Pearce and Conger, 2003:1)

Distributed leadership is described as a collective and emergent process, which is contextually situated (Carroll et al., 2008). In a review of the literature it is difficult to find a clear distinction between 'shared' and 'distributed' leadership. My argument is that there is a distinction if we consider that collective leadership extends beyond the traditional intra-organizational networks and takes account of the wider networks that exist beyond the organization. Collective leadership in this sense is becoming more widely accepted (Brookes, 2011) and it is where leadership becomes the property of a community rather than an individual (Grint, 2005). Collective leadership – through networks – is focused on shared beliefs, values, and identities (Western, 2007). I consider this more in depth in the following two chapters.

Viewing leadership as a process holds promise. In particular, by engaging with wider stakeholders a number of benefits emerge. First and foremost is that a leadership 'community' can mitigate the flaws of individual leaders (the 'who'), the way in which they lead (the 'what'), and the limitations of an individual leader's position (the 'where'). It can also take account of the best time to intervene (the 'when') and in defining the steps that need to be taken (the 'how'). Pearce and Conger's work in relation to shared leadership has emerged as an important contribution to the leadership debate, and I agree with their contention that demands on leaders have changed as a result of how the performance, which is the subject of leadership, has changed. Particular leadership skills include creativity and problem-solving based on enhanced cross-organizational dialogue, including learning conversations. At the core is the acceptance of relational processes, as there is nothing that a leader or group of leaders does that does not involve relationships in one form or another. There is an emerging leadership research approach that focuses on relational leadership (Uhl-Bien, 2006). This approach argues that, while leadership writing has focused on the traditional meaning of relationship, new approaches view the term relational as describing something quite different for leadership: A 'view of leadership and organisation as human social constructions that emanate from the rich connections and interdependencies of organisations and their members' (ibid:655). This is akin to the view adopted in this book of relationships within the role of leaders.

This collective approach to leadership is not easy, as the later discussion will illustrate. Business and public service is not undertaken between companies, but between people. There is a need to address competing values, and it remains a huge challenge to get over what can be described as the 'WIFM' factor (what's-in-it-for-me). In such cases:

> [W]hether people are open enough to say it or not, every one of us in every relationship or interaction is focused on a single question: 'What's in it for me?' (Bonfante, 2011:83)

Sixth, the 'Why' Question

Finally, the emphasis of other theories aligns to the question, **'why'** do leaders lead? A straightforward explanation is one that suggests aims of inspiring, motivating, or stimulating others to achieve a given end (Bass et al., 2008). Contemporary theory talks about transforming individual efforts towards a shared vision.

We briefly return to James McGregor Burns's work, which is consistently identified with what is now commonly described as transformational leadership. Burns described transformational leadership as occurring when 'one or more persons *engage* with others in such a way that leaders and followers raise one another to higher levels of motivation and morality' (Burns, 1978:20) within the context of a 'higher purpose'. In asking the 'why?' question, this is important. Transformational leadership is distinguished from transactional leadership and is widely considered as a new paradigm for the study of leadership. Research indicates that a transformational culture is more successful than a transactional one when measured in terms of organizational vision, information sharing, quality assurance, customer satisfaction, and working with others (Avolio and Bass, 1994).

However, a review of the literature invariably finds references to leadership once again linked to the traits of individual leaders (for instance, with an emphasis on charisma and inspiration rather than integrity and consistency), and, further, that most studies were US-based and focused on 'distant' leadership, generally ignoring the impact of 'nearby' leadership (Alimo-Metcalfe and Alban-Metcalfe, 2005:32). I cannot stress the importance of this point in preparing our discussion for the remainder of this book in exploring the benefits of collective leadership as a form of leading through 360° intelligent networks, knowledge, and skills. Respectively, Bass, Alimo-Metcalfe, and Alban-Metcalfe were influential in taking the discussion of leadership to the next level in understanding *why* leaders lead. In particular, the Transformational Leadership Questionnaire (TLQ) has been widely influential in supporting cultural-change programmes focusing specifically on the nature of 'nearby' leadership (day-to-day behaviours of line managers) and the importance of engagement.

Collective leadership focuses on the alignment between both 'distant' and 'nearby' leadership. As Bass and Avolio argued the 'founders' and successors' leadership shape a culture of shared values and assumptions, guided and constrained by their personal beliefs' (Bass and Avolio, 1994). Bass also said that what is needed is for leaders to promote and live a strong vision and sense of purpose, based on long-term commitments and mutual interests and developing shared norms that are adaptive, responding to changes in the external environment. In a later seminal and influential discussion, Kotter refers to the need to transform individual efforts towards a shared vision (Kotter, 2012).

CONCLUSION

This chapter has sought to describe thousands of years of thoughts on leadership in just seventeen and a half pages. We started our journey – quite naturally – at the beginning, briefly exploring both primate and early human development and thoughts on leadership from the silverbacks to the OWLs (Old World Leaders), the NWLs (New World Leaders), and, in setting the scene for the future of leadership thinking, the GWLs (Global World Leaders).

A common characteristic throughout our journey has been the obvious prominence given to the individual nature of leadership rather than its collective properties. I have already argued that leadership thinking (and later theories) are cumulative and that we should not discount the importance of the individual leader (as, in reality, we are all leaders in our own ways). What we do need to distinguish is the emphasis on values and behaviours. History and current examples show all too clearly the significant impact that the dark side of leadership can have when individuals follow our innate sense of selfishness. The next chapter will explore in some detail the importance of values in shaping behaviours and why and how shared values can actually mitigate the flaws of individual leaders through collective leadership.

In developing this sense of collectivity, we need to address the **'who'** and the **'what'** questions. It is by asking these questions that we can get an insight into the impact of individual leaders (whether positive or negative).

For example, Zimbardo sought to 'better understand the how and why of the physical and psychological abuses perpetrated on prisoners by American Military Police at the Abu Ghraib Prison in Iraq' (Zimbardo, 2007:18).

Grint has made a similar journey in considering the 'who', the 'what', the 'where', and finally, the 'how' of leadership. Respectively, Grint considers (Grint, 2005:4):

Leadership as person: is it who 'leaders' are that makes them leaders?
Leadership as result: is it what 'leaders' achieve that makes them leaders?
Leadership as position: is it where 'leaders' operate that makes them leaders?
Leadership as process: is it how leaders get things done that makes them leaders?

In addition, this chapter has argued that the 'when' and the 'why' questions are equally relevant in assisting leaders to understand when to lead, when to enable, and when to follow, and in providing a much stronger and more transparent understanding as to why particular leaders lead.

A reflective activity is provided below for this chapter.

Chapter 1 Activity

Think about a leader whom you have either admired or not admired.

Using the six honest serving fellows, what is it about that leader that either inspired you, or demotivated you?

Is it:

WHAT the leader did that made her a leader?

WHY the leader did what he did that made him a leader?

WHEN the leader led that made her a leader?

HOW the leader led that made him a leader?

WHERE the leader leads that made her the leader?

WHO the leader is that made him the leader?

1. Which was the key influencing factor, and was it positive or negative?
2. Why was this the case?
3. What would you want to either replicate or avoid?
4. Which of these attributes, if any, are the most important for good leadership?

2 Rediscovering the Lost Values of Leadership

A QUESTION OF VALUES OR VIRTUES?

During our journey through the ages in understanding leadership, our ancient forefathers were more focused on 'virtue' than 'values'. Plato considered the importance of virtue, believing it essential to the ultimate well-being of mankind, including skills, gifts, traits, etc. In a review of Plato's work, his scholar Socrates, and later Aristotle, had somewhat different views. Nevertheless, human beings are said – for the most part – to simply grow into a form of life with its pre-established standards and values (Frede, 2013).

We looked at Aristotle's notion of practical wisdom as an intellectual virtue and explored some of his other notions of virtues in the previous chapter. These included virtues such as happiness as a public good, self-mastery, friendship, and partnership. He also talked about impediments to virtue such as evils or vices (which he saw as the opposite of virtues), not being able to exercise self-restraint, and beast-like or brutish behaviour.

In more modern times, having 'virtues' has been replaced by having 'values'. However, the two terms are not synonymous. From the birth of religion, virtuosity was seen as a God-given gift or as a natural state of law. Well before the birth of religion as we know it today, Aristotle described the impediment of being beast-like or brutish. He saw this as the opposite of something more than human, being heroic or god-like. We can therefore infer that Aristotle also viewed virtue as something inherent in a divine being.

Aristotle argued that virtue is not only a matter of being the sort of person who performs right actions, but one who does so with the right motivation; this is what I define as the 'why' question of leadership. In the Nicomachean Ethics, Aristotle said that there is a need to achieve the right balance between action and feeling: 'at the right times, about the right things, towards the right people, for the right end, and in the right way, is the intermediate and best condition, and this is proper to virtue' (Aristotle et al., 2009:II.6). An interesting point made by Potter is that being trustworthy is best understood 'as a virtue of character, where both feeling and action over time are constitutive of the sort of person one is' (Potter, 2009:120).

Trustworthiness (at the individual level) has also been described as the precursor of confidence and legitimacy at the institutional level (Llewellyn et al., 2013).

Let us now consider what we mean by values. In literal terms, a value describes relative worth, usefulness, or importance of a person (or artefact). The perceptions of others are more important than that of our own. This was put well by Thomas Hobbes in 1651:

> [Let men] rate themselves at the highest Value they can; yet their true Value is no more than it is esteemed by others. (Hobbes and Smith 1909)

The term value can also be applied to the estimation or opinion of or liking for a person or thing, or an instance of this. A third meaning relates to the quality of a thing considered in respect of its ability to serve a specified purpose or cause a particular effect. Finally, when considered as a collective term, it relates to the principles or moral standards held by a person or social group: the generally accepted or personally held judgement of what is valuable and important in life. In this sense, the definition of 'values' moves from an individual/subjective meaning to one that is collective/objective.

Values (in the plural) reflect those things that are important to us; our motivations (whether individual or reflective) are driven by our values and our beliefs. It is these values and beliefs that will determine how we act towards others and how (and why) we make decisions. As with most things, values can be both positive and negative, driven by either a sense of the common good or from a sense of selfishness, greed, or blind ambition. It is here that we can get a sense of the difference between value and virtue. Value is a personal and subjective concept. Some of the most despotic leaders in the past had values but not necessarily the right ones! Conversely, virtue is more of an innate general inclination and can thus be described as objective.

Having mapped out an historical perspective on the terms, from here on the book will consider values from a virtuous position! In other words, it is about values that support the collective and is thus about shared values.

SHARED VALUE

It has been argued that never before have the values of leadership been under so much scrutiny. This applies globally, as in the case of Enron and the banking crisis that led us all on the road to economic austerity measures. What values were driving these senior leaders? Was it to do with bottom line profit for the sake of shareholders rather than the greatest good for the greatest number in terms of social responsibility?

We know only too well that it is not just in the private sector that the values of our leaders have been brought into question. The introduction of what is called 'New Public Management' – some 30 years ago now – has left a lasting legacy for public services, and not one that has been wholly positive. Of course we want to know how well our organizations and leaders are doing, but not at the expense of the common good and the values that our society holds dear. We can only make inroads to creating a desired culture if we work together in identifying our own values, understanding the differences and gaps and then develop a sense of shared values in defining a vision and mission that will create the form of leadership that our society both demands and deserves.

'Values' in the plural is used most often in an organizational context to refer to organizations' institutional standards of behaviour. This is helpful as we start to consider the development of 'shared values' – something that we explore in Part II of the book. The concept of values extends beyond just one organization. We must therefore consider personal values, organizations' values, and those of society.

I had an interesting discussion with a colleague when I described the title of this chapter as he remarked, 'Are there any leadership values to rediscover or do we have to create them?' This is an interesting point and one that is worth exploring. We could, of course, return to the classics, but having discussed these in the previous chapter, I would prefer to acknowledge the clear link between values and that described by our ancient forefathers as virtues, but bring it more into the (relatively) 'modern world'. By this, I mean the period in which we moved from the Enlightenment to modernity from the late 1700s through to the mid 1950s.

CHARTING THE COURSE OF LEADERSHIP VALUES

The period of the Enlightenment brought a number of key values to the fore from a range of philosophers and reformers whose work is still widely used and quoted today. These included tolerance, reason, democratic argument, progress, and the drive for social betterment as cornerstones of society, although it has recently been argued that these values are in danger of being lost (Hutton, 2012).

An interesting perspective is given on the virtues underpinning the signing of the declaration of Independence in the US by Benjamin Franklin. He argued that only a virtuous people are capable of freedom and that, as nations become corrupt and vicious, he further said that they have more need for masters (Lynch, 2010). This quotation can be interpreted in different ways and some common principles can be drawn from it:

- People need to respect each other.
- Trust can be given to those who act virtuously and intentionally do no harm to each other.
- When people become more selfish, greedy, or focused on themselves, more restrictions may be necessary through law.
- Corruption requires *more* masters to create freedom for society as a whole.

Why were the founding fathers so successful in creating what is arguably today the world's strongest nation, particularly as history shows that there were huge differences of opinion and conflict between them?

Although heavily reliant on the French in their war of independence against Britain, the Founding Fathers limited constitutional governance, unlike the French Revolution which sought a new order for all things. Keenly aware of the abuses of power elsewhere (notably in Britain), the Founding Fathers initiated clearly defined limits on the federal constitution. There was also the need to allow for creativity and innovation to flourish based on a strong ethic of personal responsibility among the citizens of the new USA. Influenced strongly by free market theorist Adam Smith, the Founding Fathers knew that government should not overtly interfere with the natural creativity and innovation of the American people. Finally, they laid the foundations for traditional American values and recognized that a free society would not be achieved if the passion and pride of the American people were restrained. These traditional values were rooted in religious virtues.

Returning to the question of why the Founding Fathers were so successful, it has been argued that they acted as a team and, at different times, when individual skills, knowledge, and expertise were required, those with the appropriate qualities stepped forward. They then stepped back again when a different set of qualities were required. In an interesting review of the leadership principles employed by the Founding Fathers, it was said that their story is one of 'unselfish, genuine leadership' and that this was their legacy (Phillips, 1997a:13).

Interestingly, Kenneth and William Hopper provide a fascinating insight in relation to the way in which a managerial culture which can be traced back over the course of the last three centuries turned the 13 American colonies into the nation that it is today. They argue that this can be traced back to the values and virtues of the first wave of European immigrants: the Puritans. However, they also warn that the core values of the 'great engine companies' are being eroded in favour of profit and a shift towards generic conceptions of leadership in which MBAs float from business to business (Hopper and Hopper, 2009). For the Hoppers, this trend – beginning in the 1950s and 1960s – is putting its commercial and economic success at risk and having a significant impact on the specialist knowledge of particular industries.

The position described by Hopper and Hopper was indicative of the pursuit of efficiency that had resulted from the popularity of scientific management. Ironically, it was in the 1950s that the notion of 'values' was discussed within the management and leadership literature. Philip Selznick in his seminal work 'Leadership in Administration' (1957) described the leader as 'an agent of institutionalization, offering a guiding hand to a process that would otherwise occur more haphazardly, more readily subject to the accidents of circumstance and history' (1957:27).

Philip Selznick was an early proponent of values. Throughout his work (Selznick, 1957) Selznick extolled the importance of institutional leaders setting a clear sense of values to be achieved (as opposed to the pursuit of organizational achievement, in resources, stability, or reputation) as the criteria of success. He also delineated between the institutional leader and the interpersonal leader. The latter, Selznick argued, contributes mainly to the efficiency of the enterprise, whereas the institutional leader is 'primarily an expert in the promotion and protection of values'.

Although articulated over half a century ago, Selznick's views still have merit in understanding and shaping the role of leaders as we move towards the middle of the second decade of the millennium, and mapping his thoughts – alongside the challenges of twenty-first century leadership challenges – is helpful.

The concept of 'statesmanship' was central to his argument but moving beyond its traditional provenance, namely that of political statesmanship. Common to all forms of statesmanship is the need to reconcile idealism with expediency, and freedom with the organization. The world of leaders was even then characterized by powerful agencies, which operated on their own initiative and were largely self-governing but becoming increasingly public in nature, in what we would describe today as the 'wicked issues' of society.

Although central to Selznick's argument, some have suggested that the term of institutional leadership was not really explored further within his work and offer some further insight (including those of Selznick himself) as to why he did not pull his moral punches.[1] This included the strong links (at that time) with the founding fathers of the USA and the question of scientific management which was still prominent at the time that he was writing. It is quite interesting that the debates between Selznick and his contemporaries were similar to those in the modern world in relation to the debate concerning competitive and collaborative advantage and – within the public sector – the private sector inspired focus on 'new public management' in the delivery of public services. As Heclo argues (Heclo, 2002:300), statesmanship was a term that had acquired several layers of meaning by the middle of the twentieth century. Selznick fought against the tendency for short-sighted technique to triumph over larger purpose, and efficient organizational management over true institutional leadership.

Selznick was writing at the time of scientific management (which had led to many of the ills that Selznick described) and the increasing interest in the development of a theory of organization; you may recall, from the previous chapter, the increasing attention of contingency theory on the organization, rather than the individual, during this period. The focus was on administrative efficiency. Selznick asked – quite prophetically – whether this preoccupation with administrative efficiency gets in the way of what really matters for institutional leaders. He sought to answer this question by focusing on the nature of critical decisions and of institutional leadership.

Issues of efficiency lose force as one ascends the echelons of administration. Mechanical metaphors such as that of the organization viewed as a smooth running machine are unlikely to represent the image at the top of the pyramid. Again writing at the time of the emerging human relations approach (such as that of John Watson, also reviewed in the previous chapter) – at the more senior level of leadership – Selznick saw a need to look beyond personal relations to the larger patterns of institutional development. He saw the problem as that of linking the larger view to the more limited one, to see how institutional change is produced by, and in turn shapes, the interaction of individuals in day-to-day situations. The closer we get to the areas of far-reaching decisions, the greater is the need for this deeper and more comprehensive understanding of social organization.

Selznick's articulation of the need for leadership involved giving direction by virtue of long-term objectives, creating a sense of mission and purpose, and infusing groups with values. He argued:

---

[1] Robert A. Kagan, Martin Krygier, and Kenneth I. Winston (2002), *Legality and community: on the intellectual legacy of Philip Selznick*, Roman and Littlefield, Maryland, USA.

> The art of the creative leader is the art of institution building, the reworking of human and technological materials to fashion an organization that embodies new and enduring values. (1957:152)

An institutional leader is more concerned with governance than management, and Selznick did forewarn of the possibility of some institutional leaders becoming too influential and powerful (leading to what is described in this book and elsewhere as the 'dark side of leadership'). It has been said that this distinction is critical to Selznick's argument.

Selznick argues that a responsible leader 'steers a course between utopianism and opportunism' (1957:149). The statesman always puts the interests of the institution above his own interests and the interests of particular groups. But the point is that leadership – statesmanship – is about ensuring longevity, which rests on the infusion and perpetuation of institutional values.

GIVING A GUIDING HAND: WHAT ARE THE INSTITUTIONAL VALUES THAT SELZNICK ADMIRED?

It is actually quite difficult to specifically identify the values that Selznick admired, and it is quite possible that this was not his aim. I have followed in the footsteps of many in analysing Selznick's work. I believe that we can speculate with some confidence how his thoughts translate into the values that organizations would still find worthy today, and we begin with looking at how Selznick saw values determining the mission and its underlying purpose. In the next section, I want to explore what these values could represent and also draw on other classics in the area of leadership (Collins and Porras, 1994) and (Heifetz, 1994; Heifetz et al., 2009; Heifetz and Linsky, 2002) in relation to what companies are 'built to last' and the principles and values of 'adaptive leadership', respectively.

Values to Vision

We can draw on three key steps from Selznick. The first step is to define the institutional mission; the second is the institutional embodiment of purpose; and the third is about defending institutional integrity.

In relation to the first step, he asks; 'how may immediate practical goals be joined to ultimate values?' (Selznick, 1957: 66).

His advice is worth quoting in full:

> The aims of large organizations are often very broad. A certain vagueness must be accepted because it is difficult to foresee whether more specific goals will be realistic or wise. This situation presents the leader with one of his most difficult but indispensable tasks. He must specify and recast the general aims of his organization so as to adapt to them, without serious corruption, to the requirements of institutional survival. This is what we mean by the definition of institutional mission and role. (1957:69)

The second step concerns the institutional embodiment of purpose, which 'is shaping the character of the organization, sensitizing it to ways of thinking and responding' (ibid:63). This purpose is fulfilled by creating and maintaining a social structure that embodies key institutional values based on the building of an institutional core, creating and reinforcing a set of beliefs and ensuring participation of all members in the decision-making process.

The final step relates to the 'defense of institutional integrity'. Selznick explains the meaning and importance of institutional integrity. He suggests that it is the responsibility of the leader as statesman to protect the 'institution's distinctive values, competence and role' (ibid:119). Selznick contends that an institution's integrity is vulnerable to corruption when its values are 'tenuous or insecure' (p.120).

Understanding the past as part of the mission setting process is important. In particular, Selznick points to certain problems that often characterize the phases of an organization's life history. This included the selection of a social base, closely related to the definition of mission, including the selection of a 'clientele, target, allies, or other segment of the environment to which operations will be oriented' (ibid:95). Building the institutional core represents a second challenge that calls for the members of the core group to mature in the role and indoctrinate newcomers to generate a shared general perspective.

Selznick also tells us that 'Even in business, where self-definition may seem less important than in political and other community enterprises, there is a need to build a self-conscious group that fully understands the "kind of company this is"' (ibid:97). Collins and Porras suggest that the right question to ask (in responding to a changing world) is 'What do we stand for and why do we exist?' (1994:xiv) and that a visionary company distinguishes their timeless core values and enduring purpose from operating practices and business strategies.

In the foreword to the paperback edition of their bestselling book Collins and Porras (Collins and Porras, 1994) said:

> We've met executives from all over the world who aspire to create something bigger and more lasting than themselves – an ongoing institution rooted in a set of timeless core values, that exists for a purpose beyond just making money, and that stands the test of time by virtue of the ability to continually renew itself from within.

The core function of their book is to understand the core values and core purposes that together define the core ideology:

Core ideology = Core values and purpose.

Core Values: The organisation's essential and enduring tenets – a small set of general guiding principles not to be confused with specific cultural or operating practices; not to be compromised for financial gain or short-term expediency.

Purpose: The organisation's fundamental reasons for existence beyond just making money – a perpetual guiding star on the horizon; not to be confused with specific goals or business strategies. (Collins and Porras 1994:73)

Societal Values Outlook

Social values, Selznick argued, are 'objects of desire that are capable of sustaining group identity' and 'this includes any set of goals or standards that can form the basis of shared perspectives and group feeling' (ibid:108). However, he goes on to argue that the maintenance of social values depends on the autonomy of elites (or professional groupings). Some of the barriers to this include the need to focus on the short-run benefits for large numbers, particularly political agencies that can take this sense of autonomy away from the elites. The elites tend to lose their 'exclusiveness' that insulates them from day-to-day pressures, which permit new ideas and skills to mature (i.e. innovation). Following up on this in a later work, Selznick emphasized that even more traditional business corporations have a 'moral responsibility' to attend to societal values (Selznick, 1992:349). The aim of leadership for Heifetz is also in creating socially desirable outcomes (Heifetz, 1994).

Collins and Porras (1994:71) tell us 'visionary companies attain more consistent alignment with a core ideology – in such aspects as goals, strategy, tactics, and organisation design – than the comparison companies'.

Multiple Levels of Leadership

One of the key tasks of professional associations and a host of other devices used for self-insulation by groups in society that wish to protect and promote a particular set of values is in ensuring the alignment between value maintenance and the autonomy of elites. It is interesting that Selznick does not use the term 'partnership' at all, although at different points in his work he does refer to the particular difficulties of sustaining shared values within work-based and military alliances.

Adaptive Institution

First, an institution is an adaptive and responsive organism as opposed to an organization, which portrays a sense of 'a lean, no-nonsense system of consciously coordinated activities' (ibid:5). An emphasis on defining values and purpose does not imply that technical imperatives can be ignored. However, an over-reliance on technological perspectives leads to the utopian view, which – Selznick argues – becomes the victim of opportunism as only a partial view is ever considered. This is very close to the argument professed some years later by Ronald Heifetz (Heifetz, 1994) who distinguished between technical and adaptive problems and where leadership is required in tackling the latter. We will explore this further in the following chapter, but suffice to say that adaptation is one such collective value.

Problem Focus

Selznick favoured where the problem led rather than where the discipline dictated (Krygier, 2012:278). While he emphasized the distinction between the technical and the institutional, Selznick recognized that the two systems are deeply intertwined and exist in continual tension with each other. Technical means have implications for values, and values depend on 'mundane administrative arrange-ments' in order to be maintained (Krygier, 2012:84–5; Selznick, 1957:141). 'Institutions embody values,' Selznick wrote, 'but they can do so only as operative systems or going concerns. The trouble is that what is good for the operative system does not necessarily serve the standards or ideals the institution is supposed to uphold' (Selznick, 1957:244). It has also been suggested that Selznick's writings on leadership serve as a pragmatic guide for how leaders can guard against the tendency to lose sight of institutional values and succumb to technical imperatives (Mesharov and Khurana, 2013:9).

Undertaking a problem-solving focus relies upon creativity, a point supported by Selznick, including strategic and tactical planning in analysing the environment (Vanebo and Murdock, 2012) and (justified) judicial reasoning (Krygier, 2012:124). Collins and Porras suggest that the first part of creating alignment is a creative process. This requires the introduction of new mechanisms, processes and strategies as a means of bringing the core values and purpose to life and to stimulate progress towards an envisioned future.

Systems

The question of systems featured early in Selznick's work. Referring back to what Chester L. Barnard called 'cooperative systems', he said that – for Americans – the lesson of cooperation has been hard to learn. Acknowledging that America had depended on other advantages (such as innovative talent and the sheer weight of resources) and within a context where low levels of efficiency could be accepted, he said 'That time is past, however, and in the absence of a supportive culture American management will depend more than ever on self-conscious application – and patient testing – of organizational theories' (Selznick, 1957). A further problem that organizations face when building an institutional core is that of formalization of procedures. This, Selznick argued, limits the open-endedness of organizations thus reflecting more of a technical rather than an adaptive challenge. Historical sensitivity is an important element of leading change if one is to move to the future and deliver the mission that has been developed. Collins and Porras suggest that alignment between systems and structures is an important characteristic of vision-ary companies.

Structures

As part of building the institutional core, Selznick reminds us that 'As always, the "openness" of decision-making calls for leadership, in this case to build a social structure that will induce a spontaneous regularity of response' (ibid:96). In the case of a technical challenge, he argues that leadership is more readily dispensable. The more fully developed its social structure, the more will the organization become valued for itself, not as a tool but as an institutional fulfilment of group integrity and aspiration.

Selznick argues that institutionalization is a process and that the degree of institutionalization depends on how much leeway there is for personal and group interaction. The more precise an organization's goals, and the more specialized and technical its operations, the less opportunity there will be for social forces to affect its development.

We earlier discussed the need for alignment, the first step of which is a creative process. The second part outlined by Collins and Porras is an analytic process. This requires a disciplined analysis of the organization, which includes its processes, structures, and strategies that will help in identifying those aspects of the organization that are misaligned and which promote behaviour inconsistent with the core ideology or progress. I discuss this in detail in Part III.

Skills

This was a gap for Selznick, who believed that the preoccupation with administrative efficiency led to what he described as the 'knottiest and most significant' problem of leadership in large organizations. He asks whether we are truly getting at the basics of the experience of institutional leaders: the improvement of self-knowledge. This he saw as key to the development of leaders and an increase in their leadership competency. Management of efficiency lies with subordinate units and it is at this level, Selznick argues, that scientific techniques of observation and experiment are likely to be the most successful (recall that he was writing at a time that Fredrick Winslow Taylor's scientific management was a dominant method of studying organizations and efficiency). This does not apply at the higher levels of leadership when he again refers to the metaphor of an organization as a 'smooth running machine' (p.27) as unhelpful. This results in a trained incapacity to observe the critical elements of organizational leadership, which includes the decision-making processes. Interestingly, in his analysis of the potential causes for this, one that he points to is what he describes as coolness undoubtedly stemming from reaction to change and the threats against vested interests. This brings us close to the notion of the self*ish* leader. Heifetz says that if leadership is to become more socially oriented, old patterns of relationship, balances of power, and customary operating procedures may be threatened and old skills may be rendered useless.

Behaviours

In considering the skills gap, Selznick also said that no social process could be understood other than the way in which it is located in the behaviour of individuals. In his view, there is a need to link the bigger picture (what he describes as the larger view) to the activity on the ground (the more limited view). In the practice of leadership, Heifetz had much to say here with his notion of moving between the 'balcony' and the 'dance floor', which I also return to at a later stage.

Behaviours are also impacted by the wider organization. Collins and Porras say that the second part of alignment is an analytic process. This requires a disciplined analysis of the organizations. They highlight how an organization's processes, structures, and strategies should uncover misalignments that promote behaviour that is inconsistent with the core ideology of the organization or impedes its progress.

I want to conclude this section with Selznick's main argument of his essay, which he says is quite simply stated as:

The executive becomes a statesman as he makes the transition from administrative management to institutional leadership.

This requires a balance between the reassessment of a leader's own tasks and the need of the enterprise. It is marked by:

- A concern for the evolution of the organization as a whole.
- Its changing aims and capabilities.

The key message of this book, I hope equally stated, is that it is the collective values and behaviours of leaders that will both determine the appropriateness of the vision, purpose, and goals and how these are going to be achieved. We will consider this further before we move on to the outline of systems thinking, but from a nontraditional perspective, in the final chapter of Part I.

PURSUING COLLECTIVE VALUES

Social Value

In this final section I want to bring the discussion of values up-to-date and to suggest that the time may now be right to pursue collective values. Before doing so I ask for your indulgence as I again paint a brief historical account of the notion of social value, which I argue acts as a foundation for the consideration of leading in the public interest and in understanding this as an objective rather than subjective measure. Although social value is taken to be more relevant to the leadership of public services, I also argue that it is of equal relevance to the private sector in what is becoming popularly referred to as 'shared value'.

As with the earlier historical accounts of organizations generally and leadership values specifically, social value as a concept appears to have first come to prominence as the developing world was coming to terms with the onset of modernization through the industrial revolution and the rise of communism. Writing in 1908, Joseph Schumpeter referred to it as a 'modern' as opposed to 'classical' concept but that the founders of 'modern' theory rarely spoke of social as opposed to individual value, although in 1908 he argued that leaders of economic thought generally approved the term (Schumpeter, 1908).

'Social value' suggests that it is society – and not the individual – which sets a value on things, although we must of course acknowledge that society comprises individuals and, as we know, individual values are more subjective. The key test – particularly within the context of mass media in contemporary society – is how to capture the collective spirit of social value because, in general terms, society does not meet to find out the wants of the community. A more recent means of both identifying and responding to social needs is through the concept of social entrepreneurialism that spans both the private and public sectors and, with the exponential increase in social media, the growing interest in crowdsourcing; but, more of this in Part III!

In a review of prominent literature (including Schumpeter) the Emerson et.al. point to the work and correspondence of Gregory Dess (1998), who suggested that social entrepreneurs play the role of change agents in the social sector, by:

- Adopting a mission to create and sustain social value (not just private value).
- Recognizing and relentlessly pursuing new opportunities to serve that mission.
- Engaging in a process of continuous innovation, adaptation, and learning.
- Acting boldly without being limited by resources currently in hand.
- Exhibiting a heightened sense of accountability to the constituencies served and for the outcomes created. (Emerson et. al, 2001)

As the crisis of leadership continues to dominate much of the discussion in today's world while the economic environment challenges leaders, private sector commentators are expressing similar views; in fact, Porter and Kramer tell us that a focus on shared value is the only way in which business can rebuild its legitimacy which they describe as having 'fallen to levels not seen in recent history' (Porter and Kramer, 2011:4). Although there has been a push by many companies to demonstrate social responsibility, the authors argue that this is at the periphery rather than the core of business and that the concept of shared values 'recognises that societal needs, not just conventional economic needs, define markets' (ibid:5). This represents a significantly new challenge for private sector companies and an opportunity for leading in the public interest.

The public and third sectors are also being encouraged to work towards the creation of social value. The Public Services (Social Value) Act 2012[2] requires public authorities to take into account the wider social and environmental value when they choose suppliers and to put a value on the knowledge, connections, and expertise of community and social enterprises. At the time of writing, the introduction of the Social Value Act provides some promise that citizenship will be at the heart of this legislative provision. It provides a statutory requirement for public authorities to have regard to economic, social, and environmental well-being in connection with public services contracts and for connected purposes. In particular, Section 1(6) of the Act says that when considering how proposals to be procured might improve the economic, social, and environmental well-being, the authority must consider only matters that are relevant to what is proposed to be procured and in doing so the extent to which it is proportionate in all the circumstances to take those matters into account. Although the Act does not give preference to social enterprises and charities, it must take into account the views of potential users, suppliers, and other stakeholders before commencing the procurement process. However, one of its weaknesses is that there is not an absolute power to consult, and social value can still be relegated to a position below that of cost considerations.

---

[2]Published by HMSO on 12 March 2012.

Public Value

Public value appears to be a wider framework for considering the outcomes of leading in the public interest, and I will argue that social value is one of three values that underpin the overarching public value framework.

There are three key elements to the concept of public value (Moore, 1995). The first is what is described as social goals, the second relates to the way in which those goals are secured through organizational capability, and the third relies upon this delivery building both trust and legitimacy. This is illustrated in Figure 2.1.

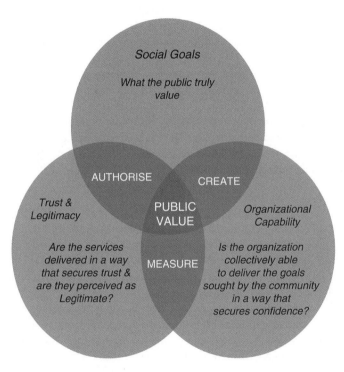

Figure 2.1 *Public value framework*

It will be apparent that the concept thus seeks to incorporate and integrate into public management aspects of performance that may be harder to measure. This includes those that deliver a social, economic, or political value that is not always immediately quantifiable through other means. It also aims to identify and measure how services are currently delivering added value, how this might be improved, and the potential obstacles to improvement by engaging users, citizens, public managers, and stakeholder organizations in an iterative process. This provides an opportunity to incorporate citizen, user, and stakeholder needs and visions through participation and engagement in a dialogue with public managers alongside the interest of the latter in efficiency, economy, and effectiveness.

A Framework for Collective Values

I have already suggested that social value is one of three wider values inherent within the concept of public value. The other two – to be discussed shortly – are those of economic and political value.

In support of this view, some argue that public value addresses issues such as legitimacy and support, as well as such factors as social capital, advocacy, client services, and channels for self-expression (such as volunteerism, board participation and other forms of engagement) (Emerson et al., 2000). While social value (and frameworks to assess the social return of investment) focuses primarily upon understanding socio-economic value, the authors refer to Moore's work, which is nevertheless considered to be complimentary.

Social value, when integrated with economic and political value, thus comprises public value.

As we explored earlier, there are three key elements to the concept of public value (Moore, 1995); social goals, the way in which those goals are secured through organizational capability, and delivery that builds both trust and legitimacy. It will be apparent that the concept thus seeks to incorporate and integrate into public management aspects of performance that may be harder to measure. This includes those that deliver a social, economic, or political value that is not always immediately quantifiable through other means.

Economic Value

Emerson et al. (2000:173) argue that economic value is created 'by taking a resource or set of inputs, providing additional inputs or processes that increase the value of those inputs, and thereby generate a product or service that has greater market value at the next level of the value chain'. They tell us that examples of economic value creation may be seen in the activities of most for-profit corporations, whether small business, regional, or global. Measures of economic value creation have been refined over centuries, resulting in a host of econometrics, including return on investment, debt/equity ratios, price/earnings, and numerous others. These measures form the basis for analysing most economic activity in the world.

Social Value

Social value is created when resources, inputs, processes, or policies are combined to generate improvements in the lives of individuals or society as a whole. It is in this arena that most non-profit organizations justify their existence, and unfortunately it is at this level that one has the most difficulty measuring the true value created. Examples of social value creation may include such 'products' as cultural arts performances, the pleasure of enjoying a hike in the woods, or the benefit of living in a more just society. Emerson et al. quote J. Gregory Dees who says that social value is 'about inclusion and access. It is about respect and the openness of institutions. It is about history, knowledge, a sense of heritage and cultural identity. Its value is not reducible to economic or socio-economic terms.'

Political Value

This is the least understood of the three public values. As has recently been argued, politicians fulfil a different role to those of organizational or institutional actors. Within a democracy, political value also has importance. Moore argues strongly for political management in mitigating the various wants and needs within the resources available and in securing delivery that is perceived as legitimate and trusted by the public. Public value (Figure 2.2) then can be illustrated as follows:

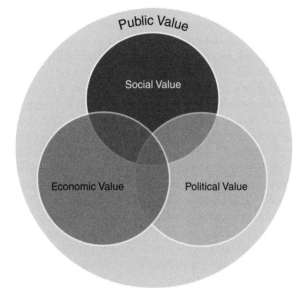

Figure 2.2 *Elements of public value*

REDISCOVERING LOST PUBLIC VALUES: A QUESTION OF PRINCIPLES

We began this chapter by asking whether we need to rediscover the lost values of leadership or whether we need to create them within the context of leadership in the twenty-first century. We considered this proposition by exploring three further substantial questions.

First, we asked whether it is possible to understand the meaning of value within the context of leadership generally and collective leadership specifically.

Second, we asked to what extent values were implicit in leaders through the ages, mapping some of the historical literature along the way. We briefly looked at our ancient forefathers, reformers during the age of Enlightenment, and the Founding Fathers of the United States and then, finally, from the 1950s through to the turn of the millennium, based on the work of Selznick and others.

Third, we sought to identify the tensions that are inherent for leaders in trying to balance competing values ranging from individual to shared values in seeking to lead in the public interest and examined some of the classical work in supporting this assessment.

The combination of these questions and the responses that we considered have illustrated that there are clearly some values of leadership that appear to have been lost over time. We looked at the early pre-religious thoughts on virtues from Platonic and Aristotelian perspectives and then aligned these thoughts on virtues with the more modern concept of 'values'. In considering the importance of values, we saw more emphasis on values rather than virtues.

In further exploring the values-based challenges presented to leaders, we can point to Selznick, Heifetz, and Collins and Porras in understanding that different leadership problems will result in different approaches and outcomes dependent upon either the individual or shared values that are at play. All these authors identify the close relationship between values and the core purpose of the business, institute, or enterprise and how this core purpose determines the way in which either those who work within or those who engage with the institutions will shape their practice. Institutional integrity, core purpose, and societal outcomes appear to be inextricably linked. Ultimately, skills and behaviours will be influenced by the way in which the core purpose is underpinned by core values and the extent to which the processes, structures, and systems support these values. We also considered the difference, but close connection between, shared and public value and concluded that the latter encompassed the former in equal measure with economic and political value.

A common denominator that was inherent in our discussion was the importance of principles, whether through virtue – represented by principles of morality, which could be argued is a given – or values, which are subjective and can change.

I conclude that the use of the term principles holds promise in helping leaders to understand the association between values (as a personal and subjective concept) and virtues (as a collective and objective term) and that principles (as with ancient conceptions of virtues) is a given, and one that refers directly to given facts or laws (such as gravity) which are immutable. This leads to the basis of the next chapter where I explore briefly the importance of understanding knowledge, research, and reality before moving on to outline the collective leadership framework that the remainder of this book concentrates on, taking us from principle to public value through effective leadership practice.

A reflective activity is provided below for this chapter.

Chapter 2 Activity	

Values and Virtue	Aristotle said that there is a need to achieve the right balance between action and feeling:
	
	'[A]t the right times, about the right things, towards the right people, for the right end, and in the right way, is the intermediate and best condition, and this is proper to virtue.'
	
	Think of a leadership example that involved both 'feeling' and 'action'.
	
	What was it about this example that involved:
	
	FEELING:
	
	ACTION:
	
	In your reflective journal, make a note of:
	
	  i. Was it the 'right time' to employ this leadership?
	  ii. Did if focus on the 'right things'?
	  iii. Was it aimed at the 'right people'?
	  iv. For the 'right end'?
	  v. In the 'right way'?

3 Understanding Knowledge, Realism, and Research and Its Impact on the Practice of Leaders

THE GRATUITOUS GREMLINS

Things or facts exist. We know this. However, do we *really* know it or is it merely a perception? More worryingly, do those who want us to perceive it in a particular way construct our knowledge and thus render it as a self-fulfilling fact or prophecy? This is an interesting way to consider how research underpins the practice of anything. For the purposes of this chapter, we will stay with leadership!

The existence of things or facts is the study of ontology; the study of our knowledge of these things or facts is called epistemology, and the theories underpinning both can be *among other things* either realist or idealist. Both philosophies accept existence, but each differs in terms of how this knowledge is gained or perceived. Ultimately, the way that we seek to build knowledge is determined by how we go about it, and this is the role of methodology, which is important if we are serious about evidence-based practice. What does the evidence say? Why does the evidence (or the evidence-bearer) say this? When does this evidence apply and in which circumstances? How does the evidence manifest itself and how is it applied? From where does it originate and, last (but certainly not least), whose evidence is it?

On the surface, the existence of things is straightforward; they either exist, or they don't, right? However, under the surface lurk some gratuitous gremlins! Certainly free and readily available, sometimes done without good reason, and often granted without claim or merit and perhaps habitually used by those who are embodiments of mischance in many of our worldly activities. Language is powerful, and this is most certainly the case with leadership. What people say is not necessarily what they mean or, more importantly, representing what the reality is. The language of leadership is replete with such utterings!

My intention is not to subject the reader to a wealth of philosophical and methodological underpinnings. Many other texts, over many hundreds of years, have done this. What I do intend to do is to give you a glimpse of my own philosophical and methodological premises if only to give some confidence that I have traversed this long and winding road. In the true spirit of collegiality, I will leave it to other researchers and philosophers to critique this approach in more appropriate media and will keep my focus firmly on the ground in aligning this to practice of leadership. However, first, I turn to a brief philosophical and theoretical underpinning.

Knowledge is the faculty of understanding or knowing, represented by intelligence or intellect. It is about having a clear and certain perception of fact or truth. Critical realism is a way of understanding the nature of both natural and human social sciences (Benton, 2004). It is one version of realism, which views the objects of scientific knowledge as existing and acting independently of our beliefs about them. The term 'critical' represents an orientation to existing social forms through normative (standards-based) analysis. Critical realists distinguish between independently existing real beings, relations and processes, and socially constructed theoretical frameworks and knowledge claims. Critical realism tends to reject the experimental approach to research, which favours the isolation of causal mechanisms from other external influences through closed systems. Critical realists argue that scientific knowledge exists within open systems in which mechanisms interact, sometimes in unseen ways and often as the result of human interaction. More importantly, they continually morph.

There are areas of disagreement among critical realists, although a common theme is that of a strong acceptance of the distinction between social structures and human agency. It represents either a vicious or a virtuous cycle (whichever way one views this) in which agents produce, reproduce, and transform social structures through their activities. In turn, social structures both enable and constrain social action (Archer, 1995). In gist, critical realism argues that there is a reality that can be scientifically studied. However, the way that we view the world will differ and realities will differ dependent upon how we construct the social world and the way in which we respond in what has been called this time of 'late modernity', in which the concept of risk has become important (Beck, 1999). Reflexivity is defined as 'the regular exercise of the mental ability, shared by all normal people, to consider themselves in relation to their (social) contexts and vice versa' (Archer, 2012:1). At this point, it is important to distinguish reflexive from reflective, with the former associated with 'looking through the mirror', as opposed to the latter, which is merely studying its reflection. In particular, as Archer continues, there is an increasing imperative for reflexivity in which a new conjuncture between cultural (ideationally based) and structural (material) order shapes new situational contexts 'within which subjects find themselves and whose variety they have to confront in a novel manner'.

There is an important point to consider here in relation to leadership. The manner of responding to these new orders will differ dependent upon the 'place' in which each individual finds herself or himself. Some will respond with vigour, enthusiasm, and entrepreneurial spirit (as opposed to traditional, inward looking spirit) whereas others will merely struggle (at best) or yield to the more dysfunctional aspects of new order (at worst). Leaders need to understand this and more positivist approaches to research and evaluation are unlikely to be able to identify these emerging changes in contextual conditions. Leaders thus need to be reflexive and not just reflective. This concerns looking 'through the mirror' rather than just seeing its reflection. Society is in a continual state of flux and adaptation, and leaders lead in this context of morphogenesis. Individuals have to decide what they are going to do in these differing situations. There are pluses and minuses. Archer tells us that the positive face of the reflexive imperative is the 'opportunity for subjects to pursue what they care about most in the social order; in fact their personal concerns become their compasses. Its negative face is that subjects can design and follow courses of action that are inappropriate to realizing their prime social concerns and whose negative outcomes rebound upon them.' Archer's definition of reflexivity is helpful: 'the regular exercise of the mental ability, shared by all normal people, to consider themselves in relation to their (social) contexts and vice versa' (Archer, ibid:1). This involves both interpersonal and intra-subjective exchanges. As Archer suggests, these derive from the absence of social guidelines indicating what to do in novel situations.

Think of this in relation to leadership; individual leaders will experience both the positive and negative of opportunities on one hand and dysfunctional outcomes on the other. Those who are led will also experience this. Collective leadership concerns a collective compass in which the personal compasses, referred to by Archer, are taken into account by collective leaders.

Let us explore this more in practice. It is often 'leaders' who appoint new 'leaders'. Moreover, many 'leaders' will appoint in their own image, described as a social construction that does not necessarily tell us the type of leader required, thus reinforcing the notion of the 'who-question' of leadership. Individual bias will inevitably be constructivist. Realism thus requires a view of perceived reality within our social world to be informed by other scientific and non-scientific evidence in order that the overall body of knowledge is cumulative and ongoing.

In a practical sense, this brings us back to Kipling's six honest serving men (from now on referred to as fellows!) discussed in the previous chapter. One cannot just create a closed experimental system in which we look at the who-question. Trying to 'bottle' the leadership skills that exist in a particular individual, such as the classical efforts of Thomas Carlyle or the charismatic calling of a leader that you may have experienced, is not often going to be successful. First, that individual will have her or his view of the social reality of the leadership context and can easily shape and adapt that so-called social reality through her or his agency. Second, the what-question is not just about what a leader achieves, but, rather, what is important (and to whom); what is achieved may just be grounded in the wrong values, no matter how well articulated. Third, the where-question is not just about position or station; it is equally about 'place' as well as 'person' (in their wider sense). Fourth, the how-question extends beyond an examination of the activities of the individual agent; the focus should also be on the processes that underpin the *leadership* beyond individual agency. Fifth, the when-question is not just about the individual leader's notion of situation or contingency (which may also be a socially constructed reality) but is also about temporal factors, which, in many cases, will outlive the individual leader agent. Finally, we can look to the why-question. Arguably, it is a neglected area in the study of leadership but one which offers a real opportunity to get below the surface of the leadership debate and determine why different forms of leadership work in different ways, for different people, and at different times. Why are leaders motivated to lead (whether for selfish or selfless reasons) and why do others either co-produce that leadership or simply follow? It is about context and realism in its many forms and holds some promise in being able to unpack the black box of leadership within this complex social world of interacting contexts.

Having said that realism – in its widest sense – and, more specifically, critical realism, holds promise, there are too many forms of both to be so confident of this potential promise. In this sense, I am with Pawson in both acknowledging and critiquing the critical aspects of realism. Equally, I favour more of a focus on realist inquiry (Pawson, 2013), and the underpinning approach to realistic evaluation (Pawson and Tilley, 1997). A realist is a person who tends to regard things as they are, rather than how they can be imagined or desired to be, sometimes to the point of cynicism. Realism takes many forms, of which critical realism is one. Critical realism is a useful way of describing and analysing social complexity, such as that of public health interventions (Connelly, 2007). However, it is not – and never can be – the be-all-and-end-all of dealing with complexity. We need to understand the different approaches to realism, something that Pawson addresses reasonably well.

Complexity is the glue that appears to bind the different approaches reviewed by Pawson. He first explores the augmented trials perspective, which is considered to closely resemble randomized control trials but within a limited conceptualization of complexity. Second, a systems perspective encompasses a variety of approaches that seek to deal with complexity but is viewed to embellish rather than deal with the burden of complexity. The critical realist perspective represents Pawson's third comparison which he views as somewhat different to the former inasmuch as it represents a philosophical solution in which indisputable experiments are replaced by indisputable theories, but where critical realists – as it says on the tin – criticize ideas generated outside of the fold while generating pure schemes for understanding 'what exists'. Finally, and more positively, albeit cautiously, he reviews the pragmatist perspective, emanating from the labour of evaluation practitioners rather than an abstract, preconceived model of complexity. Although pragmatist approaches have a number of benefits, Pawson tells us that the main shortcoming of them is that solutions remain piecemeal and thus do not constitute an answer to the overall challenge of complexity.

It is the point that Pawson makes in arguing that practical significance is only revealed by explanation-building that leads me to suggest that realist inquiry is just as helpful in supporting the development of collective leadership as well as evaluating it. Pawson also tells us that – as part of explanation-building – 'one needs to superimpose the why question'. One further addition can be added to Pawon's reasoning; the concept of precessional effect (PE), defined as the effect of bodies in motion on other bodies in motion and *then* applying the all-important why-question. PE is more commonly known in natural science. The easiest example to explain is Mother Earth, which is in regular orbit around the sun, tilted at an angle of 90 degrees. It has followed this orbit for many millions of years and we can thus predict with almost absolute certainty that it will continue to orbit the sun on this axis once every 365 days. Put this into a laboratory setting and it will inevitably be proved beyond (almost) total doubt (and I would not wish to hazard a guess as to how many 9s appear after the decimal point of '99.'). Why do I say almost? Consider a rogue meteorite that is heading to earth and enters our atmosphere at anything between 25k and 160k miles per hour. Dependent upon the size of the meteorite, once it hits the earth, our planet is very likely to be knocked off its axis with catastrophic results. Physical science protects us to a degree in that an early warning is much more likely than it was at the time of the dinosaurs! This cosmic intervention is an example of a PE in the natural world.

I refer to PE further below and, in much more detail, in Chapter 6, but let us now consider this within the context of social science, and leadership more specifically. Fuller argued that PE is also a human response and, just as it would be easy to knock a spinning top off its axis by a slight touch of the finger, so it is easy for humans to knock social events off their axis. Reflect on your experience as a leader in a reflexive manner. Can you recall instances where you have been quite clear what you need to do to achieve a particular goal, only to have this changed by your boss who flies in (at the same relative speed as the rogue meteorite) and changes the direction by spinning you and others off your axis? I certainly can, and with alarming regularity. Now superimpose the why-question; what does it tell you? Was this sub-cosmic interjection (preferred to intervention) undertaken for purely selfless motives? Probably not!

I am confident that Pawson would agree with me in saying that PE is unlikely to emerge in a patterned way within a traditional experimental evaluation. This is one of the reasons why Pawson focuses just as much on inner workings of a programme rather than just its outcome patterns and why cumulative research is going to achieve these far more than single or minimal replications of evaluation efforts.

A Realist Manifesto for Leaders

I have outlined why a realist evaluation approach (Pawson and Tilley, 1997) was preferred, for the reasons explained well by Pawson in his further work on proposing a realist manifesto for scientific evaluation (Pawson, 2013). The approach still pursues the high scientific objectives of objectivity and generative causal explanation. Pawson also tells us that it emphasizes that evaluation research has 'a different cause from other social sciences, namely to have realistic ambitions to inform real-world policy and practice' (ibid:xix). Leadership is a social process and, as argued by Campbell (quoted in Pawson, ibid:10), objectivity derives from a social process rather than from the dependability of a single experimenter, sometimes resulting in conclusions that 'are not only wrong, but often wrong in socially destructive ways ... Qualitative knowledge is thus essential as a prerequisite foundation for quantification in any science.' Reason and cumulative testing are thus the hallmarks of realist evaluation and, from a critical perspective, as Campbell states 'organized distrust produces trustworthy reports'.

Realism starts from the premise that scientific inquiry extends beyond mere collation of precisely measured facts. Realism acknowledges complexity and, indeed, embraces it, but not from the naïve view that complexity can be removed altogether; complexity morphs, and one impact on the current complex situation will often result in creating another complex set of circumstances that need addressing. It still needs to be theory-driven but within this wider understanding and appreciation of the complexity. If leadership tasks are not complex, then – as is rather provocatively argued – surely it is a management task?

Patterns represent a key component of this book. Realism also acknowledges that our social world, just like the natural world, is patterned. While events can take place in regular sequences, the uniformities are discovered through identification and observation of the generative mechanism in much the same way as physical science. In social science, the generative mechanism is more about the why-question; why does a particular mechanism or series of mechanisms result in persuading change in terms of the outcomes within particular contexts? This takes a reflexive rather than a reflective approach. The individual leader may, therefore, respond to an event or challenge in a particular way, but what impact does this have in differing contexts? What impact did the earlier reflexive example have on your original goal?

I finish this section with a final nod in Pawson's direction. He said, 'In all cases, the outcome patterns come to be as they are because of the collective, constrained choices of all stakeholders' (ibid:18). Leaders produce outcome patterns, not all of which are positive outcomes. Apparently alcohol is good for helping to lift the veneer off wooden surfaces. Perhaps a more sober form of RE can help to lift the veneer off leadership and expose the gratuitous gremlins!

How Does This Work?

We return to the opening theme of this chapter concerning 'the knowledge of everything' and align this to realist inquiry. The study of existence (known as ontology) of the social world in critical realism is the relationship of person-to-person (agent-to-agent relationships) and agent-to-structure relationships. Structures are socially constituted institutions. Everything that we do in our work roles and in leading others involves a relationship; such actions are not reducible to experiments in the laboratory. This argument brings to the fore the importance of a conducive context (C) and its interactions with generative mechanisms (M) and the observable outcomes (O) (Pawson and Tilley, 1997). Pawson and Tilley describe these as context-mechanism-outcome (CMO) configurations. CMOs can be positive or negative (in terms of the mechanisms triggering the right outcomes within a conducive context or, conversely, the triggering of the mechanism which obstructs or hinders what it is that the social action is seeking to achieve).

From a theory of knowledge perspective (epistemology), it begins with a theory of causal explanation (why things happen) based on generative principles (why things keep happening). This, in turn, relates to the theory of existence (ontology), which suggests that regularities in the patterns of social activities (why things look the way that they look) are generated by underlying mechanisms (the devices, tools, or contrivances that may make those things happen or look the way that they do). People's reasoning (that can, of course, be socially constructed) and the resources available to them in a particular context often define the underlying mechanisms. Such mechanisms are also subject to precessional effects. As with natural effects (where objects are knocked off course from its axis), so the same can occur in the social world, where intended mechanisms are knocked off course by the intervention of a particular leader or group of leaders such as that of the brief example discussed earlier. We explore this further in later chapters; suffice to note at this stage that realism has the potential to look for such precessional effects and to determine whether the motives were selfless or selfish.

Returning to the research process, we can suppose that the task for researchers is to test theories of how particular outcomes are generated by the triggering of specific mechanisms within differing contexts. These CMO configurations thus view interventions as an attempt to identify 'what works for whom in what circumstances'. It could apply, for example, through marketing strategies, public policy programmes, or, indeed, business alliances, mergers, or acquisitions. What we will explore throughout the remainder of this book is how this applies in relation to the practice of leading in the public interest.

Pawson says that single instances (such as a laboratory experiment) are unlikely to provide the knowledge being sought. Research results thus accumulate over successive trials and other forms of empirical research. Returning to our leadership example, the precessional effects will differ in different circumstances and at different times and, particularly, by different people. We identify the key potential families (or typologies) of successful/non-successful CMOs. The overall benefit of this is that knowledge is generated through a teaching and learning process in which individual stakeholders' expertise is facilitated and marshalled by the researcher (Pawson, 2013), a further reason why RE is of equal utility in supporting the development of leaders.

Leadership follows similar arguments, which is why I have chosen realist inquiry. We begin with our initial theory of leadership (refer to the activity at the end of Chapter 1 – supported by the six honest serving men (fellows)). Classically, we have considered the 'whom' of leadership as the critical mechanism, as opposed to the collective. Your example may have shown that this form of leadership just keeps happening with alarming regularity; why is this? To use Oshry's analogy, why does noxious 'stuff' still keep raining down on the squeezed middle leaders? If the patterns emerging from this leadership continue to happen, what is it that makes this so? Reflexive thinking can help here. At a simplistic level, this may be due to the personal demeanour of the present incumbent of our 'whom' example through selfless or selfish reasoning or a combination of the resources available to that person. This may have worked in this particular context, particularly if the leadership challenges need this form of leadership in dealing with a leadership crisis that might just require a command-and-control form of leadership. It is unlikely to work in all circumstances and is likely to require different forms of leadership (a combination of what, who, where, how and when) but – at all times – supported by the important 'why' question and being critical in considering research findings.

DEVELOPING THE COLLECTIVE LEADERSHIP FRAMEWORK

Background

The research underpinning the collective leadership framework was grounded in the arguments presented in the preceding sections, informed also by my own experience of leading in different situations for over 30 years, supported by almost ten years of reflective and reflexive activity. The realistic evaluation methodology is undertaken within a case study strategy (Yin, 2009). In line with the principles of realistic evaluation there are three areas that I investigate in seeking to answer my overall research question, which the title of this book encapsulates: can collective leadership be selfless? My research question and aims were consistently applied throughout all of my research projects in relation to these three areas:

i. **Context:** This concerns the conditions that are needed for a measure or intervention to trigger mechanisms to produce particular outcome patterns.
ii. **Mechanism:** What is it about a measure or intervention, which may lead it to have a particular outcome in a given context?
iii. **Outcome patterns:** What are the practical effects produced by causal mechanisms being triggered in a given context? (Pawson and Tilley, 1997)

A realist inquiry – nested within a case study strategy – is entirely appropriate to a study of leadership actions (mechanisms) within differing conditions of leading in the public interest (context) and in determining the impact that these leadership actions have on improving service delivery or products (outcomes).

Realistic evaluation is a generative model of causality and holds that 'to infer a causal outcome (O) between two events (X and Y), one needs to understand the underlying mechanism (M) that connects between them and the context (C) in which the relationship occurs' (Pawson et al., 2005). It has an explanatory rather than a judgemental focus and develops a multilevel approach to CMO configurations, thus lending itself well to a case study strategy. It has proved to be entirely appropriate to this evaluation of leading in the public interest. The focus of the basic evaluative question changes from 'what works?' to 'what is it about this programme or intervention that works for whom in what circumstances and why?' (ibid:22).

By comparing case studies, a rich picture emerged of the research *contexts* of leadership across a range of organizations where different *mechanisms* (leadership actions, behaviours, and relationships) generated different *outcomes* (in terms of programmes and resulting patterns of behaviour as assessed by personal impact and product) and why. Pawson and Tilley (1997:217) argue:

> Programs cannot be understood as undifferentiated wholes, as 'things' with some simple brute facticity. They fire multiple mechanisms having different subjects in different situations and so produce multiple outcomes.

As Tilley argues, the evaluation of leadership is unlike the evaluation of programmes (which can in fact be seen as a public leadership outcome), but I argue that the realistic evaluation framework is of equal relevance to the study and practice of leadership as it is to the programmes that such leadership generates (Tilley, 2010), and it thus defines the resultant collective leadership framework.

During my research projects I used a range of different methods. This included analysis of strategic documents. This is important, as it is often through the written word that the leadership's intentions are communicated and, as argued earlier with our gremlins and further below, where they can be manipulated! I also conducted interviews and focus groups across a range of organizations and at different levels. This gave me the opportunity to explore the alignment between the 'written word' and its impact in practice. I was keen to determine whether the 'theories in use' mirrored the 'espoused theories'.[1]

The first research commenced in 1994 within an action setting. The research sought to identify the conditions that helped or hindered the development of community based policing. At this particular time, I was a Divisional Commander of a large policing division that was home to first, one of the most affluent areas in England, second, one of the most deprived, and third, one of the most ethnically diverse communities. This provided an excellent, but challenging, foundation for examining differing contextual conditions and to explore the mechanisms that were likely to lead to or defeat the intended outcomes focused around community safety. During this time, I was developing a unique approach to community based policing that brought community representatives into the decision-making process in deciding locally based policing priorities and engaging the community in the coproduction of community safety. In 1997, I was appointed to lead the force's response to the (then) impending implementation of the Crime and Disorder Act 1997 which, for the first time, inter alia, was to give statutory backing to consultation between the police and the community.

In the following three years, I worked with Sir Keith Povey (then Her Majesty's Regional Inspector of Constabulary) and, on his behalf, led the inspections of regional police forces, which included their visions, strategy, and practice in relation to crime reduction and community safety. At this point – and with his full support – I had started my PhD study, which provided rich access to strategic document analysis and a wide range of interviews and focus group opportunities. In the final year (1999/2000), again on behalf of HM Inspector, I led a cross cutting national inspection of community safety following the introduction of the Crime and Disorder Act. The rich data that was obtained from all of these reviews and studies formed the basis of my final doctoral thesis (Brookes, 2004). Leadership emerged early during these realistic studies as a major (and overarching) critical success factor (Brookes, 2006).

In August 2000, immediately following the publication of our national review of community safety (HMSO, 2000), I was appointed as a founding Home Office Regional Director (HORD) in one of ten Government Offices for the Regions, with responsibility for working with the five chief constables, 40 local authority chief executives, and a range of other public, private, and voluntary organizations in

---

[1]For a further insight in relation to 'theories in use' and 'espoused theories' see Chris Argyris and Donald A. Schon, *Organisational Learning and Culture Change: A Theory of Action Perspective* (Reading, MA: Addison-Wesley, 1978).

relation to crime and community safety specifically. In the final 18 months, I had additional responsibility for overseeing cross cutting government policy ranging from crime and community safety to education and economic enterprise in one of the counties within the region. These responsibilities gave me a unique insight as a key participant in relation to the strengths and weaknesses and opportunities and threats of collective leadership across widely diverse organizations and institutions, including the for-profit sector.

I will use a number of examples from both my operational and strategic leadership roles, and these various studies, to exemplify some of the points that I make in Parts II and III. The year 2006 represented a significant watershed for me as I 'retired' from my 30-year police and civil service career and took up an appointment at the University of Manchester at the Business School. I was able to build on my career as a senior practitioner and take the opportunity to further research leadership in the public interest. My research, teaching, and engagement during these ensuing years will also form the basis of my arguments in Parts II and III.

Shortly after my appointment as an academic (or, what I prefer to refer to as a 'pracacademic'[2]) in 2006, funding was secured from the Economic and Social Research Council (ESRC) for a seminar series entitled the 'public leadership challenge'. Five seminars were held between 2006 and 2008, and they involved a range of senior practitioners, senior academics, and policymakers engaging in dialogue about the leadership challenges in the public sector ranging from services as diverse as defence through to health, local government, and policing. A final report was published in 2008 including the first iteration of the 20P collective leadership model that follows and the publication of the 'New Public Leadership Challenge' (Brookes and Grint, 2010).

During this time, I also undertook detailed research with all local authority areas and a range of partner organizations in the North West of England. The focus of the research was to determine how leaders worked together in support of local area agreements[3] through local strategic partnerships (LSPs) (Brookes, 2010). I was again very keen to examine the alignment between the 'written word' and 'practice' in considering the differences, if any, between the espoused theories and the theories in use. A number of peers from across the authorities assessed strategic documents in the first stage of the research. These were then analysed and followed by a series of interviews with director and policy leads in five areas. Focus groups with senior officers from other public services in the same local authority areas supported this. The interviews with directors and policy officers focused on the extent to which the Local Authority plays its part in leading improvement. Focus groups took place with senior representatives of partner organizations. They represented their organizations on the LSP (or similar named body). Some also led action groups (for example, health and well-being, education, community safety, and diversity). Further research was also undertaken in 2008 and 2009 in a large metropolitan

---

[2] With due acknowledgement to Professor John Benington, who used this term during the ESRC seminar series meetings (referring to the dual emphasis of senior practitioner and academic).

[3] The primary objective of a local area agreement is defined as that of delivering 'genuinely sustainable communities through better outcomes for local people' (Brookes, 2010:308).

police force in relation to the focus given to what is described as the outcome of effective public leadership, namely public value (Brookes and Fahy, 2013), and is described in the previous chapter.

As a consequence of the ongoing research for almost 20 years, alongside my practical experience as a leader, I have continually developed and modified a frame of reference for collective leadership. I have also developed supporting collective leadership inventories, which were applied across a number of organizations (including the private sector) in support of executive education programmes. It was applied at different levels of leadership but with an overriding focus on the strengths and weaknesses of collective leadership. The framework is based on an understanding of the language of leadership, which is informed by my experience of leadership, the literature reviewed in the earlier chapters, and the research described above. The next chapter focuses on this framework and then applies this to its practical application in Parts II and III.

A reflective activity is provided below for this chapter.

Chapter 3 Activity		
Knowledge	Go back to the example that you used in the previous chapter's activity and describe briefly (in the box) what this involved and the knowledge that it sought or seeks to generate.	
Realist	Can you say that you know the answers to the following questions concerning this example:	
	In relation to this project, I know:	
	WHAT conditions currently exist in relation to the wider operating environment	
	WHY we are doing it and the choices that have informed it	
	WHEN achievements have already been made, when they will be made and the long term benefits	
	HOW the project is going to be achieved	
	WHERE it will be achieved and at what levels	
	WHO will lead the project and who is involved in delivering it	
Impact	Given the intended outcome of this project, to what extent do you think that the complexity of its context has been identified and appropriate responses designed? Taking account of the seven contextual factors, provide your reflection.	• PESTLE • Principles • Purpose • Processes • Problem Profiles • People • Power • Partnership • Phronosis

4 Understanding the Language and Reality of Leadership

FRAMEWORKS AND MODELS: HOW DO WE MAKE SENSE OF THEM ALL?

The point of introducing this somewhat cryptic question here is to consider the difference between a framework and a model. This is absolutely fundamental in understanding how my argument progresses for the remainder of this book. I am not going to bog you down in minute detail on theoretical propositions and debate, but it is important to leave you – as the reader – in no uncertain doubt as to the differences and how this was developed and refined by my research methodology, but from a practical rather than a theoretical perspective. The framework and model have been developed far more through my analysis and modelling than during the actual research itself, which has been an iterative and cumulative process. I describe this in more detail in the following chapter, but it is useful to begin with an accessible description of the differences between a framework and a model, which I summarize as follows:

- A framework is a way of representing the empirical relations between every aspect of inquiry when considering a scientific theory or research. It describes the general direction and the constraints of the theory or research and provides an explicit explanation why the research problem exists by highlighting how the variables relate to each other.
- A model is something used to represent or explain the operation and mechanism of something else. A conceptual model exists in one's mind and can often consist of symbolic representations through symbols or diagrams. A model is useful because it relies less on words and language (which can be either ambiguous or socially constructed) and is less reflective of the reality, and relies more on mechanisms and images. It assists in interpreting the phenomenon within its contextual setting (i.e. the framework) and can be more universally applied within different organizational and cultural settings.

Thus, the framework gives the overall structure of my research whereas the model explores my specific methodology and its application in practice. The framework enables me to paint a rich picture of the contextual conditions for collective leadership and focuses on interconnectedness, dependency, and the structure of my research and its findings based on my research aims, the literature, data collection, and analysis. It is in this respect that I use the Realist Evaluation contextual dimensions. It provides an overview of the leadership concepts and the practice of leadership that I have seen during the course of my work and my research.

The 20P framework originated from a final report published through the Economic and Social Research Council (Brookes, 2008) and the publication of the 'New Public Leadership Challenge' (Brookes and Grint, 2010). It built on this earlier framework and comprises three elements. The first element is that of 'context', which includes Ps 1 to 11. This begins with P.E.S.T.L.E (Political, Economic, Social, Technical, Legal, and Ethical) external conditions in addition to Principles (2), Paradigm (3), Phronesis (or practical wisdom)(4), and Places (5). Internal contexts are represented by Purpose (6), Problem Profile (7), Processes (8), People (9), Problem Solving (10), and, finally, Partnership (11).

Four further Ps represent the 'mechanisms', namely Policy (12), Practice (13), Pedagogy (14), and Problem Solving (15). The remaining five Ps are those that define the 'outcomes' of public leadership: Programmes (16), Personal Impact (17), Patterns (18), Product (19), and the key outcome that represents all is that of creating and demonstrating Public Value (20). Each of these will be discussed and illustrated further below. In support of this framework, I apply a theoretical concept of synergetics, which serves this purpose well. I explain this in the next chapter.

Having considered the contextual conditions through my conceptual framework for collective leadership, I then introduce a collective leadership model that equates to Realist Evaluations' mechanisms. You will recall from my earlier discussion that contexts are difficult to influence, whereas mechanisms can have a direct influence on the prevailing contexts. Whereas the framework described below is explicit, my operational model (if I may call it this) existed in my mind's eye and the Collective Leadership Inventory (which has developed from this model) is its visible manifestation. In this sense, I call upon a further theoretical and practical concept, cybernetics, also discussed in the next chapter. This concept works well in helping to understand the underlying patterns of collective leadership, based on both qualitative and quantitative relationships between the contextual conditions and the mechanisms. The model thus brings the framework to life and is both testable and practical. I believe that part of the problem is that we have been trying to 'square the circle' of leadership which, as many eminent geometric and mathematic experts have told us, is impossible – hence its use as a means of indicating an impossible task. I have called on the wisdom of Bucky Fuller, who, in describing the importance of synergetics, prefers a triangle (or, to be more precise, a tetrahedron (which is a pyramid shape with four sides, including the base)). The strength of his work is his assumption that there is in nature a vectorial, or directionally oriented system of forces that provides maximum strength with minimum structures, something that I argue is closely akin to the notion of shared and distributed leadership.

Let me provide two examples to illustrate this:

i. We often refer to being 'weightless' in space. This is not the case, as it is the strength of the various 'forces' – working in synergy – that keeps an astronaut 'floating in space', and it is speed and the various forces that keep the astronaut (and his space station) in orbit.

ii. Fuller's expertise in both engineering and geometry resulted in his designing the geodesic dome. This is a spherical form in which lightweight triangular or polygonal facets consisting of either skeletal struts or flat planes, largely in tension, replaced the arch principle and distribute stresses within the structure itself. It was revolutionary.

So, what does all this have to do with leadership? This is a question that I am sure many of you will ask. I will explain this as succinctly as I can in the following chapter, but first I introduce the conceptual framework that consists of what I will hitherto describe as the context of leadership.

THE CONCEPTUAL CONTEXT OF LEADERSHIP: FROM PRINCIPLES TO PUBLIC VALUE

The Language of Leadership

One thing that has been quite clear to me for a number of years is that the meaning of 'leadership' is a very slippery eel! Just as you think you understand it, along comes another interpretation that deserves attention. During my research I have been compiling a leadership language inventory in much the same way, as I will later advocate a collective leadership inventory. I have a long-standing interest in etymology as a means of exploring the origins of words and the way in which their sense has been modified over time. The collective public leadership framework, although primarily developed through the research, is supported in all respects by an etymological analysis, using primarily the *Oxford English Dictionary*.[1] Unless otherwise stated, my definitions originate from this valuable source.

Language is important. Ludwig Wittgenstein is one of the foremost philosophers in relation to the meaning of language, which he saw as a communication tool that people should use to describe the world in words that make sense and which do not distort. Moreover, he argued that we should try and understand what is being said by reference to its context. There is a need to make connections, associations, and differentiations, not to manipulate or bend the picture to construct an ideology (Wittgenstein and Russell, 1922). Language is thus a social construction and should be considered as such.

---

[1] I have used the OED Online as it presents the complete *OED* in its most recent version. It is updated regularly and therefore a very informative source.

Understanding Context

In the introductory chapter I said that the word 'context' stems from the Latin word *contextus* which comprises the two words *con* ('together') and *texere* ('to weave'). It describes the circumstances that form the setting for an event (i.e. leadership), and helps understanding. In this sense, context is not something that is directly controllable but one that does have a clear impact on intentions.

The term context appears to have first entered the English language in a quotation from a manuscript circa 1425 in describing the construction of language; it appears to have originated from the historical chronicler Ranulph Higden who referred to the '*contexte historical*', thus, 'what went before'. Its material (or concrete – as opposed to abstract) literal meaning has been described as 'The whole structure of a connected passage regarded in its bearing upon any of the parts which constitute it; the parts which immediately precede or follow any particular passage or "text" and determine its meaning'. In its transferred sense, the term has been applied to 'the moral context of the day gone by', and the 'position of facts in the context of experience'. In other words, what a word means depends upon its connection in past experience with some other thing. Context-free is obviously the absence of context, although an interesting argument has been applied to this compound: 'Context-free measurement of symbolic forms which are instrumentally manipulated is apt to be misleading' (Pool, 1959). In a later work, it was argued that 'nothing is more often manipulated instrumentally than expressions of evaluation' (Pool and Etheredge, 1998). Context is thus important in understanding the intended meaning of writing and has been equally identified as important to an understanding of leadership. In relation to leadership, it can be argued that 'context' concerns the environment in which leadership occurs and how it is perceived. In other words, it concerns 'what goes before' or 'what exists'.

It is not simply good enough to identify the contexts. What is also needed is the ability to identify the contextual conditions that either help or hinder the development of public leadership through collective endeavours.

From Principles to Public Value

I will begin where I left off in Chapter 2 in further considering the important leadership components of value and principles, because all other components rest on these. I discussed the difficulty of distinguishing between virtues and values. In considering this distinction, we saw more emphasis on values rather than virtues and, further, that values bear a close relationship with the core purpose of the business, institute, or enterprise. In turn, the core purpose determines how leadership is practised. The common denominator is that of principles which also serve well as a modern understanding of virtues in the sense of it being a 'given' or 'the moral high ground'; values – as a collective term – relates to the principles or moral standards held by a person or group of people.

I use the term principles as a means of helping leaders to understand the link between values (as a personal and subjective concept) and virtues (as a collective and objective term). The leadership analysis – based on its language – thus begins with principles, which is the second P of the framework. As a given, principles are non-negotiable, as is the end result of those principles, that of creating public value (P20). This is illustrated in Figure 4.1, in which the importance of principles as a contextual given is highlighted alongside the physical (external) operating environment for public leaders, the first P, namely the political, economic, social, technical, legal, and ethical contextual conditions and the paradigmatic (internal) environment that determines 'how we do business here' (the third P). There is no direct influence over either the external physical conditions or the internal paradigmatic conditions, certainly in the short to medium term. The problem with acknowledging that we can all have an influence on these conditions in the long term is that external physical and internal paradigmatic conditions cannot be realistically changed except within the longer term (and, in this sense, we are talking about a period of between at least 15 and 30 years). This could take a generation. This raises the second difficulty; if we are innately selfish, as I argued in Chapter 1, then why should leaders take account of 15 to 30 years hence? This is a particular challenge in a democracy where the electoral cycle is no more than five years or in a commercial environment where the leadership challenge is about keeping the shareholders happy (and that invariably means short-term profits rather than longer-term shared value).

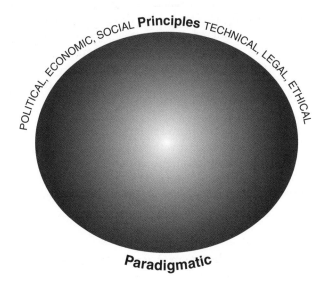

Figure 4.1 *External contexts of public leadership*

Stephen Covey described a similar scenario in relation to tackling what he called 'areas of concern': concerns that we have, including health, family, work-related problems, or even national or international problems or threats. This contrasts with 'circles of influence', which are concerns that we have but in which we can do something about, unlike wider areas of concern. Covey suggests that it requires a proactive approach, which he describes:

As human beings, we are responsible for our own lives. Our behaviour is a function of our decisions, not our conditions. We can subordinate feelings to values. We have the initiative and the responsibility to make things happen. (Covey, 1989:141)

This is contrasted with a reactive approach, in which people often neglect issues under their control and influence. In terms of leading in the public interest, I have argued for a coactive approach, a term that I first used during my PhD studies in the 1990s, based on work in relation to the professional development of community police officers (Oettmeier and Wycoff, 1997) and which I adapted to the leadership of community policing and defined as a strategy based on the police working cooperatively with other agencies to identify and address the conditions needed for improved community safety (Brookes, 2006). I argue that a coactive approach can be adopted as part of collective leadership in tackling some of the higher contextual concerns.

Everything in between the principles and paradigm of the internal context and the physical conditions of the external context and the public value outcomes is not a given and is subject at all times to the creativity and interpretation of all of us (as individuals) and – as I argue in the next chapter – can be either intentionally or unintentionally disrupted through a process that I describe as precessional effects. This is what Covey would refer to as a circle of influence. This can be considered as a way in which we practise as individual leaders and as a process (as a collective) representing the way in which the *ship* of leader*ship* is practised collaboratively. It is in this context that leaders can increase their circle of control and have an influence on the organizational and network context that presents itself; again, these influences can be either positive or negative.

These external (physical environment) and internal (principled and paradigmatic environment) 'given' contexts interact with the organizational and network 'non-given' contexts through the organization's or institute's core purpose, which is the fourth P and which describes the first of the internal contexts. First, a vision defines the differences between the 'what is' of these environments and the 'what ought to be'.

How Do We Differentiate between Organizational Vision, Mission, Purpose, Goals, and Objectives?

These words trip off the tongue so easily in organizational life, but are the words really saying what the leaders mean *to* say and, more importantly, do the leaders mean *what* they say? Unfortunately, the literature and practice of leadership/management and organizational discipline often uses terms in different ways. This is not much help! From this point on, it would be useful to think in terms of your own organizational or institutional context as we work through the detail. Let us begin with Activity 4.1 and consider the importance of purpose.

ACTIVITY 4.1: FIND OUT IF YOUR ORGANIZATION HAS AN ORGANIZATIONAL VISION. DOES IT RELATE TO THE FOLLOWING COMPONENTS OF A VISION?

A Purpose

Mission statement	
Goals	
Objectives	

If you work with other organizations through partnerships or alliances, repeat this activity.

A Partnership Purpose

Mission statement	
Goals	
Objectives	

If you couldn't find a vision statement or the components above, briefly write a vision that encapsulates your organization and then complete the activity above as you work through the next section.

So, let's begin from a vision!

As we move closer to the organization, a number of other contextual elements are present. In much the same way as principles and public value go hand-in-hand (as a given), so do the underlying values and the vision of the organization and its networks (less of a given!). The origin of the word 'vision' goes back to the earliest biblical times and, in modern parlance, still describes something that exists beyond physical sight, such as a dream, an appearance of a prophetic happening or character, or a revelation. A vision represents the ability to conceive what might be attempted or achieved. In other words, it concerns statesmanlike foresight in the way that Selznick suggested. A vision statement makes this 'desired future state' explicit. You can visualize the future and have a real sense and, in some cases, an image of what you see in the future, but you have yet to define it or indeed communicate it. The vision asks, 'what are the organization's strategic ambitions and aspirations and what should the future look like?' Similarly, values (which underpin the organization's vision) also asks the 'what' question: 'What does the organization see as important?' To what extent did your example vision statement reflect these characteristics, whether it exists within your organization or one that you have created?

Purpose

The role of the core purpose of the organization, as the fourth P, which interacts with the external context, is to take the 'what' questions further. The core purpose states the reason for which something is done and its intended effect and takes due account of the underpinning values and the overarching vision. It asks '*why*' does the organization exist and '*who*' will carry it out? *Purpose* thus has three levels:

- **Mission:** The way the vision is taken one step further by entrusting it to others as a mission. It provides a high-level statement of the 'how' question.
- **Goals:** A clear statement of intent in relation to future results or expectations in the short term. The goals ask, 'Where and when can we take steps to achieve the mission?'
- **Objectives:** Something that needs to be pursued to achieve the organization's goal.

The core purpose and its mission, goals, and objectives define the relationship between the vision and the underpinning values. This is illustrated in Figure 4.2.

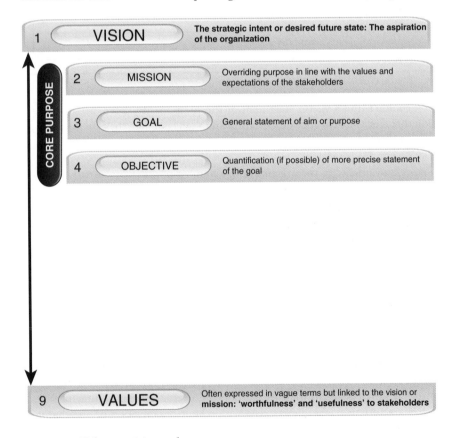

Figure 4.2 Values to vision and core purpose

A mission statement may be viewed as the commissioning of an undertaking to people who are destined to do this and who feel strongly about their aims and ambitions in life. A mission statement generally comprises three components:

- Who is the target client, customer, or community?
- What product or services are provided to the client, customer or community?
- Why would the clients, customers, or community choose your product or your service?

It is the first step in responding to the questions 'why we are doing what we are doing' and 'who will help us in bringing this about'. The leadership role here is in mobilizing others to line up behind the vision and to collectively take forward the mission to achieve it. The mission statement reveals the purpose, motives, and broad intention and provides the foundation for the organization to consider *how* it goes about achieving its vision. It starts to draw out the values of the organization, building on the values of those who work within or engage with the organization. It allows us to ask questions of the organization, such as 'is there a purpose?' and 'how does my role fit with this?'

If the purpose helps in defining 'why the organization exists' and 'who will help us in bringing this about', then the mission is about considering 'how we do it' at a higher macro level.

Processes

If *purpose* represents the first internal contextual condition (and acting as the conduit for aligning the organization to its external 'givens'), then the second internal contextual condition is about *processes*, the fifth P. A process describes a 'series of actions or steps taken in order to achieve a particular end'. This includes a series of changes, a systematic series of operations 'that are performed in order to produce something and a multitasking operating system'. In taking steps to achieve a particular end, then the core purpose should support the mission by stating goals.

The term 'goal' is often confused with the term 'objective' whereas it actually represents the cumulative result of a number of objectives. A goal describes a clear statement of intent in relation to future results or expectations and is a statement of direction primarily in the short term. Goal attainment is linked to activity whether it is at the societal or organizational level. Procedures for establishing goals and deciding priorities become institutionalized through a clear statement of intent. Talcott Parsons referred to the goal-directedness of action (Parsons, 1952) and we can thus see how the internal processes play a key role in translating the vision to action. Objectives align the goals to those who are likely to play a role in achieving them. The goal thus asks, '*Where* and *when* can we take steps to introduce our change' and the objective asks, '*What* do we have to do to achieve our goal?'

The aim of the vision, mission, and goals is to encourage the appropriate behaviours that reinforce the underpinning values. The core purpose determines the why, where, and when of the organization's aims. This is illustrated in Figure 4.3 and Table 4.1.

The terms, descriptions, explanations, and intelligent questions can be summarized:

VISION:	WHAT – are the organization's aspirations and ambitions?
Core Purpose:	WHY – does the organization exist?
	WHO – will carry it out?
Mission:	HOW – is the vision taken forward?
Goal:	WHERE and WHEN – do we need to action?
Objectives:	WHAT – do we have to do to achieve the goals?
VALUES:	WHAT – does the organization see as important?

Figure 4.3 *Values to vision questions*

Table 4.1 *Values to vision*

Term	Explanation	The intelligent questions
Vision statement		
The ideal desired future state. A vision of the strategic aspirations and ambitions your organization wants.	A vision is the ability to conceive what might be attempted or achieved. So a vision statement represents the organization's foresight.	**What** are the organization's strategic aspirations and ambitions and what should the future look like?
Core purpose		
The reason for which something is done and its intended effect. Purpose has three levels: Mission, Goals, and Objectives.	The role of the organization is to set out its purpose clearly and it is the role of the employees to serve this purpose.	**Why** does the organization exist and **who** will carry it out?
Mission		
The way the vision is taken one step further by entrusting it to others as a mission.	A mission mobilizes people in organizations by identifying and building on collective values. It reveals the purpose, values, and broad intention of an organization and tells us what is most important to us in our work. It draws out the values of the organization and builds on the values of staff and partners.	**How** does the organization go about achieving its vision?

Goal		
A clear statement of intent in relation to future results or expectations in the short term.	A goal is the cumulative intended result of a number of objectives.	**Where** and **when** can we take steps to change the world?
Objective	Objectives need to be **SMART.**	
Something that needs to be pursued to achieve the organization's goal.	*Specific*: be clear and unambiguous. *Measurable*: Measuring progress toward the attainment of the goal. *Achievable*: be realistic and attainable. *Relevant*: be objectives that matter to the team, department, and organization. *Time-bound*: have a deadline for completion.	**What** do we have to do to achieve our goal and by when?
Values		
The principles or moral standards of the organization which govern the behaviours and conduct of its staff.	The way that the organization, through the behaviours of its staff, goes about achieving its mission, purpose, goals, and objectives.	**What** does the organization see as important in terms of its impact?

Problem Profiles

The sixth P is that of the problem profile. The original meaning of a 'problem' can be traced back to the classical Latin *problema*, which is a question proposed for academic discussion and also the title of a work by Aristotle (second century AD). Its post-classical Latin meaning related to a puzzle or a riddle and, in ancient Greek, a question proposed for a solution. These meanings are now rare in contemporary language. In modern terms it can be considered as 'a difficult or demanding question; a matter or situation regarded as unwelcome, harmful, or wrong and needing to be overcome; a difficulty'.

The term 'profile' (as a noun) originated partly from the Italian term *profilare* meaning 'to draw in outline' (interestingly, either by spinning or threading) and partly from the French term *profiler* meaning to represent in profile. It also represents a summary description or set of salient characteristics, or an organization. A profile is a means to investigate or record the way a physical quality varies, a record or summary of data or, in technological terms, an analysis (through a profiler). One of the critical challenges for leaders is to identify 'patterns'. This will be discussed in detail in Parts II and III.

In the context of leadership, if we put the two terms together, 'problem profiles' underpin and inform the purpose. An intelligence-led approach to leadership provides the context for understanding the problems, the ongoing changes to the patterns, and the range of solutions. If a solution is already known, it is not necessarily a leadership problem. This is a point made by Grint (Grint, 2008b) who equates a 'puzzle' with a 'tame' problem whereas a wicked problem is (usually) unsolvable. A problem profile concerns the framing of the problem. If the problem is framed wrongly, then this is likely to lead to the wrong solution being chosen. A key aim of the problem profile is thus to frame the challenge that the organization or its networks are facing and, if it is framed correctly, then there is less opportunity for individual leaders to re-frame it.

People

The seventh P represents people. The term originates from Middle English through Anglo-Norman French from the original Latin term of *populace*, namely people in the plural and 'considered collectively'. Within a democracy, 'people' are described as the primary principals, and it is with people that agency exists. I have already made the point that there is nothing that we do within our workplace that does not involve relationships. This is the role of agency. In modern usage, the first and most obvious meaning of agency is 'a person or organization acting on behalf of another, or providing a particular service' or the process of so acting. However, the term originates from the classical Latin, *agent*, *agēns*, or *agere*, meaning to drive, lead, conduct, manage, perform, or do, and the post-classical Latin *agentia*. This translates in modern language to the second meaning, which is 'the ability or capacity to act or exert power through active working or operation by means of action or activity'.[2] It is thus an action or intervention that produces a particular effect.

There is often a debate in the social sciences in relation to the importance of either agency or structure in shaping human behaviours, which is important in relation to collective leadership behaviours. If agency concerns the capacity of individuals to act independently and to make their own choices, then structure is the recurrent patterned arrangements, which influence or limit the choices and opportunities available (Barker, 2012), often reflected through policy and processes. People, as with processes, are therefore part of the contextual conditions for collective leadership.

Power

Closely aligned to the context of people and, in particular, the meaning of agency is that of power, the eighth contextual 'P'. Many will have agency, but not power. If a person has power, then the ability to reconstruct both agency and structure is present. The literal definition of 'power' is considered to represent 'the ability or capacity to do something or act in a particular way; to direct or influence the behaviour of others or the course of events and – in terms of governance – is closely related to the notion of legitimacy'. Power will always have a role in determining the success or otherwise of leadership.

---

[2]'agency, n.' OED Online. Oxford University Press, June 2015. Web. 27 July 2015.

There are several different taxonomies of power with that of French and Raven's classifications of coercive, reward, legitimate, referent, expert, and informational power (French and Raven, 1959) representing an early (and influential) one; Mintzberg's five bases for power, namely resource, technical skill, body of knowledge, formal power, and access to those who possess it (Mintzberg, 1983) as a further development; and Hofstede, who considered power as a multidimensional concept that differs from culture to culture in terms of its 'power-distance' measured by means of the style and perceptions of decision-making by 'bosses' and the extent to which 'employees were afraid to disagree with their manager' (Hofstede, 1980:82).

The traditional notion of power is that relating to position or station, although there is now an increasing recognition that power (in directing or influencing the behaviour of others) can be both informal (and 'softly' applied) rather than formal (and 'directly' applied). The former term is preferred by Handy (Handy, 1993:125); he views it as a verb (in terms of influencing) rather than a noun, describing it as one that is 'elusive' in terms of operationalizing and measuring it: 'the focus should be on looking at power as a "bargaining relationship" over time within a framework of constraints which the actors cannot easily change' (Crozier, 1971:118).

Both forms of application have their advantages and disadvantages, with the 'soft' use of power generally more effective in collaborative arrangements in tackling the 'wicked' problems described earlier whereas the 'direct' use of power is often used in command and control situations, particularly where immediate and urgent action is needed.

Partnership

The ninth 'P' within the context of leadership is one that interacts with the (external) social environment in the same way that purpose interacts with the (external) physical environment: partnership. This is a relatively recent term and describes an association between two or more people as 'partners' or the state of being a partner. The third sector and community groups are increasingly recognized as a key element of partnership working as public leaders, although strategic alliances are an increasingly important element of commercial enterprises.

The development of partnerships is particularly important because it draws together both agency and structure and is where the 'battle for power' is often fought. The notion of corporatism (sometimes also known as corporativism) is the principle or practice of corporate action or organization, especially a corporative system. Corporatism is related to the sociological concept of structural functionalism (Adler, 1995) which, in turn, views society as a complex system whose parts work together to promote solidarity and stability (Macionis and Gerber, 2011). Corporatism is often viewed pejoratively, for example in terms of swamping individualism[3] or as a wedding of the public sector to the private sector, described quite starkly as a form of collectivism that is evil and in which public/private partnerships are seen to represent unholy alliances (Rhyne, 2014).

---

[3]1890 *Advance (Chicago)* 13 November, from 'corporatism, n.' *OED Online*. Oxford University Press, June 2014. Web. 24 August 2014.

The difficulty with this debate comes back to the construction and self-construction of meaning. I have previously said that collective leadership is a means of defining a shared purpose and made the following distinction:

> Collectivity is preferred to collectivism as the former infers a quality or condition rather than the latter which denotes a movement (Allen, 2004). Collectivism was described by Bevir et al. (2003:8) as 'irresistible yet unwelcome' in the late nineteenth century. The two terms do share common features (the public good, social justice and the idea of positive government) but the role of individual agency remains prominent within a collective response, mitigated by responsible followers exercising constructive dissent (Grint, 2005) within the context of collective leadership. (Brookes, 2011:177)

Phronesis (Practical Wisdom)

There are two remaining contextual Ps that I believe are the most important of the 11 contextual Ps because they draw all the others together; the first is 'phronesis' (practical wisdom), discussed here, and the second is 'place', discussed below.

As discussed in Chapter 2, phronesis originates from Aristotle's ancient Greek, φρόνησις (meaning thought, sense, judgement, practical wisdom, and prudence) and φρονεῖν (to think, to have understanding, to be wise). In modern language it is taken to represent practical understanding, wisdom, prudence, sound judgement. Aristotle has been quoted as saying that 'all the virtues were forms of phronesis' (Ferguson, 1958:iii. 30). Interestingly, and in direct comparison, Parel (1992:157) suggests that Machiavelli's political philosophy 'rejects the relevance of the traditional notion of moral virtue and phronesis'.

Phronesis – as practical wisdom – thus represents a key element of the collective leadership framework through the development and application of intelligent leadership. This will be discussed in both Parts II and III in relation to intelligent leadership. One of the critical aims of practical wisdom is to not only understand the presenting context but to also identify and understand the dynamic interrelationships between the contexts. An important aspect of our definition of context is the notion of 'weaving together'.

Place

The term 'place' is generally taken to mean an open space or senses relating to a particular part or region of space or a physical locality. This is the eleventh P. It has an interesting etymology. Its Old English and post-classical Latin origins certainly reflect space and locality but, from the end of the thirteenth century, were viewed as a position, employment, or office. It is also contrasted with time: a sense of space as a 'continuous or unbounded extension in every direction' or 'the amount or quantity of space actually occupied by a person or thing; the position of a body in space, or in relation to other bodies; situation, location'.

In terms of 'place' as a contextual condition for collective leadership, you can change your place (or space) but it is not necessary to change your purpose. As

Shakespeare[4] argued: 'Though you change your place, you neede not change your Trade.'

For the purposes of this book, Heifetz's conception of the holding environment (discussed earlier) – whether virtual or physical – will be considered as both an absolute and a relative contextual condition (place) of collective leadership, alongside its wider meaning of 'place'. What this helps us to do is to understand that we can 'create space' for collective leadership as a holding environment in determining how we align both the external and internal contextual conditions in the process of developing appropriate mechanisms that will lead to the public value outcomes that leading in the public interest requires. Phronesis (practical wisdom) and place can thus be viewed as mediating contextual conditions and will form the basis of my argument in Part III in arguing for intelligent leadership as the practical application of collective leadership.

A reflective activity is provided below for this chapter.

Chapter 4 Activity	
A Purpose	
Mission Statement	
Goals	
Objectives	
If you work with other organizations through partnerships or alliances, repeat this activity.	
Partnership Purpose	
Mission Statement	
Goals	
Objectives	
Reflect on the Strengths and Gaps and insert your comments below:	
STRENGTHS	GAPS

---

[4] *a*1616 Shakespeare *Measure for Measure* (1623) i. ii. 99 (from 'place, n.1.' OED Online. Oxford University Press, June 2014. Web. 25 August 2014).

5 From Vision to Delivery

CONTEXTUAL DYNAMICS OF COLLECTIVE LEADERSHIP

The analysis of the literature and the research findings offered an insight in relation to potential dynamic interrelationships between the internal contexts of collective leadership, as represented by the first 11 Ps of the Collective Leadership Framework discussed in the previous chapter. This highlighted the potential for identifying the various contextual dimensions that assist in identifying appropriate values and behaviours of leaders and leadership with seven possible combinations shown in Table 5.1. Each of the seven combinations is described in terms of the leadership behaviour that each contextual dimension seeks to influence and the wider leadership values that describe each such dimension in terms of its leadership outcome. I argue at the conclusion of this chapter that the collective leadership values encompass all elements of the foregoing described research framework and that it provides a unique opportunity to evaluate the effectiveness of collective leadership as well as the outcomes that the vision and mission seek to achieve. Each of the seven contextual domains comprises three dimensions of which both the first and the third act as a link with, respectively, the preceding and the following domains. For example, the first domain (collective vision) comprises 'purpose', 'partnership', and 'problem' – with 'problem' acting as the link with the next domain (outcome focus), which comprises 'problem', 'purpose', and 'process', and so this pattern continues.

The leadership narrative thus starts and ends with purpose and progresses through a focus on the 'problem', the 'processes' in dealing with those problems, and the 'power' to deal with them (linked by the 'partnerships'), and finally through the development of people in supporting the purpose. The problem profile as a contextual link is evident at the beginning of the cycle in linking the purpose to other internal contexts, and similarly at the end of the cycle.

We can align these internal contexts to the external contexts, previously explored, in Figure 5.1.

Table 5.1 Leadership contexts, behaviours and values

Leadership Contextual Dimensions	Leadership Behavioural Elements	Collective Leadership Values
PURPOSE/ PARTNERSHIP/ **PROBLEM/**	This very much emphasizes the collective nature of the people through partnerships, within a sense of shared purpose in tackling wicked problems	**C**ollective Vision
PROBLEM/ PURPOSE/ **PROCESS/**	Developing a framework and culture that aligns the shared purpose to public value needs through realistic goals and objectives	**O**utcome Focus
PROCESS/ POWER/ **PARTNERSHIP/**	Sharing and distributing authority, capacity and capability to target time based goals within an environment of clarity and ownership across networks at all levels	**M**ulti Level Leadership
PARTNERSHIP/ PROCESS/ **PEOPLE/**	With particular reference to the sharing of information and resources this is viewed as the heart of network activity relying on trust and legitimacy in the delivery of publicly valued outcomes in a way that achieves mutual benefit	**P**artnership Working
PEOPLE/ PURPOSE/ **POWER/**	Together with adaptive approaches (below) this is considered to represent the 'tipping point' in turning vision and aspiration into outcomes and reality through tasking and coordination based on intelligent leadership	**A**ction Oriented and Adaptive
POWER/ PEOPLE/ **PROBLEM/**	Encouraging 'learning networks' that enable innovation and improvement within a framework of governance that enhances legitimacy across those networks	**S**ystems and Structures
PROBLEM/ PEOPLE/ **PURPOSE/**	Ensuring that domain knowledge and skills combine in creating the capacity and capability to improve through reflection and with demonstrable impact on problems underpinning the shared purpose	**S**kills and Behaviours

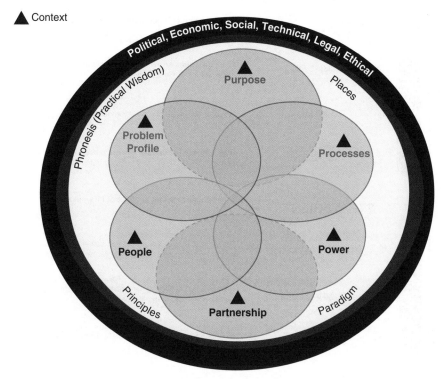

Figure 5.1 *Collective leadership framework: Internal and external contexts*

THE MECHANISMS OF LEADERSHIP: FROM POLICY TO PRACTICE

Understanding Mechanisms

The vision and values of leadership (which bring together the strategic intent of the organization and its underpinning principles and moral values) are shaped by the context, but both are supported by the organization's strategies in setting its long-term direction within the conditions defined by the internal and external drivers. In Covey's terms, we could thus describe the vision and values as setting out the high-level areas of concern that the leadership seeks to influence whereas the strategies are about increasing influence within those areas of concern and, moving beyond Covey's emphasis on proactive approaches, in encouraging a coactive response which is shaped and influenced by co-production and collective action. If the context is primarily focused on the core purpose (through its mission, goals, and objectives), the mechanisms concern the strategic activities (by virtue of its capability, business model, and control processes). This is illustrated in Figure 5.2.

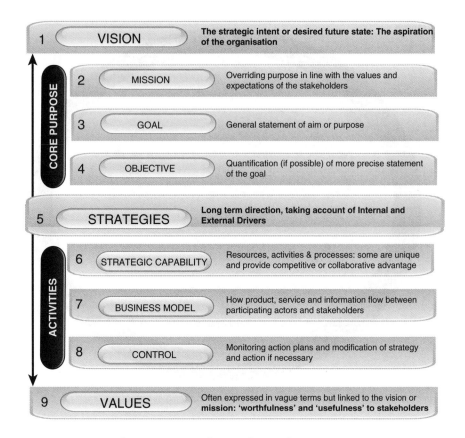

Figure 5.2 *From values to vision, with everything in-between*

Source: Johnson et al. (2011)

In this section, I explore the mechanisms that emerged from the research and illustrate how these mechanisms interact with the contextual conditions (based on what I describe as COMPASS 360° values) in seeking to achieve the high-level outcomes that the vision and values seek to aspire to. It is the mechanisms that act as 'triggers' to 'fire' particular actions that are aimed at achieving the outcomes within differing contextual conditions. In keeping with the theme of this book, I will explore the definitional and etymological background to the four Ps that represent the mechanisms.

I argued in the introductory chapter that the term mechanism is used in answer to 'how' questions, whereas context concerns drawing upon Kipling's remaining five honest serving fellows ('what, why, when, where, and who'). The term mechanism relates to the structure or operation of a machine or other complex system: a theory or approach relating to this or a process comparable to a machine. In more general usage, it relates to the interconnection of parts in any complex process, pattern, or arrangement through mutually adapted parts working together. Of particular relevance to the realistic evaluation approach is the description of a mechanism as part of a kinematic chain of which one link is fixed or stationary. It is the mechanisms that act as 'triggers' to 'fire' particular actions that are aimed at achieving the outcomes within differing contextual conditions. In this sense, one can consider the 'fixed' (or given) as the context with the mechanism representing the moving (non-given) actions including unconscious, structured sets of mental processes underlying a person's behaviour or responses and conscious actions taken as part of the overall strategy (both reflective and reflexive). In general usage, mechanisms are described as the means by which an effect or result is produced (representing 'outcomes' within a realistic evaluation framework).

Mechanisms refer specifically to what is done and how it is done. They focus on the behaviours and actions of individuals and the actions taken on behalf of organizations, thus representing both agency and structure. Mechanisms are aimed at ensuring that the desired outcomes are achieved within the given contexts.

Let us explore the four Ps that represent our mechanisms.

Policy

The first of the mechanisms, and our twelfth 'P' is that of policy. The provenance of the word dates from Middle English, derived from the Old French *policie* (civil administration), via Latin from Greek *politeia* (citizenship), from *politēs* (citizen), from *polis* (city). One can thus view this from the collective perspective. In modern usage it refers to a course or principle of action adopted or proposed. The policy mechanism is closely related to the overarching context of purpose and can be considered as the means by which the purpose is put into effect.

Given its original meaning in the sense of civil administration, and 'citizenship', a question to determine is whether this also applies to for-profit enterprises as well as not-for-profit and public institutions. Business is clearly affected by government policy (such as taxation, registration, regulation, etc.), but businesses also develop their own policies, which will have an impact on customers, clients, and the community. The scope within which decisions can be taken will be defined by business policies, defining the limits within which decisions can or cannot be made and setting out the business model to be pursued, and the acquisition of resources, including mergers, alliances, and take-overs.

The term policy should not be used in place of strategy because both differ, the former representing a blueprint and setting out roles, responsibilities, and procedures in accordance with the purpose whereas strategy is more to do with mobilizing others to achieve the purpose, for example through its mission statement.

Practice

Closely aligned to the 'P' of practice, policy often seeks to influence a particular pattern or a pattern of practice, and it is in this respect that I argue that strategy takes its place. The definition of practice relates to 'the actual application or use of an idea, belief, or method, as opposed to theories relating to it'.[1] It can also describe the customary, habitual, or expected procedure or way of doing of something, or

---

[1]'practice, n.' OED Online. Oxford University Press, June 2015. Web. 28 July 2015.

in the repeated exercise in or performance of an activity or skill so as to acquire or maintain proficiency in it.

Strategy and tactics thus represent the way in which practice is applied, and while both are considered an art, the original meaning of the two terms derives from the military stage (i.e. strategy as the art of a commander-in-chief, whereas tactics is the art of handling forces in battle or in the immediate presence of the enemy). However, the same sentiments can be applied within the art of collective leadership, in which the aim is to achieve goals that represent the public interest rather than success on the battlefield.

Problemitization

Policy and practice may together rely on the extent to which problem solving occurs, particularly in aligning practice with the contextual problem profiles that underpin the purpose of leadership, as described earlier.

The fourteenth 'P' thus defines problemitization as 'to make into or regard as a problem requiring a solution'. In relation to leadership and the role of leaders, we take into account the distinction between critical, tame, and wicked problems. A 'tame' problem is one in which there is a 'tried-and-tested' solution whereas a 'wicked' problem is one that does not. This is discussed in detail in Part III, as is the final mechanism, to which I now turn, that of pedagogy.

Pedagogy

Practice, based on appropriate problemitization, and theory go together in defining and supporting relationships within networked environments. If one does not inform the other, a complete cycle of leadership development cannot take place. Invariably, these two ideas occupy attention in separate directions.

Throughout my research, one of the key issues to emerge is that learning and development most often take place in complete isolation from the workplace and the day-to-day challenges faced by leaders at all levels. I discuss this also in Part III and, in support of intelligent leadership, propose an approach in which leadership development and leadership practice are aligned and applied in unison.

The four Ps representing the mechanisms are now added to the framework illustrated in Figure 5.3.

OUTCOMES: CREATING AND DEMONSTRATING PUBLIC VALUE

Understanding Outcomes

The *Oxford English Dictionary* defines an outcome as 'a state of affairs resulting from some process; the way something turns out; a result (of a test, experiment, measurement, etc.), a consequence; a conclusion or verdict'. It is also described as the 'product, which results from an action, process, or system'.

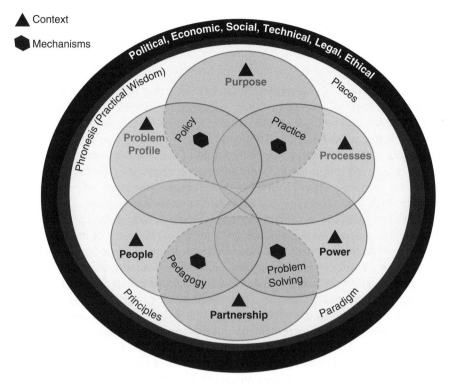

Figure 5.3 *Four Ps representing the mechanisms of collective leadership*

Programmes

Programmes are 'a planned series of future events or performances, a set of related measures or activities with a particular long-term aim'. The term originates from the early seventeenth century (in the sense of 'written notice'). It thus helps to bridge the gap between the shared purpose (context) and policy and practice (mechanisms) in delivering public value.

A programme is a deliberate means of taking forward a course of action and each can be evaluated. Programmes can thus be viewed as a public statement of intent, with an itinerary, plan, and schedule of what will be definitely undertaken.

Patterns

Of relevance to leadership is the meaning of 'patterns' as 'an arrangement or design regularly found in comparable objects; a regular and intelligible form or sequence discernible in the way in which something happens or is done ... a model or design or an excellent example for others to follow'.[2] In the first chapter of Part II, I will discuss in some detail the relevance of patterns and will argue that everything that

---

[2] 'pattern, n. and adj.' OED Online. Oxford University Press, June 2015. Web. 28 July 2015.

we do, and everything that we see, is determined by patterns. This is reinforced in Chapter 3 in the discussion of the intelligent leadership process.

Personal Impact

A further outcome of effective public leadership is that of 'personal impact'. As we know, traditional leadership theory and language has tended to focus on the individual whereas public leadership focuses more on the collective. However, the individual lies at the heart of collective activity, and another aspect of collective leadership is that of relationships. The concept of performance holds more weight when considered within the individual domain as opposed to the collective (patterns and products). The difficulty, I suggest, is in the assessment of performance of individuals to the prevailing patterns or products/service outcomes.

As I have argued above, the non-alignment between pedagogy and practice is not helpful and represents a major opportunity for the development of improvements in favour of the public interest. In assessing the outcome of this, of course we want to see the knowledge transferred into the product/service delivery outcome, but we also want to know the part that individuals have played within the whole, but not through the easy-to-collect and easy-to-measure process targets, through measures that are meaningful to the public interest. This includes self-development more generally and specifically for leadership. This represents some major challenges, not least of which is how do we assess an individual's propensity to self-develop?

You will recall in Chapter 1 that I said that you could not read all the books that existed in relation to leadership within your lifetime; the same applies within many professions. This is particularly the case within the context of health, something that affects us all. It has been argued that most clinicians 'can barely keep pace with the rapid advances in health-care knowledge' and 'that general internists would need to read 20 articles a day all year round to maintain present knowledge. Although the availability of systematic reviews and guidelines reduces the need for doctors to read original studies, they still find it difficult to keep up with such syntheses' (Grol and Grimshaw, 2003:1224). It would be naïve to suggest that we can achieve such comprehensive knowledge within individuals, but what we can do is ensure that we take a much greater collective approach to, and alignment between, organizational/network and individual learning. This forms the focus of the final chapter in Part III.

Product

A product is defined as 'an article or substance that is manufactured or a thing or person that is the result of an action or process' (for example, an outcome from a particular mechanism).[3] In terms of leadership within the not-for-profit sectors, the product is likely to be more about the result of an action or process rather than its production, as opposed to manufacturing where the product is likely to be a tangible and visible outcome. But there are no clear rules and there is no 'barbed wire' around outcomes, whether as services or products.

---

[3] 'product, n.1.' OED Online. Oxford University Press, June 2015. Web. 28 July 2015

Being 'fit for purpose' is one of the ways of defining quality, and this is a good starting point in understanding the common denominators between physical products and less visible services. The origins of the word quality go back to Anglo-Norman and Old French, *qualité* (of things), an attribute or property. It can represent a personal attribute, a trait or a feature of a person's character, an attribute considered desirable and, interestingly, a virtue. In terms of non-personal attributes, it relates to the 'standard or nature of something as measured against other things of a similar kind; the degree of excellence possessed by a thing'.[4]

Quality thus relates to both personal disposition as well as actions taken, and highlights the importance of balanced performance measures. This brings me to the final P, that of public value, which represents the all-embracing outcome of leading in the public interest.

Public Value

I have discussed the importance of public value in the earlier chapters and will revisit the concept throughout this book. However, in concluding Part I, the key message is that leading in the public interest considers the creation and demonstration of public value as the outcome of effective public leadership. There is a wide and increasing emphasis on public value, principally through the work of Mark Moore (Moore, 1995). Public value concerns social goals and ensures that those goals are delivered in a way that secures trust and legitimacy and where organizational capability and capacity exist to deliver these goals. Trust is particularly important in securing good relationships across a range of differing contexts.

The full collective leadership framework, including the desired outcomes, is illustrated in Figure 5.4.

CONCLUSION: TOWARDS SHARED VALUES THROUGH WHOLE SYSTEMS?

This chapter has outlined the research approach that I undertook and the modelling that followed. I have briefly outlined why and how the realistic evaluation framework was used and the benefits that this had. Quantitative analysis of the qualitative data was also applied, and this assisted in identifying the interrelationships that I subsequently explored and which I have presented here and build upon subsequently.

The Collective Leadership Framework that emerged was developed over a considerable period of time and has been tested in a number of different settings. I have to say that the analysis and modelling has been a continuous and iterative process, very time consuming but very exciting and rewarding. It certainly has the potential to be a very useful and appropriate way of assessing and developing collective leadership based on the shared COMPASS 360° values that I have briefly introduced here.

---

[4] 'quality, n. and adj.' OED Online. Oxford University Press, June 2015. Web. 28 July 2015.

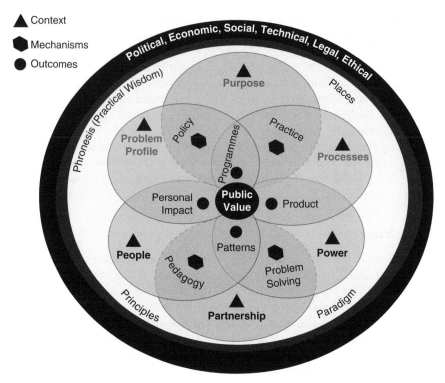

Figure 5.4 *Completed collective leadership framework with desired outcomes*

This will form the basis for the remainder of this book in terms of both assessment and development of collective leadership, but before doing so I want to create my link between the theoretical and research background and its practice by sharing with you another fascinating intellectual journey that I have experienced in terms of cross-disciplinary symbiosis! I again go back in time and consider some the of the ancient classics, but, on this occasion, my journey – just like the Walt Disney character Donald – took me through Mathmagicland, starting with Pythagoras and the birth of mathematics (Disney, 1959) through to Buckminster Fuller and Stafford Beer in the twentieth century.

This journey will form the first chapter of Part II and will suggest that the Collective Leadership Framework is fully consistent with how Buckminster Fuller described mathematics as giving both structure and direction, and, in particular, that it considers the magic of geometry in the identification of synergy. The most exciting aspect for me is that this was purely unintended and was an alignment that I came across in applying my research and analysis to the modern concept of whole systems thinking. I came to realize that this was not a modern organizational or lifestyle phenomenon at all, and that geometry can help us in charting the course for good collective leadership in the public interest. It was a second Damascus moment!

A reflective activity is provided below for this chapter.

Chapter 5 Activity	
Long-term Strategy	
Strategic Capability	
Business Model	
Controls	
If you work with other organizations through partnerships or alliances, repeat this activity.	
Partnership Strategy	
Strategic Capability	
Business Model	
Controls	
Reflect on the Strengths and Gaps and insert your comments below:	
STRENGTHS	GAPS

Part II
Leading in a Complex World

6 Exploring Contexts and Mechanisms as Whole Systems

ALL SYSTEMS GO?

In Chapter 5, I introduced the notion of complexity and drew on Pawson's work that describes this as the glue that binds the various approaches to critical realism. A characteristic of complexity is that it is unlikely that the issues or problems underpinning it are unlikely to be fully resolved. In this sense, it shares these characteristics with those of wicked problems.

Whole systems thinking concerns the identification of various elements of a system and the links and relationships between them. To what extent do we actually practise this? It is one of those areas where words and actions do not always match. I have had an active interest in whole systems thinking for over 20 years. It was during my continuing literature review and my exploration through our dear old friend the *Oxford English Dictionary* (OED) that I had my second 'Eureka' moment. I was researching the term synergy and came across a reference to the work of R. Buckminster Fuller[1]:

> Synergetics is the exploratory strategy of starting with the whole and the known behaviour of some of its parts and the progressive discovery of the integral unknowns.

This is almost akin to what could be described as the black box of leadership. The word synergetics originates from the post-classical Latin word *synergeticus* (which was first used in 1673 or earlier), itself from the ancient Greek word συνεργεῖν (which means to work together, to cooperate). However, synergetics has still been identified as a new interdisciplinary field of science which studies the origins and evolution of spatio-temporal structures, thus highlighting again the importance

---

[1]1975 R. Buckminster Fuller & E. J. Applewhite Synergetics i. 13 (from 'synergetic, adj.' OED Online. Oxford University Press, June 2014. Web. 3 August 2014).

of time and space; Bushev described synergetics as 'a very rare bird in textbooks', partly, he argues as 'a consequence of its interdisciplinary nature, owing to which no scientific field regards it as its own part' (Bushev, 1994:3). This accords with the discussion in the last chapter in terms of the applicability of either positivist or interpretativist/realist research.

Referring to the absence of references to this field, I found it most interesting, however, that Bushev made no reference to the work of Fuller, whose ideas are discussed in detail within this chapter in relation to his work on synergetics. This is particularly surprising as the OED suggests that the use of the term as a 'noun' seems 'first to appear in the name of Synergetics, Inc., a U.S. company formed in 1954 or 1955 with Buckminster Fuller as president'[2]. As you will discover, this was preceded by some remarkable and comprehensive thinking and innovation.

I have also explored the close links between synergetics and cybernetics. Cybernetics is not a term that you will ordinarily hear in the workplace as you would 'synergy' and 'whole systems'. Ask the proverbial 'ordinary person on the Clapham Omnibus' what is meant by 'cybernetics' and you will get some interesting responses! I have done this, and many, not surprisingly, refer to the Internet and, in particular, cyberspace and cybercrime. This is not entirely wrong, but given that its provenance goes back, as is so often the case, to our ancient Greek forefathers, it is certainly not a new phenomenon.

As with synergetics, the provenance of the word cybernetic originates from ancient Greek (κυβερνᾶν, to steer), hence its association with the verb 'governs', from the French *cybernétique*; this French word appears to have been translated into English from 1948 by Wiener:

> We have decided to call the entire field of control and communication theory, whether in the machine or in the animal, by the name Cybernetics. (Wiener, 1948:19)

This is also an interesting distinction between the 'machine' and the 'animal' and, as Bushev reminds us, the idea of control plays an important role in synergetics as well but the difference lies in the way the control is being exercised. Referring also to the work of Wiener, he draws upon the closeness of the concept of cybernetics to the idea of morphogenesis, originating from the Greek *morphê*, meaning shape and *genesis*, thus, creation, literally together meaning the 'beginning of the shape'. Morphogenesis was also used by the famous father of the modern computer, the mathematician Alan Turing (Bushev, 1994:7). No surprise, of course, but this term originates from the biological process that causes an organism to develop its shape, namely morphological characters such as those that refer to structure or form which includes, as well as shape, length, or colour of the body or, in geomorphogeny, the formation of landscapes, landforms, and rock types. This, of course, is akin to another concept that I discussed right at the beginning of this book, evolution, and morphogenesis also takes time, in biological terms, over thousands and even millions of years. Turing suggested that even though such systems may originally

---

[2]'synergetic, adj.' *OED Online*. Oxford University Press, June 2014. Web. 3 August 2014.

be quite homogeneous, due to instability of its equilibrium, 'which is triggered off by random disturbances' changes occur (Turing, 1952:37). This is also akin to the notion of precessional effect, discussed in the preceding chapter. Reflect for a moment on the example of the meteorite in a natural setting and the interjection of a particular leader in relation to your earlier example.

The random disturbances can be considered a part of the mathematical theory of catastrophe theory which, Bushev tells us, 'stays frequently on the agenda of conferences on synergetics' (Bushev, 1994:8) and describes 'transitions from one into another stable state of a system, where a catastrophe is a sharp change in the equilibrium state resulting from a smooth change of the external conditions' (ibid:9–10). In other words, slight external change causes huge change internally.

Some years after the term cybernetics appeared, *The Listener* magazine observed that 'the claim of cybernetics is, that we can treat organisms as if they were machines' (BBC, 1960). Building on this, the OED describes the primary meaning of cybernetics as:

> The field of study concerned with communication and control systems in living organisms and machines.

In extended use, it is also viewed as 'a field of study concerned with the integration of living organisms and electronic or other technological devices; robotics' which, the OED explains, is closely associated with the term bionics. How many of us remember Steve Austin – the bionic man in a TV series during the 1970s known as the *Six Million Dollar Man*? This originated from the novel published in 1972 by Martin Caidin entitled *Cyborg*. It is interesting that the original film (from which the TV series developed) started with a computerized text scroll explaining the term cyborg. Here, of course, we can begin to see the links between Turing's longer-term focus on biological morphogenesis and the more modern and less time-intensive gestation period of technological or social morphogenesis. As Wright argues, technological innovation 'could be considered under the rubric of "significant events"' (Wright, 2013:94), although such 'events', it is suggested, are best considered as developments rather than events. In terms of social morphogenesis, Wright offers some useful key points which are applicable to wider public leadership challenges in its application to the analysis of social change at the global level:

1. Social life is prone to change.
2. These transformations result from forces at different levels of social life, including the international level.
3. Social relations are multidimensional, so that the process of social change involves complex combinations of political, economic, cultural, psychological, and material forces.
4. A wide range of actors can shape the course of social history in a global setting.
5. Structural forces play an important role in terms of the production of social change. (Wright, 2013:95, *reproduced with permission*)

What Is the Relationship between Synergetics and Cybernetics?

Bushev made an attempt to distinguish the two, while acknowledging the similarities. Both, he seems to suggest, relate to self-organization phenomena, but he distinguishes cybernetics on the basis of maintaining a definite level of organization, or the self-improvement of systems, which are capable of accumulating past experiences and making use of it, based also on the principles of feedback. He said, 'Cybernetics sets itself the task of developing algorithms and methods of *control* (original emphasis) of systems' (Bushev, 1994:7). He argued that this makes a fundamental difference from synergetics, which concerns a wider environment. Another strong proponent of cybernetics is Stafford Beer, who argued that cybernetics is done by comparing models of complex systems with each other, and seeking the control features which appear common to them all (Beer, 1981).

Turing considered this within both biological systems and machine code, including the famous Turing machine; developed by Turing in the 1930s, the Turing machine is a mathematical tool equivalent to a digital computer and has since been the most widely used model of computation in computability and complexity theory. It is in this sense that I want to distinguish between synergetics (more long term, such as biological and physical morphogenesis) and cybernetics (more medium and short term, such as technological or social morphogenesis). I will now discuss the relevance of each to the development of collective leadership, considering synergetics as context and cybernetics as mechanisms, but both within the whole. I further suggest that cybernetics represents more of a reflective approach whereas synergetics focuses on reflexivity.

What We Need Is Some Synergy!

I am going to indulge once more in drawing upon some interesting theoretical perspectives that lie well outside of the discipline of leadership but which, I believe, have real resonance to understanding the complexity of leadership. I do so on the implicit understanding that cross-disciplinary theorizing and application is often not well received in the academic world, as Bushev told us. This is part of the need to think differently, not just about the discipline of leadership, but across all academic and practitioner domains. The study and practice of leadership, like so many other complex issues, lends itself well to its reliance on what some describe as 'whole systems approaches'. This is a popular phrase in both the management and leadership literature today, but I prefer to view it from both a synergetic and cybernetic perspective; bear with me! It is more about looking *through* the mirror rather than *at* the mirror.

'Synergy' itself is a popular byword in organizational management and leadership, but, as with the term 'leadership', do we really understand what it means? Popular management articles, books, and blogs abound with suggestions. One definition considers it as the 'concept that the value and performance of two companies combined will be greater than the sum of the separate individual parts'. It is suggested that synergy is a term that is most commonly used in the context of mergers and acquisitions (Investopedia, 2014), others suggest that it is important to the idea of comparative advantage (Sherf, 2010), and that widely read blog – known affectionately as '*Businessballs*' – views this from within a context of networking which the authors describe as a very helpful way to find cooperative and collaborative partnerships – based on mutual interest; synergy, they argue, is a way of understanding this (Businessballs, n.d.).

More recent academic journal articles use the term synergy in diverse contexts, including as a means of understanding 'stakeholder synergies' in relation to the role of public participation in wind power project development (Jami and Walsh, 2014), greater synergy and improved collaboration for complex partnerships in countries emerging from armed conflict (Pishchikova, 2014), and, from the commercial sector, the synergy effect of internationalization and firm size on US performance in the hotel industry (Lee et al., 2014).

It is a universal law that to achieve synergy, the whole system should be the first focus of attention rather than examining the individual parts of the whole.

> **Reflection**: Using your chosen example, reflect back on your experiences. To what extent was it dominated by a focus on the whole system rather than its individual parts?

It is at this point that I introduce the final observation of Fuller from the quotation at the beginning of the chapter, following his suggestion that it involves 'exploring the progressive discovery of the integral unknowns': he added to this, 'and their progressive comprehension of the hierarchy of generalized principles'.[3] With support from Edmondson, we can assume that what Fuller was arguing here is that the law of synergy 'dictates a basic strategy of starting with a whole system and then investigating its parts. The most painstaking study of its separate components will never reveal the behaviour of a system. All other generalized principles (the identification of which, was Fuller's main goal) therefore must be subsets of this fundamental truth: the whole is not equal to the sum of its isolated parts' (Edmondson, 1992:41).

This is also akin to the notion of double-loop learning rather than single-loop learning (Argyris and Schon, 1978). An example of single-loop learning is when values, goals, plans, and policies are operationalized rather than questioned. Double-loop learning is to take these organizational givens and scrutinize them critically.

To improve health and well-being requires a good knowledge of the environment in which we live and the impact of the environment on health. Referring back to my introductory narrative on social morphogenesis and its links with catastrophe theory, the sudden change of the industrial revolution had a dysfunctional impact on public health. During the last 30 years, the focus of attention in health and all other public services has been on outputs through measurable targets, rather than improved well-being through the creation and demonstration of public value, behaviours that are not necessarily conducive to the wider well-being. The financial crisis is yet another example, with an almost single-minded attention in the commercial sector on making money rather than considering the impact on both the national and global economy.

---

[3]Also from 1975 R. Buckminster Fuller & E. J. Applewhite Synergetics i. 13 (from 'synergetics, n.' OED Online. Oxford University Press, June 2015. Web. 28 July 2015).

> **Reflection**: Can you think of any other examples in which your organization or enterprise has focused on single-loop rather than double-looped responses and/or learning?

Let us return to the original meaning of the term synergy by referring to its wider discipline, that of synergetics, defined by the OED earlier as:

The phenomenon of synergistic activity or behaviour, as a field of study, especially an empirical discipline that seeks to deal with the overall behaviour of systems (typically social or conceptual systems) in flux, in so far as it cannot be inferred from the behaviour of components of the system.

The definition is a bit wordy, but it is perhaps more revealing and relevant than the descriptions given in the blogs and management journals. Let us break this down into some of the key components of synergetics:

- Synergy is considered to represent an activity or behaviour.
- It is a field of study that looks at overall *systemic* behaviours.
- These are generally social or conceptual systems that are in a change of flux.
- Synergy cannot be inferred from looking at individual *systemic* behaviours.

I have italicized the term *systemic* because it is interesting to consider whether behaviours can be ascribed to systems. I believe that it relates more to conduct (of systems) and the impact of this conduct on the performance of the system. Fuller's account of synergetics can be aligned with the earlier arguments in relation to a realistic science of evaluation compared to the more classical, positivist form of research; both are empirical except that the former includes experiential observation whereas the latter is primarily undertaken through experimental observation. I have also emphasized the focus on *systemic* behaviours as these are often the 'givens' – i.e. it is the context within which the organization and its networks function, in the sense that the systems can be difficult to influence, as opposed to human behaviours. I distinguish this from non-systemic behaviours, which can more easily be influenced because they are within the gift of a collection of individuals to do so. It is in this respect that I look more closely at the concept of cybernetics as a means of understanding behaviours and the interaction with mechanisms within the context of collective values.

In this sense, then, we can start to give some consideration to the 'unknowns'. It is also helpful to repeat the rather unfairly derided comment of Donald Rumsfeld. In February 2002, as the then US Secretary of State for Defense, he stated at a Defense Department briefing:

There are known knowns. These are things we know that we know. There are known unknowns. That is to say, there are things that we know we don't know. But there are also unknown unknowns. There are things we don't know we don't know. (Rumsfeld, 2002)

Although not the first to acknowledge the presence of 'unknown unknowns', the rationality of the comment has been as much acknowledged by academics as some of the more popular press has ridiculed it. As Logan argues, in this case within the context of the propagation of scientific enquiry in biology and botany 'careful examination of the statement reveals that it does make sense' (Logan, 2009:712). Pawson (2013) also recognized 'the importance of acknowledging "unknown unknowns"' viewing this as part of the continuum from the steady conversion from one state to the other, from incomprehension to unfamiliarity to understanding' (Pawson, 2013:160). We can thus begin to see an alignment between realistic evaluation (my methodology) and synergetics (theoretical framework), supported by the concept of cybernetics as the operating model of leading in the public interest.

If we align this discussion on the 'unknowns' to what Fuller describes as the hierarchy of generalized principle, which has been interpreted possibly as governing all of the physical universe's inter-transforming transactions (see Fuller and Dil, 1983:94), we gain further insight. Fuller defined a consistent approach to modelling the universe as spatial systems composed of events and relations. We note that most of human's interventions do not follow these principles (for example, money is a man-made invention, as is its exchange). There is an emerging difference between systemic and non-systemic (human) interventions, which I argue reflects the differences between synergetics and cybernetics, respectively.

It would be helpful to discuss this distinction a bit further. Fuller further argued that synergy is the behaviour of the whole system unpredicted by the behaviour or integral characteristics of any parts of the system when the parts are considered only separately. I argue that this would include human intervention that lies beyond systems and processes, acknowledging, of course, that humans can shape these systems and processes – more on this later!

Edmondson reminds us that Fuller suggested that the isolation of systems enables the descriptions of local processes and relationships without reference to an absolute origin (Edmondson, 1992:39). In this particular instance, reference to an absolute origin is indispensable; in other words, it is indispensable to ask (leaders) 'why are we doing this?'

What Are the Benefits of Distinguishing between the Whole and Its Parts?

The first benefit is that the distinction draws upon physical science as well as social science. Considering whole systems can be considered a science, and 'Bucky' Fuller, as he was affectionately known, starts with the universe using synergetic geometry.

A second benefit is to assist us in identifying the impact of either transformational or transactional interventions. The basic nature of interaction is the process of action/reaction/resultant. Figure 6.1 provides a good illustration:

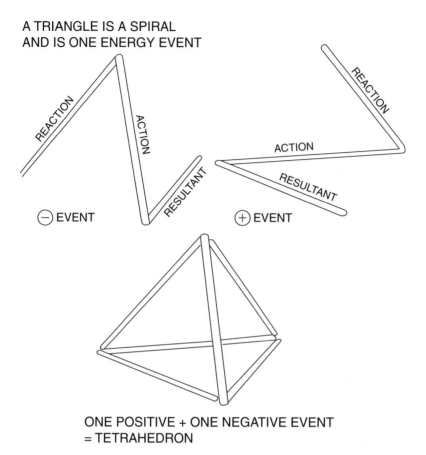

ONE POSITIVE + ONE NEGATIVE EVENT
= TETRAHEDRON

Figure 6.1 *Triangular energy events*

Source: 'Two Triangular Energy Events Make Tetrahedron: The open-ended triangular spiral can be considered one "energy event" consisting of an action, reaction, and resultant. Two such events (one positive and one negative) combine to form the tetrahedron.' Fuller, R. Buckminster, (1975) *Synergetics*. New York, USA: MacMillan. Figure 511.10. Reproduced with the permission of the Buckminster Fuller Institute.

A further important element of Fuller's work was his conceptualization of the 12 degrees of freedom, with a balance between six positive and six negative degrees. The first important point is to understand that these 12 degrees of freedom always exist in any motion or effects on motion, and it can thus help us to take account of how different mechanisms are fired, with what effect, in differing contexts to produce patterns of outcomes.

The basic rules of the 12 degrees of freedom are illustrated in Figure 6.2. Triangulation is fundamental to structure, but it takes a plurality of positive and negative behaviours to make a structure. The six positive/negative degrees of freedom are summarized as follows:

Axial rotation: This relates to coexisting axial rotation poles. One of the prime motions of our universe is axial rotation; it is fundamental to the universe. In

Basic Rules of the 12 Degrees of Freedom (df)

There are four fundamental corners in every system
and each must be triangulated:
4 x 3 = 12

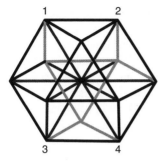

Components:

* This assists in measuring the extent of a system's
  (partnerships) mobility

* It shows how many alternative directions of motion
  must be impeded before the body in space is
  completely restrained

* There are 6 positive and 6 negative df in the Universe
  in respect to which all structural systems in the Universe
  must abide:

  - Axial Rotation
  - Orbital Rotation
  - Expansion/Contraction
  - Torque (twist)
  - 'Inside-Outing'
  - Precession

Figure 6.2 Basic rules of the 12 degrees of freedom

relation to the earth, the North Pole and the South Pole are two (imaginary) points where the earth's axis of rotation intersects the celestial sphere. *I consider this to represent what I describe as distributed leadership. We are traditionally conditioned to look up and down in 180 degrees from the top of the organization to its grassroots (and, occasionally, back up again).*

Orbital rotation: Similarly, orbital rotation is fundamental to the universe and is 'the norm'. An example given by Fuller is that aircraft fly at 40,000 feet. This is only 10 miles out. Multiply it by 10 and it is in its own orbit. The diameter of the earth is 8000 miles, and 100 miles respectively is a very small amount. People refer to the sun 'going down' in the evening and using the words 'up' and 'down' instead of 'in', 'out' and 'around', and, according to Fuller, such words are used by the few who are working in cosmic realism (Fuller, 1973). *Is* *this the way in which our leaders work, in a hierarchical 'top-down' way rather than looking in, out, and around?* At this point I invite you to think of a very popular song that describes this. You will find out at a later stage if you got this right!

Expansion/Contraction: A further fundamental motion of the Universe, this represents the rationale of evolutionary expanding capacity and contraction of needs. Tension and compression are complementary functions of structure but with tension, for example when pulling a tensional rope its girth contracts in compression. When we load a column in compression its girth tends to expand in tension (Fuller, 1998). Fuller used the buildings of antiquity as an example. Put a beam between two walls and, as the load comes on top, the bottom tries to open up – the top goes into compression and the bottom goes into tension. This is why the ancient Greeks built columns very close to each other; *can we equate this to the way in organizational structures are built to support a top-heavy hierarchy?*

Torque/Twist: Torque is defined as 'the twisting or rotary force in a piece of mechanism (as a measurable quantity); the moment of a system of forces producing rotation' (OED, 2014). Citing an example from the *Daily Chronicle* in 1906 (21 April), torque was described as the amount of force in a rotary direction – the power of the twist. If you hold one end of a rod and I hold the other, and I twist it round in your hands, that is because I am giving it a torque greater than you can resist. A disturbing torque or twist can alter the rotational axis or orbit in which an object is in motion. *This could be considered in terms of the twists and turns undertaken by management in organizational change, resulting in a changed direction – often a negative direction!*

Inside-outing: This means inverting the arrangement of the tension and compression components of a structure. Fuller referred to this as to evolute, which is to cause to perform an evolution. In one of his many lectures, Fuller used an illustration of a 'little child' who 'learns' these forms of motion from axial through to inside-outing. A practical example of this is provided in relation to designing houses from the inside out on the basis that dealing with 'growth, unfolding, transformation and reproduction leads from the living creature and nature to the cultural techniques and artifacts' (Chu and Trujillo, 2009:66). Fuller suggests that we should consider changes from the inside rather than the outside. *To what extent do leaders develop their vision and priorities from the outside in?*

Precession: This is the least understood of Fuller's 12 degrees of freedom but one that is arguably the most important. He views precession as a generalized principle (which is true in all instances) and makes links between precessions in three areas: the physical universe, nature, and human-socio behaviour. Let me just remind you at this point of similar distinctions made in relation to biological, technical, and social morphogenesis and the time and space dimensions. In the physical universe, the earth orbits the Sun precessionally. Although being pulled towards the sun by a gravitational force at 180 degrees, the earth precesses at 90 degrees from the direction of pull, in much the same way as a spinning top does when you spin it. In terms of nature, when you drop a stone into a pond, the stone sinks to the bottom whereas the waves precess outwardly – in perfect circles at 90 degrees, and the honeybee – in seeking its goal of honey – cross-pollinates other plants by touching vegetation at 90 degrees to itself. In transferring this to the human dimension, precession is of the strongest importance. *In terms of the practice of leaders, the main tendency has been to look up and down (at 180 degrees) rather than inward and outwards or horizontally and often, to react accordingly. These reactions often knock the organization's direction off its course.*

Aligning the Basic Rules of the 12 Degrees of Freedom to Human Behaviour and Leadership: The Precessional Effect

Fuller's work on precession is very closely associated with the notion of putting 'the greatest good for the greatest number' ahead of personal motivations. It also accepts that there may be a positive side effect for you as an individual in doing so. It is what he called the 'precessional effect' (PE). In simple terms, this means 'the effect of bodies on motion on other bodies in motion' (Fuller, 1975). Precession (which does not necessarily follow the universal generalized principles) can thus have an effect on what nature intended (think of global warming as one rather controversial subject).

As with Darwin before him, Fuller refers to man's fight for survival and considers the precessional effects as the unintended side effects of this fight for survival. It is how human reason leads to intervention within the wider context of the physical and metaphysical world, ranging from the point at which humans first inhabited the earth, naked, hungry, and frightened but determined to survive through to the contemporary world of space travel. Fuller argues that one thing that has remained throughout this history is human preoccupation with the sense of static and fixed 'space' rather than thinking in more geometric terms in which 'space' is not tuned-in to the physical sensorial range of what he termed 'tunability', making reference to the electromagnetic sensing equipment with which we personally have been organically endowed.

Fuller has clearly challenged many of the classic theories, embracing many, building on others, and being critical of a few. There is much to bring to the discipline and practice of leadership.

Fuller's notion of thinking as a systemic process involves aligning experiences into three broad sets, which he describes as the macroscopic irrelevant, the microscopic irrelevant, and the lucidly relevant set. It has been said that most geometrics are either microscopic or macroscopic, either too tiny or too huge for us to encompass without microscopes or telescopes (Medford, n.d.). Macroscopic study concentrates on large-scale aspects of phenomena. Can this really be irrelevant, as argued by Fuller? Its literal translation is to be 'Visible to the naked eye (as opposed to *microscopic*); (also) using the naked eye'[4] associated with the nature of being general, comprehensive, and/or concerned with large units, hence the popular term in management – the 'macro' level. Fuller also describes the microscopic level as irrelevant. It is clearly the opposite of macroscopic, and thus it can be regarded as being

---

[4] 'macroscopic, adj.' OED Online. Oxford University Press, June 2015. Web. 28 July 2015.

a bit closer to an understanding of its irrelevancy. Let us explore this a bit further and then consider the 'lucidly relevant set'. Using his original words, Fuller argued:

> For instance, we find that all irrelevancies fall into two main categories, or bits. One set embraces all the events that are irrelevant because they are too large in magnitude and too delayed in rate of reoccurrence to have any effect on the set of relationships we are considering. The other set of irrelevancies embraces all the events that are too small and too frequent to be differentially resolved at the wavelength to which we are tuned, ergo, in any discernible way to alter the interrelationship values of the set of experience relationships we are considering. Having dismissed the two classes of irrelevancies, there remains the lucidly relevant set to be studied. (Fuller, 1979:509)

His description of the 'lucidly relevant set' takes some time to digest (page 509.04), but when broken down, is deceptively simple. I have taken the liberty of paraphrasing my interpretation of his meaning:

> Our experience is vast and thus our ability to remember is unpredictable. Indeed, we can easily forget the questions that we have asked ourselves. There is a need to finely tune our considerations to the special set of events that relate to the vividly emergent pattern under immediate priority of consideration.

In other words, too much detail should not bog us down, whether at the macro or the micro level. However, a very important part of the lucidly relevant set is patterns. The lucidly relevant set therefore appears to sit at what we can call the 'meso' level. The word meso originates from the ancient Greek word $\mu\varepsilon\sigma o$- and is a combining form of $\mu\acute{\varepsilon}\sigma o\varsigma$ (middle). It is therefore a chiefly scientific term for middle or intermediate and is used in a range of disciplines to denote this. In relation to the leadership of organizations, where we appear to be heading is to concentrate our efforts at the meso level (mechanisms) while taking account of the wider macro level (context), keeping an eye on the micro level (outputs and outcomes). Having temporarily dismissed the irrelevant, it is then possible to consider the lucidly relevant from both outside and inside the set. It is perhaps, for this reason, that Fuller's geometric preference was for the tetrahedron, a simpler geometric structure than the Metatron and more robust than the single tetra (triangle).

This argument thus has resonance with the challenges that face leading in the public interest. First, it has been suggested that the dynamic nature of synergetics implies that we need not get stuck permanently in paradigms, as Kuhn argues (recall the discussion of Kuhn in Chapter 1), and that, perhaps, synergetics is trans-paradigmatic. A key question here is the extent to which leaders are caught up in their own views of the 'way we do things around here' and who may be unable (or unwilling) to step out of their paradigm or comfort zone. A second and equally important point, given the emphasis of this book, is the importance of Fuller's concept of precession, which he refers to as nature's way of getting the job done at 90 degrees to human selfishness and ignorance (as opposed to 180 degrees). Taking account of precession is an evolution that Fuller anticipates in encouraging us to start to do the right things for the right reasons, a point also argued a couple of thousand years ago by Aristotle!

Geometric Foundation for the Concept of Synergy

Before moving on to the practicalities, let us briefly consider the geometric foundation for Fuller's concept of synergy. This extends back to the beginning of life itself. I will then progressively relate this to the more practical aspects of leadership when I begin to discuss local processes and relationships that can be influential within a collective leadership arena, with the support of cybernetics.

Geometry is the branch of mathematics concerned with the properties and relations of points, lines, surfaces, and solids and which is often referred to as sacred geometry. From the nineteenth century the term has also been generalized to spaces of more than three dimensions. Metatron's cube is one of the earliest and well-known of platonic solids which itself is defined as a regular, convex polyhedron (a solid in three dimensions with flat faces, straight edges, and sharp corners (or vertices)). It has been argued that all systems are polyhedral, initially from Fuller (discussed earlier and below), but also by Stafford Beer (discussed in the next section) (Baldwin, 1996); real systems are always multidimensional (ibid:218).

Named after the angel Metatron, a spiritual being, it is often referred to as 'the flower of life'. It is made up of 13 circles, and when straight lines are drawn to interconnect all 13, the pattern delineated by the lines portray the first three platonic solids including projections of a double tetrahedron (two triangles), a cube within a cube, and an octahedron (eight equilateral triangles, four of which meet at each vertex). Metatron's cube is illustrated in Figure 6.3.

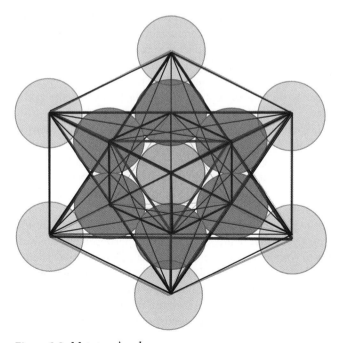

Figure 6.3 Metatron's cube

Figure 6.4 *Tetrahedron within Metatron's cube*

The tetrahedron encompassed within Metatron's cube is highlighted in Figure 6.4 and comprises what is known as the tetrahedron star (double tetrahedron). Considering both the Metatron cube and the tetrahedron is helpful in considering the dynamic interaction between the external and internal contexts of collective leadership.

This is illustrated further in Figure 6.5 in which the six external contexts of collective leadership in the public interest are shown to represent the six outer circles, whereas the six inner circles within the tetrahedron star represent the six internal contexts. In all cases, public value as the outcome of public leadership sits at the heart of the framework.

The external (PESTLE) context coexists with, and influences, the six internal contexts. You will recall from my earlier discussion in relation to the 20 Ps that the first P of the internal context was identified as the 'problem profile'. Following my review of Fuller's work, I argue that this relies on 'pattern integrity', coexisting with policy, partnership, processes, people, and power. The link between the external and internal contexts are mediated by four further contexts (representing four dimensions of a hypercube): the prevailing paradigm ('the way things are done around here'), its principles (the givens that define the values and purpose), place (which will differ from context to context), and, finally phronesis (the practical wisdom), all drawn together through the process of intelligent leadership (discussed briefly in the final chapter). This relationship is illustrated in Figure 6.6.

The four mediating contexts together influence the mechanisms that will be adopted by an organization and its networks, taking account of the internal and external conditions.

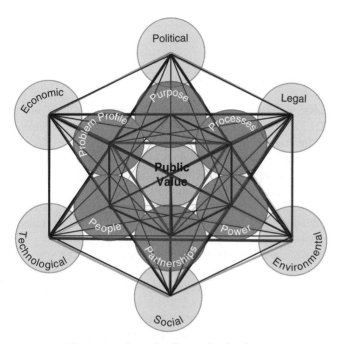

Figure 6.5 *Metatron cube and collective leadership*

I suggest that Aristotle's original concept of phronesis (practical wisdom) – shown as the base of the internal 3D cube – aligns with the first two Ps, representing the mechanisms of policy (what the organization sets out as its model for delivery) and practice (how leadership is applied in aligning context to outcomes), supported by the two remaining 'P' mechanisms, pedagogy and problemitization. It is in this respect that we begin to look at local processes and relationships and can do so through what I describe as shared and distributed leadership (taking account of both

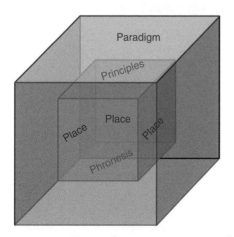

Figure 6.6 *Hypercube representing internal and external contexts*

axial and orbital rotation). Let us move on to a discussion of cybernetics to explore the leadership role in its more specific relationship with the mechanisms.

CYBERNETICS: FROM CONTEXT TO MECHANISMS

Following on from geometry, attention now turns to Stafford Beer, himself influenced by Fuller. Baldwin tells us that Beer used the icosahedron as a model for organizing projects for much the same reason as Fuller used for structure: efficiency (Baldwin: 219). The regular icosahedron is a solid contained by 20 equal equilateral triangles.

Although Beer and his colleagues used this in relation to members of a decision-making team with a specific goal, this book contends that it can also be used to bridge the gap between the 20 Ps reviewed in the earlier chapters and the development of collective leadership values and behaviours in tackling wicked problems through cross boundary leadership.

The 20 triangular faces of the icosahedron, which each have equal sides, represent the 20 Ps, and there are 30 edges. We saw in the earlier chapters how the seven internal contexts interact (on a 3×4 triangulation basis) to create seven potential collective leadership values.

We can now start to consider realistic evaluation in terms of a 3D model – drawing on both geometry and relationships – to bring together synergetics and cybernetics in identifying a range of collective leadership behaviours that can create the appropriate balance of precession in achieving desired outcomes.

The seven collective (COMPASS360) values are underpinned by a range of collective behaviours that equal 30 (represented by the 30 edges of the icosahedron). When equated to the 360° compass for leadership, this further coincides with 12 degrees of freedom for each collective leadership behaviour (six positive and six negative, from axial rotation to precessional effect). Within the icosahedron, the 12 degrees of freedom can be considered as the 12 vertices, thus:

30 (edges) × 12 (vertices/df) = 360, which forms the basis of leading through 360° intelligent networks, knowledge and skills (**LINKS**[360] ®). This is illustrated in Figure 6.7.

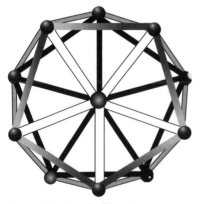

Figure 6.7 *Icosahedron*

Before We Move on Again, a Brief Recap Is in Order!

Chapter 3 set out the brief theoretical perspective and action research underpinning the collective leadership framework and its operational model, adopting a realistic evaluation methodology. This chapter has considered whole systems thinking and has drawn on both synergetics (in support of the conceptual framework) and cybernetics (in terms of the operational model). The importance of the 12 degrees of freedom – both negative and positive – encompassed within six factors (axial rotation, orbital rotation, contraction and expansion, torque and twist, inside-outing, and precession), and based on the tetrahedron star, illustrates how the external (PESTLE) context interacts with the internal contextual conditions based on the first 11 Ps of the 20P collective leadership framework.

In terms of cybernetics, Stafford Beer was influenced by the work of Bucky Fuller and adopted the icosahedron as a means of understanding control and communication within organizations. The 20 faces represent the 20 Ps aligned with the 7 COMPASS[360] values, and its 30 edges represent the mechanisms that trigger leadership behaviours. If the 12 degrees of freedom are applied to the 30 edges, this represents true 360° leadership. It is again coincidence that my modelling (from the 20Ps) equalled 30 dimensions. I would like to think that this is due to strict adherence to the universal laws, as referred to by Fuller, but I would not be so arrogant to claim this! However, I am confident that there is synergy between the two!

In terms of the Collective Leadership model, the alignment between the model and the icosahedron is illustrated in Figure 6.8. This model, and the supporting Collective Leadership Inventory (CLI) will form the basis of the remainder of Part II of this book.

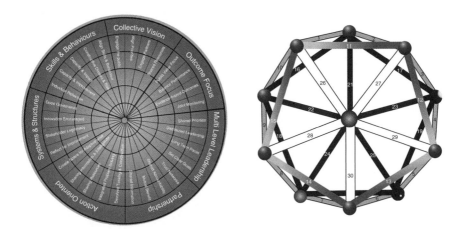

Figure 6.8 *Compass 360 framework and icosahedron*

The Benefits of Securing Collaborative Advantage

In an excellent account of what collaborative working needs to achieve collaborative advantage (a form of synergy), Lank (Lank, 2006) tells us that it is often implicitly positioned as an optional extra, something that is in addition to the day job. The challenge is that most resource allocation processes are generally designed to support a department or function within one organization and not the allocation of resources across different organizations. The implications of this – no matter how small the lack of resources may initially be – can have a significant impact. She suggests that the children's nursery rhyme may ring true:

For Want of a Nail
For want of a nail the shoe was lost.
For want of a shoe the horse was lost.
For want of a horse the rider was lost.
For want of a rider the message was lost.
For want of a message the battle was lost.
For want of a battle the kingdom was lost.
And all for the want of a horseshoe nail.

Our ego so often dominates over our desire to serve and support the whole. Instead of considering ourselves as separate or superior to others, we should consider ourselves as part of the whole. Leaders should seek to achieve synergy.

Did you get the answer to the question on page 90? It was the song 'Fool on a Hill' and some believe that this was a reference to Buckminster Fuller who was unfairly derided for his views on 90 degree perception with a footnote reference (http://www.raymondjames.com/AdvisorSitesFiles/PublicSites/davidlerner/files/FoolontheHill_052413.pdf).

A reflective activity is provided below for this chapter.

Chapter 6 Activity			
Complexity	Consider a work based example; was the whole system the first focus of attention rather than examining the individual parts of the whole? Yes ▢ No ▢		
Synergy	Was your example project subject to double-looped learning as opposed to single-looped learning?		
	Did the project focus on the 'unknowns' as well as the 'knowns'?		
	Was there evidence of distributed leadership (up and down) (axial rotation)?		
	Is there evidence of shared leadership (looking out and around) (orbital rotation)?		
	Are efforts made to relieve the tension from top-heavy hierarchy (tension and contraction)?		
	Was there a change of direction by the organization (torque and twist) that improved the conditions of success?		
	Does the leadership develop the vision and priorities from the inside-out (inside-outing)?		
	Was there any evidence of leaders knocking the project off course through intervention (precessional effect)?		
Process of Action	Every event is formed of the tripartite process of Action - Reaction - Resultant, which can be either positive or negative. Describe whether you are able to identify this process from your own example project.		

7 Understanding the Challenges of Leadership

CONTEXTUAL CHALLENGES IN THE REAL WORLD OF LEADERSHIP

Introduction

In considering the contextual challenges presented to leaders, two questions are posed: what are the key challenges for leaders as we progress through the twenty-first century, and to what extent do these challenges differ from those of the twentieth century? The early chapters explored the history of leadership thoughts and studies and considered the importance of the language of leadership and its application in the real world of leadership. During the early stages of preparing this book, one comment that was made was that the term 'the real world of leadership' is unhelpful. I would challenge this, and argue throughout the remainder of this book that there is a significant void between the espoused and the actual practices of leadership. I reiterate that both the language of leadership and 'systems' can be constructed by individual leaders within their own particular way 'of seeing the world' rather than aligning the 'ship' of leaders to systems that are in balance across the actual playing field for leaders and those who are led and the wider communities impacted by this leadership.

The real world relates to the 'practical world' as opposed to the 'academic world' and is defined as the 'world as it actually exists; the existing state of things, as opposed to one that is imaginary, simulated, or theoretical'. It is closely aligned to the term reality, which is the 'quality or state of being real; real existence; what is real rather than imagined or desired; the aggregate of real things or existences; that which underlies and is the truth of appearances or phenomena' and 'that which constitutes the actual thing, as distinguished from what is merely apparent or external'.[1] It therefore follows that a realist is a person who is 'an adherent or advocate of Realism ... (as opposed to an idealist or conceptualist) and one who occupies him or herself with things rather than words. Such a person tends to regard

---

[1]'real world, n. and adj.' OED Online. Oxford University Press, June 2015. Web. 28 July 2015.

such things as they really are, rather than how they are imagined, or desired to be, sometimes to the point of cynicism. I therefore argue for realist leaders'.[2]

Exploring the Challenges

The first challenge for collective leaders is to face the real world or – as Jim Collins argues – to 'confront the brutal facts of the reality' (Collins, 2001). This does not mean that such leaders should not have a clear vision (in Collins' terms, for example, for collective 'greatness'), but advises that the route to this should accept the brutal facts of the external and internal operating environment that leaders face. Within this context, the first step is to define a *collective vision*. This involves engaging with the wider public as well as customers and clients and other partners and potential partners, sharing each other's priorities and ideas, which represent the public interest, and working together for the common good. Sounds simple, does it not? Yet, it is the greatest challenge facing leaders.

The second challenge is to be *outcome-focused*; that is, to align the purpose of the organization (i.e. why the organization exists) to the collective vision, in answering the question 'for what purpose does our organization exist?' In some cases, and this will be certainly true if your leadership role is firmly located within the commercial sector, it is to make profit on behalf of your shareholders. We should not be naïve enough to suggest that the competitive advantage of companies and organizations should be totally overshadowed by collaboration in the public interest. However, as is often the case, it is a question of balance and, in this case, it is about balancing outcomes. Often, competitive advantage as an outcome can only be achieved by the prior achievement of collaborative advantage.

As we learned in Part I, an outcome is a state of affairs resulting from some process; the way something turns out and the overall outcome of leading in the public interest is the creation and demonstration of public (or shared) value. We can ask why this challenge exists. We only have to look at the deceptions practised by so-called leaders to satisfy shareholders (for example in the commercial sector, through Enron and elements of the banking industry) and stakeholders (in the public sector) in slavishly following process-related targets. These may be easy to count but ignore qualitative aims that are difficult to measure but critical in counting what counts, for example where some hospitals ignored quality and clinical quality as opposed to counting numbers of processes. Why does this continually occur, and why are leaders sometimes blind but often dismissive of the human dimension? You will recall my reference to Zimbardo's classic but chilling account of why 'good people' turn 'evil' when a system is created that conditions certain behaviours. What would happen, for example, if we randomly allocated people to leadership roles and others to followers' roles within a similar contextual condition to that of the Stanford Prison Environment, but within a corporate or public service delivery context? It is likely that selfish behaviours would emerge rather than selfless motivations, focused on competition rather than collaboration.

---

[2]'realist, n. and adj.' OED Online. Oxford University Press, June 2015. Web. 28 July 2015.

Being outcome-focused is thus about balancing the measurement of public as well as company, organization, and government needs, and to measure what happens at all levels.

I have made the point throughout the introduction that, no matter what companies, organizations, or government institutions do, it involves our contextual ninth 'P' – that of people – and its preceding 'P' – that of process; a key element of the dynamics between these contextual factors is that of relationships. These relationships take place at all levels and span company and institutional[3] boundaries. The third challenge, therefore, is to recognize and embrace the need for *multi-level leadership*. This encourages leaders to share their leadership across networks and distribute leadership within each company or institution, aiming to achieve clear short-term and long-term goals. One of the most important benefits is the opportunity to be transparent in relation to checks and balances, but only if this is accompanied by a climate that encourages such values and behaviours to emerge.

There is a clear link between this third and the following fourth challenge: *partnership working*. Leaders need to know and trust their networks, share information, and responsibility and actively seek to achieve goals that benefit the common good. This is an understandable aim for public institutions, but is this also the case for commercial enterprises? Partnering is not an easy task and presents significant challenges in the alignment of shared aims and values and in agreeing to share resources. However, it is increasingly being recognized as not just desirable but essential in leadership. Competitive advantage can still be achieved through collaboration.

The fifth challenge for collective leaders is to be *action focused and adaptive* in what leaders are trying to achieve. This calls for engagement in joint problem-solving and distribution of leadership through intelligence-based activities based on pattern integrity. It is in this respect that Aristotle's concept of phronesis (practical wisdom) can be really helpful, summarized as having 'the right people, doing the right things, at the right time, in the right places and for the right ends'.[4] We recall that phronesis is the intellectual virtue concerned with 'doing'.

If the action of partner organizations is aligned to the vision and desired outcomes, any initial success needs to be sustained. This represents the sixth and seventh challenges, respectively, that of developing supporting systems and structures and in building appropriate skills and behaviours. Both of these challenges are important in maximizing collaborative and competitive advantage in sustaining and anchoring success.

Developing *systems and structures* is about encouraging innovative ways of achieving joint goals and supporting continuous improvement, but in a way that takes account of the various 'forces' that are necessary to achieve an appropriate balance and acknowledging the precessional effect (PE) that leaders can introduce. The first point is to thus acknowledge that leaders can construct systems, and by applying an individualized precessional effect, the system itself can be knocked off its axis with

---

[3]From here on, I refer to 'institutions' as a 'catch-all' spanning all public sectoral boundaries (an establishment, organization, or association, instituted for the promotion of some object, esp. one of public or general utility, religious, charitable, educational).

[4]Adapted from Aristotle by Ross, W.D., Brown, L. & Dawson, B. 2009. *The Nicomachean Ethics* [electronic book], Oxford, Oxford University Press.

possible harmful or disastrous impacts. The second point, aligned to the first, is the critical need to achieve balance, which is where Fuller's 12 degrees of freedom can be very constructive in understanding the dynamics of systems.

Part of sustaining success and achieving systemic equilibrium is the role of leaders in coactively *aligning skills and behaviours* by building capability and capacity and encouraging reflective and reflexive activity for both improvement and performance. My research to date has illustrated that this represents one of the most significant gaps in the development of collaborative leadership, in which individual aims and objectives often over shadow those of the collective. In particular, there is little evidence, if any, of leadership development being directly aligned to the work place. As I argue in the final part of this book, the development of leaders in relation to leadership challenges should be directly applied to the overarching values and vision of the organization or institution and used as a means of improving the organization or institution while at the same time supporting individual leadership development.

The remainder of this and the following chapters will explore these challenges by expressing them as collective leadership values and describing how these values can be transformed into appropriate behaviours. Before doing this, I introduce the 'Leadership Values Tree', which is a useful means by which values and behaviours can be considered. It uses the high level contextual (and collective) values in illustrating this throughout this part of the book and then considers the notion of negotiated order in bringing some sense to these values and behaviours within different organizations and enterprises.

The Leadership Values Tree

The Leadership Values Tree activity has been inspired by the classic work of Einstein in relation to his theories on energy (and its link with time, space, and mass[5]). The tree relies on a number of sources of energy to sustain itself: sunlight, water, carbon dioxide, and nutrients from the soil. The same applies to leadership, and the challenges that face leaders often relate to the energy encouraged by values and their conversion into appropriate behaviours. The values represent the underpinning context of leadership (or the roots of the tree), the behaviours its outcomes (or the foliage or fruit), whereas the trunk represents the mechanisms for innovation (or the distribution of the energy from the roots to the fruit), namely the practice of leadership. The outcomes, represented by the leaves of trees, rely upon the conversion of light energy into chemical energy through photosynthesis; if the leaves are not healthy enough to absorb sunlight, then photosynthesis will not take place and the tree is likely to die. To continue this brief analogy, if leadership behaviours (as outcomes) are unable to absorb the energy from transformational leadership practice (the mechanisms), then the underpinning values (the context) are unlikely to survive and leadership efforts likely to fail.

The recent economic crisis has put the issue of leadership 'on trial' and, repeating the point argued above, we need to 'confront the brutal facts of *this* reality', as argued by Collins (Collins, 2001 – *my emphasis*). This includes confronting the dark side to leadership as well as developing new approaches. The root of what is so

---

[5]I pick up these three concepts of time, space, and mass in Part III.

often called a 'leadership crisis' is often about degeneration of values where greed and self-interest can often overshadow shared values. Times of crisis require vision, courage, and innovation.

The development of shared values is about listening and collaborating. Values are more general than behaviours and exist at multiple levels. They play a role in both setting the agenda and in the identification or evaluation of desired outcomes.

Leadership should also be measured – and one way of measuring leadership is to measure the values of leadership through demonstrated behaviours – in addition to other measures of effectiveness. In this sense, the Leadership Values Tree considers the alignment between the roots of value and the fruit of appropriate behaviours through innovation (representing the trunk of the tree).

While values are difficult to change, behaviours can be influenced and developed. Values can both predict and shape behaviours, but values need to develop the right beliefs and attitudes if the leadership tree is to bear fruit. Figure 7.1 uses four values as the basis for discussion in illustrating how they are linked to appropriate behaviours.

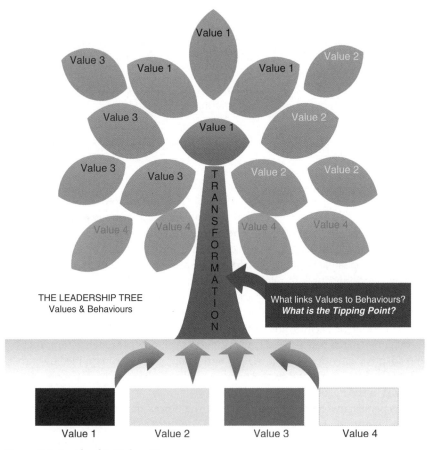

Figure 7.1 *Leadership Values Tree*

The aim of this activity is to engage your workforce and stakeholders in identifying what values are important (from a collective sense) and the four behaviours that they consider underpin each of the values. Each person is asked to select no more than four values. In the final analysis, a maximum of eight can be identified. This will be illustrated further throughout this part of the book.

In the next chapter, we will consider the leadership values and behaviours that underpin the development of a collective vision. We then explore how values and behaviours can make a direct impact on the achievement of outcomes that reflect the public interest in Chapter 9, followed by Chapters 10 and 11 in which we consider how values and behaviours assist in defining leadership across different levels of leadership and through partnership working. Chapter 12 specifically focuses on the values and behaviours that encourage an action focus through adaptive leadership, followed by Chapters 13 and 14, which, respectively, consider the leadership challenges relating to supporting systems and structures and the development of appropriate skills and behaviours. In each case, we will consider the potential tipping point to bring about transformational change, for example in the achievement of the collective vision and desired outcomes. I will draw upon behavioural dimensions that have emerged from the research underpinning this work as well as a number of case studies across the not-for-profit and for-profit sectors. You may wish to shadow my discussion by undertaking a similar analysis of your organization and its networks by accessing the online resources of the companion website (www. palgrave.com/companion/brookes).

You are now invited to undertake an activity using the Leadership Values Tree and aligning this to your work-based example or case study.

NEGOTIATED ORDER

Before moving on to the collective leadership framework, I want to briefly introduce the theoretical perspective of negotiated order, first introduced by Anselm Strauss (1917–1996). Strauss suggested that virtually all social order is negotiated order (Strauss, 1978). We can recall that one of our key Ps is that of people who, according to Strauss, chiefly negotiate with each other. Such people, according to Strauss, alternatively create, maintain, transform, and are constrained by, social structures. This will certainly apply in relation to the creation of a collective vision and how this vision is maintained through the articulation of public interest outcomes. The creation of these values and behaviours are likely to be maintained through different levels of leadership, across different organizations within networks, and exemplified through partnership activities. Transformation will occur through action oriented and adaptive activities (a triple 'A') but either supported or constrained by socially constructed structures and systems and the skills and behaviours of people who are involved in the negotiation of this order.

This perspective helps us to understand the process involved in leading change and in identifying the social contexts and conditions that shape change or that typify the prevailing stability or status quo. The perspective also assists in understanding the link between individuals, organizations, and society as a whole. It helps in identifying how people respond to changes in the internal and external contexts, identifying the extent to which they respond from an individual or collective position, and identifying the patterns that emerge from these dynamic interactions.

Strauss does not view this negotiation of order in a linear way. The process of creation, maintenance, transformation, and constraint management is likely to emerge in a dynamic and cyclical manner. The negotiation patterns that emerge from these dynamic interactions will have profound implications for the resultant vision, outcomes, and collective versus individual leadership practices and partnership activities. It will thus be clear that a leadership aim of changing systems and structure first (which, I argue, is often the first thing that a new leadership will introduce) is likely to fail if it does not first address the collective vision and public interest outcomes. Moreover, we should not underestimate the importance of developing leaders' negotiation skills, something that is almost invariably lacking in the development of leaders. This is illustrated in Figure 7.2.

Figure 7.2 *The dynamic process of negotiated order*

A reflective activity is provided below for this chapter.

	Chapter 7 Activity	
Step One	Using an example from your work place consider the seven COMPASS leadership values (described earlier and listed to the right) and select FOUR of these values that you consider would be of importance in taking the London 2012 vision from inception through to success and delivery.	1. Collective Vision 2. Outcome Focus 3. Multi Level Leadership 4. Partnership Working 5. Action Oriented 6. Systems & Structures 7. Skills & Behaviours

Step One	Make a note here, or in your electronic learning journal, which of the values you identified and why: Value 1_____; Why?_____ Value 2_____; Why?_____ Value 3_____; Why?_____ Value 4_____; Why?_____

From these four values identify up to four behaviours that you think should reflect each of these values.

Step Two	**Value 1:** Behaviour:_____ Behaviour:_____ Behaviour:_____ Behaviour:_____	**Value 2:** Behaviour:_____ Behaviour:_____ Behaviour:_____ Behaviour:_____
	Value 3: Behaviour:_____ Behaviour:_____ Behaviour:_____ Behaviour:_____	**Value 4:** Behaviour:_____ Behaviour:_____ Behaviour:_____ Behaviour:_____

8 Collective Vision

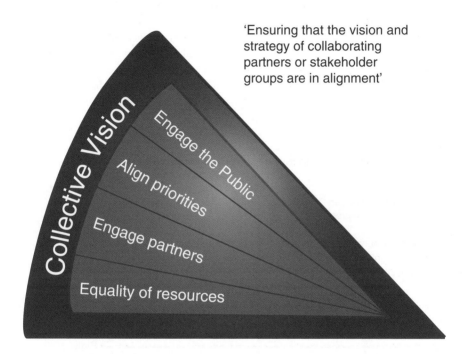

'Ensuring that the vision and strategy of collaborating partners or stakeholder groups are in alignment'

Collective Vision

Engage the Public

Align priorities

Engage partners

Equality of resources

DEFINING THE COLLECTIVE VISION

Our 360° collective leadership journey begins with a collective vision. We discussed the meaning and importance of 'vision' in earlier chapters. In this section, I also want to emphasize both the meaning and importance of the term collective in considering this first collective leadership value. The collectiveness of leadership and action is a key element of the leadership framework. Collective, as an adjective and a noun, is defined as being 'formed by a collection of individual persons or things; constituting a collective; gathered into one; taken as a whole; aggregate, collected'. This is opposed to the individual, and to distributive, further defined as 'Of, pertaining to, or derived from, a number of individuals taken or acting together; common'.[1]

---

[1] 'collective, adj. and n.' OED Online. Oxford University Press, June 2015. Web. 28 July 2015.

The OED helpfully distinguishes 'collective' from 'distributed'. The verb 'distribute' originates from the Latin *distribut* (a participial stem of distribute (the prefix *dis*, meaning 'in various directions' and *tribuere*, meaning 'to assign, grant, deliver')). In current language, it is defined as 'to deal out or bestow in portions or shares among a number of recipients'.[2] Rossi et al. make the point that 'there can be a potential ambiguity as to whether the aggregated entities are to act individually (distributive) or they are to act together as one (collective)' (Rossi et al., 2005:971).[3]

I also explored the difference between 'distributed' and 'shared' leadership and suggested that the notions of 'shared' and 'distributed' leadership are central to the definition of collective leadership (Brookes, 2008). Tilley supported this with an underlying theory, illustrated in Figure 8.1, as a two-dimensional matrix representing horizontal (shared) leadership and vertical (distributed) leadership (in Brookes, 2008:8).

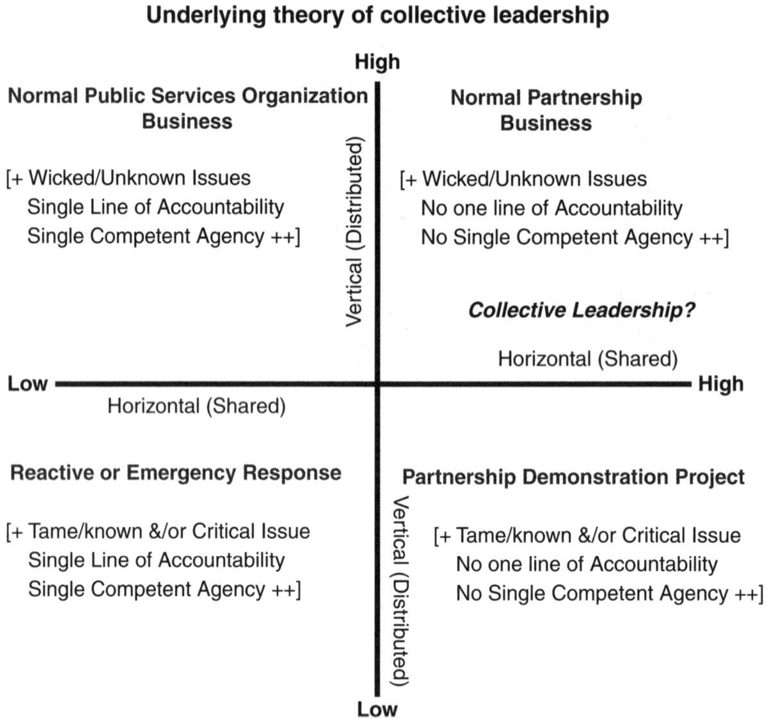

Underlying theory of collective leadership

Figure 8.1 Underlying theory of collective leadership

---

[2]'distribute, v.' OED Online. Oxford University Press, June 2015. Web. 28 July 2015.
[3]For an interesting discussion in relation to the difference between 'distributive' reading and 'collective' reading in group protocols, see Rossi, Kumar and Cohen (n.d.) 'Distributive and Collective Readings in Group Protocols', building on Clark and Carlson, 1982.

The realistic evaluation approach aligned to the theoretical framework suggests a high-level context-mechanism-outcome triad; the style of leadership representing vertical/horizontal/combination (outcome) will depend in part on the type of problem being addressed (context) and whether there is a single or plural engagement by agencies with concomitant lines of accountability (mechanism).

> **Reflection:** Think of a partnership or an alliance that you have been involved in within your workplace. Can you identify different aspects of a collective vision based on the Tilley schema in Figure 8.1?

Within the not-for-profit sector, which this particular research study was focused upon, it is argued that different styles of leadership may therefore emerge dependent upon the focus of the public agency and its relationship with others and how this is then distributed within each organization and secured through personal impact. It allows for the identification of a range of different agencies that may exhibit the four possible styles that are suggested in Figure 8.1. It may be assumed, for example, that in spite of a general tendency to a fit between leadership styles and a conducive context (such as the climate of public value and/or a climate of trust), lags are likely due to the predominance of national or corporate priorities and what may be perceived as short-term action and/or a lack of commitment in turning shared strategies into delivery. The approach seeks to identify changed leadership styles, activated by external changes in the performance climate and trust networks as well as other conditions that may be identified (hence the '++' in Figure 8.1). These factors of change may also elucidate useful evaluation mechanisms for replication purposes and the cumulating of research more generally.

I argued for a distinction between the two terms (shared and distributed) with 'collaborative leadership being shared across organizations and collegiate leadership distributed within organizations' (ibid). The combination of the two represents collective leadership with the first priority of identifying a collective vision.

I would like to offer what I see as quite a simple, but subtle, distinction that works well in understanding the complexity of leadership. Distributing leadership is about allocating leadership. As the person to whom the leadership has been distributed to, you may thus have a share of (the whole) leadership, and this is an important part of developing a collective vision – in other words, being collegiate (in the sense of, relating to, or comprising a college). Collegiate originally refers to people who are empowered members of the same organization or society who work to a common set of rules.[4] If *we* share leadership, we are collaborating (originating from the two Latin terms *com* (with) and *labore* (to work) and thus relates to the phrase 'to work with'). Thus, as the recipient of distributed leadership, you have a share of the whole (leadership), but it is only when you are engaged in the leadership that you are truly taking part in sharing the whole (leadership). It is thus about engagement and participation. This notion fits well, I suggest, with Bucky Fuller's notion of both axial and orbital rotation and his rather interesting comparison between ancient

---

[4]'collegiate, adj. and n.' OED Online. Oxford University Press, June 2015. Web. 28 July 2015.

structures (pillars and tops) which distribute mass through compression and expansion, and geometric structures (with no underpinning structure) based on sharing the mass across domes, with the minimal underpinning structure.

The collective vision seeks to draw together the aims and objectives of all partner agencies that share a common vision in a way that secures mutual benefit for all. In assessing this question, a range of behavioural dimensions has emerged from the research, the first of which is engaging the public.

ENGAGE THE PUBLIC

Leading in the public interest includes actively engaging with the public, whether it relates to private or public leadership. Remember that everything that we do involves relationships and everything that an institution or a corporate enterprise does is focused on the public (whether as Consumers, Clients, or the wider Community – the three Cs of the public). During my research, engagement with the public was described generally as 'aspirational' rather than 'actual'. One of the key leadership research questions in relation to one of the projects (including all local authorities in the North West of England) was 'how is leadership shared and distributed?' At a policy level (through analysis of the written documents), evidence of engagement was strong (in other words, what was being espoused), but at the field study level (interviews/focus groups) the experience of empowerment with citizens and users was much less. Responses from both policy officers and focus groups illustrated that this was a major weakness. At the strategic level, there was a strong sense of shared leadership and governance, as opposed to the need for significant development in relation to the empowerment of citizens and users and in undertaking the local authority role as enablers and shapers, which was much less positive (Brookes and Johnson, 2007).

In engaging the three Cs we should ask:

- Who are they, and do you and they understand the challenges in relation to the development of a shared vision?
- What needs are identified and used in developing your shared vision?

> **Reflection:** Ask these questions in relation to your own work based project or a case study.

A local authority officer who had responsibility for engaging the public gave a good example of this challenge. She said, 'Community engagement is one of those terms that we bandy about but you have got to be clear about what you are engaging the community about and make sure that the engagement adds value.' She continued, 'If we go out and ask the population as a whole what impact the LAA (Local Area Agreement) has had, most will say, "What is an LAA?" If we ask how much they have been involved in healthy living – such as the preventative agenda, active ageing or socializing, we would find hundreds of people who are now engaged'.

What we call things matters. The examples given in relation to health and well-being reflects 'wicked' or 'adaptive' challenges.

As a further example, I want to consider the changes made to the corporate vision and purpose of one of the major retail chains, Tesco PLC, and the importance given to its customers. Its former chairman, Terry Leahy, in discussing nine management lessons from transformational business experience[5] said:

> The most reliable voice is the customer. If you're prepared to listen to them, they'll tell you about their lives, what they need, what is good about your business and what's not, how your business can be improved, the list goes on.

And, in terms of leadership:

> It's all about the impact you have on other people. You need to have thousands of leaders within an organization – not just a handful. These leaders will deal with the customer, project, etc. as a leader.

In his book Leahy took this one stage further by arguing that it is not just about changing values, but that it is also about living the values to 'mobilise tens of thousands of staff to live them, day in, day out, so that every time a customer came into contact with the Tesco brand, that experience provoked a positive, rational and emotional response' (Leahy, 2012:130).

Values of society change, and so must organizations' and corporate enterprises' values. This is something that Tesco PLC recognized. In its annual report for 2013, the company described how its Core Purpose needed to reflect how much society has changed in recent years – 'more scepticism about corporations, more desire to see business demonstrate it has a purpose beyond profit, a sense that large companies should be contributing more to tackling some of the big challenges. The world has changed from a culture of "more is better" to "making what matters better".' The aim is to reflect these shifts in society in the way that Tesco thinks and behaves as a business. It is thus aiming to achieve a collective vision that puts the customer at the heart of everything it does. This is an ambitious aim, but is it one that can genuinely put 'corporate greed' behind that of the public interest?

Interestingly, this core purpose and values (which have existed for a decade) were not included in the annual report for the period ending February 2014, although they remain prominent on the company website and are implicit within the commentary. As a retailer, Tesco's business model is based on four core activities. Their statement highlights the company's *key stakeholders* and suggests that these activities will be delivered through *partnership*:

> Using our unrivalled insight to understand what *customers* want, we buy products and services from *suppliers*, move them through our *distribution network* and sell them to *customers*. Most importantly, our core purpose is at the heart of these activities. It is by improving these activities for customers each time they shop with us that we make what matters better, together. (Tesco, 2014:11)

---

[5]http://www.sas.com/knowledge-exchange/business-analytics/building-an-analytical-culture/nine-management-lessons-from-terry-leahy-former-ceo-of-tesco-plc.

We will consider the alignment of the vision with Tesco's suppliers and distribution networks shortly (as partners), but first, a brief explanation of the form of collective leadership assessment is offered.

For each of the behavioural standards, a range of statements were devised, based on the underpinning research, for the Collective Leadership Inventory (CLI) comprising a four-statement scale. The statements for the behavioural dimension of 'engaging the public' are given below. It will be noted that this ranges from 'No regard is paid to the involvement of the public and social goals are not identified' to 'Leaders not only engage with the community but actively involve them in identifying social goals'.

From this point onwards, you should consider using this inventory in terms of your own work based project or a case study. Read the explanatory notes below and then select the rating that applies (between 1 and 12). This is also available through the reflexive activity journal that can be downloaded from the book's companion website (www.palgrave.com/companion/brookes).

Does your organization proactively engage your customers or the public in deciding priorities?			
No regard is paid to the involvement of the public and social goals are not identified.	Leaders engage in discussion and consult but do not involve the community or public.	There is a strong determination to engage with the public and clear efforts are made, but social goals have yet to emerge.	Leaders not only engage with the community but actively involve them in identifying social goals.
1 2 3	4 5 6	7 8 9	10 11 12

Note of Explanation: As this is the first example (of 30 behaviours) it is opportune to provide some explanation that will serve for the remaining 29 behaviours, based on this first example. I refer back to the 12 degrees of freedom discussed earlier and the 12-point grading that is applied to each (representing a total of 360). If there was absolute perfection, then this first dimension (engage the public) for this first COMPASS value (collective vision) would score 12, and thus collective vision – if the remaining three dimensions scored the same – would be equal to the maximum of 48. If the same applied throughout the remaining 26 behaviour dimensions, the total score would be a maximum of 360! But, of course, perfection is not likely and, indeed, may not be particularly healthy. What we seek to encourage is a balanced approach across all collective leadership values and behaviours. I will discuss this in more detail at the conclusion of Part II.

ALIGN PRIORITIES

Getting 'all of the ducks lined up in a row' sounds somewhat mechanistic but is nevertheless a good maxim to follow when aligning priorities. Leahy – reflective of the advice offered by Collins (2001) – put part of the (then) success for Tesco in generating audacious goals (or big hairy ones if we listen to Collins in his use of the acronym 'BHAG'!). Too many priorities result in no priorities, and, as is often the case, we need to achieve an appropriate balance. As one policy officer told me, 'Prioritizing the priorities is thus important.' If we are leading in the public interest, the three Cs become critical: Customer, Client, or Community. In relation to the community, I found that the priorities of the public in the North West were not necessarily reflected within the priorities of the public service institutions, although this had been highlighted as a strength during the peer review of the formal partnership agreements. Only a third of policy officers interviewed and less than 20 percent of focus groups described the empowerment of citizens and users as a strength of the partnership.

A strong concern was also expressed by policy officers in relation to the bureaucratic negotiation of priorities with the regional government office. One officer commented on an additional 18 targets that were added to the existing list of 35 and yet none of these took account of their core business:

> How wide or narrow that becomes with the 35 + 18 we will have to see but it does not cover everything that we deliver – the LAA is part of the process but the wider aim is to deliver the outcomes of the wider Sustainable Community Plan, much of which is not covered in LAAs – for example, climate change.

If we again consider the Tesco case study, a large company which describes itself as 'touching millions of people's lives every day', it used its scale as a means of aligning priorities in the sense of creating opportunity to make a positive difference to some of the biggest challenges facing the world. Three big ambitions were identified in areas where it was felt that the company could make a real contribution and create value for society as a whole. Tesco introduced a new value, which was about using their scale for good, by building on the essential work that it was already doing as a responsible corporate citizen.

However, priorities change, not just for public service organizations when government's change, for example, but also for-profit enterprises. Tesco's strategic aims were dealt a serious blow during 2014 when a serious financial error occurred. Tesco discovered an overstatement in its first-half profit forecast of £250 million, due to the way in which it booked payments from deals with food suppliers, and this later rose to £263 million. This led to a dramatic decline in its stock market value ranging between 20 and 50 percent. This was alongside a decrease in market share driven primarily through the discount retailers Lidl and Aldi. As a result of this, Tesco's CEO later made an announcement regarding its changes in priorities; rediscovering competitiveness in core UK business; protecting and strengthening the balance sheet; and rebuilding trust and transparency. It was inevitable that some bad press followed, including reports of the purchase of a Gulfstream aircraft for Tesco executives (Haywood, 2014), and rebuilding trust and transparency will be a challenge. This is not unique to Tesco, as most large corporates will encounter this need at some point in their trading history, as will public service organizations at times of crisis. Responding to these challenges will require a close adherence to the priorities of the public, and Tesco will need to push its customer and community-focused values even harder.

In relation to the research and the experience of collective leadership, the behavioural conditions that emerged in relation to priorities were:

Are attempts made to broker and align policies and priorities with customer and public needs and priorities?			
The focus is entirely on internal targets.	The primary focus is on internal targets and 'lip service' is paid to public needs and priorities.	There is an increasing commitment to align public needs and priorities.	The focus is equally balanced between external and internal priorities.
1 2 3	4 5 6	7 8 9	10 11 12

ENGAGE PARTNERS

An important point of discussion is to consider the differences between not-for-profit and for-profit institutions and enterprises in relation to their respective engagement with other partners.

In relation to business, the meaning of partner can be considered as an association of two or more people as partners for the running of a business. However, it was used in a wider sense as far back as the late seventeenth century, when defined by L'Estrange in 1692 (OED, 2012) as 'Alliances, Matches, Societies; partnerships, commerce, and all manner of civil dealings and contracts'. It was even referred to by Charles Dickens when he described that he 'has been for sometime seeking a partnership in business'.[6]

In modern business, the forming of strategic alliances has become more prominent. Such an alliance is an agreement for cooperation among two or more independent firms to work together towards common objectives.[7] Such firms do not form a new enterprise but rather seek to further their aims by collaboration.

Partners also include suppliers within a supply chain with a shift away from a traditional transactional view of exchange between buyers and sellers to a more proactive, collaborative relationship approach increasingly focused on the common key themes of power and dependence, trust and commitment, cooperation, and coopetition (Fernie, 2009). Power has generally moved from supplier to retailer in terms of the ability of one entity in the chain to control the decision of another entity, with an increasing dependence of the supplier on the retailer. This is due to the increasing dominant market position (expert power) of the increasingly larger and influential retail chains, with Fernie describing this quite simply as a relationship between 'hostage' and those 'drunk with power' often resulting in a breakdown of the relationship, which has been the case in relation to the nature of competition in the UK grocery sector, focused on the possible abuse of power by retailers and their suppliers. Trust is considered as the antithesis of power, and it is trust that

---

[6]'The letters of Charles Dickens' (eds. Madeline House and Graham Storey) · 1st edition, 1965–2002 (12 vols.).

[7]http://www.businessdictionary.com/definition/strategic-alliance.html#ixzz2nxWd6Suv.

leads to cooperation but is difficult to measure – which is an important issue for the aims of this book. Coopetition – as opposed to competition – is an interesting term and means cooperation between companies that actually compete, in gaining an advantage through a mixture of cooperation with suppliers, customers, and other enterprises that produce complementary products. It is a form of strategic alliance and is practised widely by software and hardware companies in the computer industry. In all cases, relationship management is critical and, as argued, trust is an important component of this.

The case study of Tesco is interesting because the company was described as a pioneer in the supply chain, having developed a world-class logistics approach, although their movement into non-food had complicated its supply and logistics operations (Fernie and Sparks, 2009). In their early history, Tesco relied upon direct delivery to stores, often led by local managers using their own contacts, managing their own supply and demand, and, in some cases, setting their own prices. Following a substantial business reorganization known as 'Operation Checkout' in the 1970s, this shifted to a centralized approach with Tesco recognizing that they were just as much in the business of distribution as they were retailing. Smith and Sparks (Smith was a former Tesco manager) provide an interesting account of this transformation of the supply chain (Smith and Sparks, 2009) leading ultimately to the notion of value chains in terms of the chain of activities that a firm operating in a specific industry performs in order to deliver a valuable product or service for the market. Consumer service improved significantly and has been seen as one of the major reasons for the rise of Tesco in its domination of the retail market in the UK.

What occurred after this transformation of the supply chain is that the relationship between supplier and retailer changed, with the supplier being even more dependent on the retailer, with Tesco using a range of agreed performance indicators to manage its relationships and collaborations with suppliers (Smith and Sparks, ibid). At the heart of the current crisis for Tesco at the time of writing is this very relationship with their suppliers and what has been recently described as a highly aggressive approach towards suppliers from a desperate management team trying to prop up falling sales (Ruddick, 2014) with a call for a further shake-up of the supplier–retailer relationships. The revelation that suppliers pay retailers to hold promotions and place their products on prominent shelves was eye-opening in itself, and earlier scandals, such as the horse-meat scandal the previous year, have highlighted the absence of regulation of this important relationship. However, it is not just about regulation and legislation; I suggest that ethical leadership of such relationships is even more important.

These apparent concerns naturally lead to a discussion on the diverging needs of achieving either competitive or collaborative advantage. Before we consider this further, let us consider the context of partnership working within not-for-profit institutions.

At a time of fiscal crisis, public sector attention has been shifting quite significantly to the role of independent providers through partnership with the private and third sector organizations. Examples include: healthcare (private finance initiative), criminal justice (offender management), and social services (welfare-to-work). Although there is a long history of partnership working within and across public services (Brookes and Grint, 2010), the leadership challenges are now more pronounced than ever before, especially in relation to cross-sector partnerships. The notion of shared value – discussed in earlier chapters – is central to this. How do we ensure that the public interest is served through these partnerships and to what extent is the tension between both collaborative and competitive advantage likely to emerge? Are these tensions similar to those that are emerging in the supplier–retailer relationships described earlier, but in reverse?

'The strategic planning process is an example of collective action, which is critical in defining a collective vision. Collective action produces and consumes interdependences and ensures the supply and use of a public good' (Olsen, 1965); what is the role of partnership within this process?

The traditional way of managing business consists of silo-based, compartmentalized organizations, each doing their own thing with little evidence of sharing of information and data but much blaming and shaming. This emerged during the research. There is now an increasing recognition that competitive advantage is more likely to be achieved by working across boundaries and putting the three Cs at the heart of this. Boundaries between companies and institutions, suppliers, customers, and the community are being increasingly crossed by those innovative and creative organizations that seek to achieve mutual benefits through shared values. A good example of this relates to economic and social development. Business enterprises do not operate in isolation from the communities in which they exist. This applies whether we are considering the global level or a much more local public or community level. Regional approaches are also being created to bring together economic intelligence and evidence to inform the development of policy to support the region's economy, working in partnership with local authorities and a range of public and private sector partners. A good example of this is New Economy in Greater Manchester, United Kingdom and more recent changes of governance in this city region.[8] Within such partnerships, academic networks as part of a cluster with industry and public service organizations represent significant spaces where creativity and innovation can flourish. In supporting competition and growth, collaboration can provide a strengthened infrastructure, such as roads and telecommunications and access to an improved recruitment pool of local people.

We can further consider the behavioural standards that emerged from the various research projects and also apply these to the relationships described in the for-profit sector with a particular focus on ethical engagement:

Do leaders readily engage ethically with other partners in the shared delivery of mutual strategies, aims, and objectives?			
Organizations operate in isolation from others and there is no alignment between strategies, aims, and objectives.	There is linkage between partner organizations in relation to strategies etc., but it is token engagement rather than genuine ethical alignment.	Increasing efforts are being made to align respective agendas with some evidence of mutual benefit emerging.	Partners fully engage in the ethical determination of a shared vision and fully align their strategies, aims, and objectives.
1 2 3	4 5 6	7 8 9	10 11 12

---

[8]http://neweconomymanchester.com.

EQUALITY OF RESOURCES

In the previous section, it was acknowledged that partners need to achieve mutual benefit through their engagement in either strategic alliances, public service partnerships, or supplier–retailer/manufacturer relationships. One benefit that can be achieved is by virtue of pooling the knowledge and expertise of its constituent members. This brings a sense of shared purpose and values, but it also has a number of challenges that leaders face. It requires a shift in emphasis from where organizations only take responsibility for their own priorities and outcomes and pay little regard to identified public need or the development of social capital (community networks) to one in which leaders (from a number of different sectors) fully accept responsibility for delivering public value and support other leaders with their priorities. Social capital (community networks) is paramount. If we return to the revised purpose of Tesco and its aim to put its responsibilities to the communities it serves at the heart of what it does, to what extent does the equality of resources come into play, and how will the most recent setbacks act as a barrier to this? Strategic partnerships, such as those of regional economic alliances, have potential to lay the foundation for resources to be shared across a range of different organizations in the achievement of common aims.

We are becoming increasingly comfortable with the notion of shared resources in the technologies that we use in undertaking our business. From the notion of a simple local area network or intranet to networked alliances and, increasingly, through 'cloud computing' and 'open sourcing', the technological context is changing dramatically. Why is it more difficult to achieve in relation to more physical resources? Although Fernie and others tell us that for-profit organizations are increasingly collaborating in the non-visible aspects of their core business, there is much less enthusiasm for collaborating in relation to the actual core business. At the root of this reluctance may well be what I would describe as the 'corporate greed' factor; enterprises do not want to give their competitors a resource advantage or give up the resources that they already have.

If you look at most visions, mission statements, and underpinning values, there is likely to be a strong espoused commitment to collaboration and resource sharing and yet the reality is not realized. Why is this? First, trying to get people to 'sing from the hymn sheet' is difficult. Second, even if you achieve this, providing the right systems and structures to support this is equally difficult, and third, sharing resources that one has is intuitively scary! I recently overpaid a very good friend for a service that he rendered at a celebration party. Retrieval was very difficult! He openly and honestly said to me, 'Now that I have this money, it is very difficult to give it back!' Thanks George, but I know it will come back at some point and, at the time of writing, I remain very optimistic! Why? He was honest and I trust him.

Relational leadership is central to this. Perhaps there is a need to have 'skin in the game'. I first heard this term when I was co-presenting at an international healthcare leadership conference in Brazil when a colleague from Harvard was talking about President Obama's health reforms. The simplest description of this is to invest in achieving a goal (for which you have a personal interest), even if it involves a monetary risk. The old adage of 'start as you mean to carry on' comes to mind. This may have not been ethical (although it was the early 1970s), but as a young sailor, based at HMS Victory in Portsmouth, England (the shore base), some of my colleagues acted as guides on the real (Admiral Nelson's) HMS Victory. On our 'day off' we would accompany our colleagues and make sure that we were at the front of the queue at the end of the tour. We would then pass over a ten-bob note (it was also pre-decimalization – for the uninitiated, ten shillings!) and thanked our guides for an excellent tour. If other visitors followed our lead we would get our ten-bob back; if not, it was a bit like George!

Sharing resources is not just about physical resources; it is also about tasks. How often do we say, 'if you want a job done, ask a busy person'? Some people give of their time for no recompense or reward. Think of the homeless and the hungry, particularly at Christmas. Altruism comes to the fore in a very small number of very committed people who view the homeless as vulnerable and needy rather than a much larger contingent who see the homeless as 'wasters' at best and vagabonds at worst. The same applies with tasks that help in achieving a common aim. This is true social capital.

> **Reflection:** When did you last fulfil a task that supported a common aim with no intention of personal gain? Also, when did another person support you without a selfish motivation in what you were trying to achieve?

Once again, we can consider the behavioural dimensions:

Do leaders share resources and tasks equitably in line with both partner organization and public expectations?			
Organizations only take responsibility for their own priorities and pay little regard to identified public need or the development of social capital.	Leaders accept individual responsibility for their own area of responsibility but rarely coordinate activity for the public benefit.	Leaders are increasingly accepting responsibility in a coordinated manner and are demonstrably committed to building social capital.	Leaders fully accept responsibility for delivering public value and support other leaders with their priorities. Social Capital is paramount.
1 2 3	4 5 6	7 8 9	10 11 12

FROM VISION TO DELIVERY

This chapter has explored the collective leadership behaviours underpinning the definition of a collective vision. The need to engage the public and align priorities were the first two such behavioural dimensions which are critical first steps in attaining liberation from oneself or an individual organizational perspective in the case of partnership working. A similar argument is made in relation to the engagement of partners within public–private partnerships, strategic alliances, and other networks that have a shared commitment to common aims and the need for the equitable sharing of resources.

The collective vision should determine its desired outcomes and ensure that the public interest is explicit within these outcomes. This is discussed in the next chapter.

A reflective activity is provided below for this chapter.

Chapter 8 Activity
Write notes below in relation to what you can do to improve your organization or network in these areas.

Does your organization proactively engage your customers or the public in deciding priorities?

Are attempts made to broker and align policies and priorities with customer and public needs and priorities?

Do leaders readily engage with other partners in the shared delivery of mutual strategies, aims, and objectives?

Do leaders share resources and tasks equitably in line with both partner organization and public expectations?

9 Being Outcome-Focused

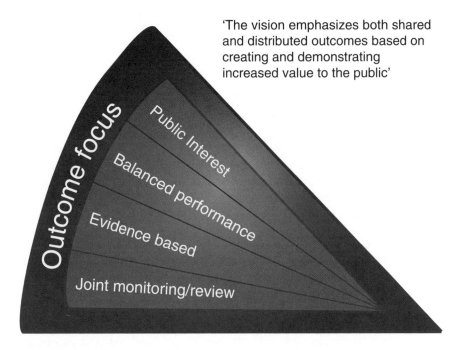

'The vision emphasizes both shared and distributed outcomes based on creating and demonstrating increased value to the public'

Outcome focus

Public Interest

Balanced performance

Evidence based

Joint monitoring/review

WHAT DO WE MEAN BY BEING OUTCOME-FOCUSED?

Outcomes can only be achieved if leadership that is shared and distributed supports efforts to do so. This is discussed in detail in Chapter 10 in describing why leadership styles need to change at all levels and how leadership through partnership can be more effective. However, the focus on outcomes also has to be shared and distributed as part of the strategic assessment and planning phase.

A key question for those who lead in the public interest is to ask whether public confidence[1] is assessed and whether action is taken to improve perceptions. Understanding the perception of our three Cs is just as important – if not more important – than assessing more traditional outcomes based on profit, growth or efficiency, and effectiveness.

---

[1]Represented by the three Cs (Customer, Client, Community).

In the Public Interest

Outcomes should provide a framework for ambitious but realistic goals across the spectrum of partners, timescales, and overall well-being targets as well as internal targets. They should be meaningful to all stakeholders. Above all they should be SMART (Specific, Measurable, Achievable, Realistic, and Time-based).

In relation to the work of leaders and their partners, we can ask:

- What are the key outcomes that the collective vision is aiming to achieve?
- How well positioned is your organization in either drawing other partners together or in being an active member of the partnership in achieving these outcomes?
- To what extent does your organization or network as a whole take both individual and collective responsibility to achieve these outcomes?

I described the notion of public value in the earlier chapters, making the point that public value represents the overall outcome of leading in the public interest. This term has only been used with reference to the not-for-profit sector, but it is equally relevant to the for-profit sector, reflected by increasing importance being given to shared value. Public confidence can be assessed through satisfaction, trust, and salience (importance) measures.

What are outcome measures that are in the public interest? Let us take health and well-being as one example, and then make a comparison with the for-profit sector.

Reducing inequalities in health has become a key desired outcome for health services in the UK and elsewhere. For example, the European Union has argued that it is becoming increasingly clear to the public health community that health is not only the responsibility of the citizen, but also of society as a whole, and, further, health cannot be dealt with by the health sector alone, because policies in many sectors have an impact on health (Wilkinson and Marmot, 2006). This requires a radical reorientation in approaches to ensuring good and equitable population health and well-being, which engages a wide range of sectors and actors in this objective.

For the purposes of this example, we will consider the outcomes sought by the National Health Service in England. A key driver for the focus on such inequalities emerged from an inquiry and subsequent report undertaken by Sir Michael Marmot in 2010. Health affects all aspects of a person's life: education, housing, employment, and safety, and individuals will have diverse needs. Health is thus unequally distributed within and between societies (Marmot, 2010). Health inequalities are preventable. It is known, for example, that people in lower socio-economic groups are more likely to experience chronic ill-health and die earlier than those who are more advantaged.

Marmot said that:

Inequalities in health arise because of inequalities in society – in the conditions in which people are born, grow, live, work and age.

The need for collective action is implicit where Marmot told us that 'Central and local government, the NHS, the third sector, the education system, the private sector, individuals, families and communities all have significant roles and responsibilities for reducing health inequalities' (Marmot, 2010:151). In terms of outcomes, an ambitious recommendation was made: 'the Quality Outcome Framework should be revised to ensure that general practices are incentivized to provide 100 percent coverage of the quality of care for all patients' (ibid:157).

While the causes of health inequality are complex, they can be predicted. The external environment conditions (political, social, economic, legal, and environmental) will influence health.[2] There is however a number of key barriers, a key one of which is that of engaging in shared outcomes. Marmot further argued:

> Common objectives and agreed priorities can be seen as key components of a partnership but these are not easy to agree in a context of different roles and responsibilities, fragmentation of funding streams and financial pressures. (ibid:3.4.1)

I now shift the focus to the concept of public interest within the for-profit sector, again using the case study of Tesco PLC. Smith and Sparks (2009) have described the continuing and significant growth of Tesco since the early days of its 'pile-"em-high"/sell-"em-cheap"' philosophy from its beginning. As the exponential growth continued, an emerging corporate concern was that of the environment. The authors point to the 'lightning rod' topics, such as plastic bags, food miles, and packaging waste, but also the internal business concern for such issues as 'reducing waste and unnecessary elements in the supply chain ... which make commercial as well as environmental sense' (ibid:166). This is one example where the achievement of collaborative advantage can also lead to a competitive advantage.

This emphasis continues, and Tesco PLC has clearly placed its corporate social responsibility at the heart of its values and strategy, as outlined below. However, these are ambitions (and, as argued by Tesco, 'big ambitions'), but what are the outcomes that are aligned to these values and strategies?

To put our responsibilities to the communities we serve at the heart of what we do

The changes we have made to our Core Purpose and Values to reflect Tesco's wider social purpose are clear signals that we put our responsibilities to the communities we serve at the heart of what we do.

Having priorities is only part of the story. Clearly, Tesco does need to prioritize its growth and profit objectives (i.e. in balancing its performance), but how are the ambitions aligned to outcomes? This is particularly important given the reputation issues that the company is now facing following the published shortfall in profits

---

[2]Institute of Public Health, Ireland.

in 2014. However, at the time of writing, there is room for optimism. A retail analyst – who argues that the growth of the large 'discounters' is slowing considerably – also suggests that the defining feature of the grocery sector in 2015 will be Tesco's recovery (Butler, 2015). The new CEO set out his vision for recovery at the beginning of 2015, which includes the reduction of overheads by 30 percent, with obvious requirements for job cuts and store closures. The immediate reaction was a 15 percent rise in the share price, following a reported 40 percent fall the previous year (Felsted and Oakley, 2015). One commentator made a point that is highly relevant to the arguments set out in this book: that it was one thing to set out a plan, but it still needed to be executed successfully. Moreover there is the need to lead at a time of inevitable low staff morale, which was clearly the case as the new CEO set out to change the decline in company performance and which needs to be balanced with the intended restructuring. This is the real challenge of collective leadership.

How can Tesco go about defining public interest measures in support of its revised social purpose and value and the latest plans of its new CEO? There is certainly no mention of public or social value in the CEO's strategic intentions. At present, this remains limited to year-on-year reductions in greenhouse gas emissions that were put forward before the current crisis. However, could such retailers make a more specific impact on improving the health and well-being of its community, and to what extent would this play a wider role in re-building the confidence of three Cs'.

Tesco's relatively new value ('We use our scale for good') offers some promise. This value recognizes that Tesco is now a large company, touching millions of people's lives every day. This scale provides an opportunity to make a positive difference to some of the biggest challenges facing the world. The company argues that the new value is about building on the essential work that it already does as a responsible corporate citizen. A good example of this is one of their 'Tesco and Society' initiatives, in helping to identify the 11 must-have skills for every 11-year-old.[3]

As we learned in the last chapter, the key message behind Porter and Kramer's notion of social value is that the competitiveness of a company and the health of the communities around it are mutually dependent (Porter and Kramer, 2011). The arguments within this article have since been supported in relation to case studies in which corporate enterprises have demonstrated this mutually dependent connection. One example from Porter and Kramer illustrates this:

> *'Since their launch, in 2005, Nexera canola and sunflower seeds, used for making cooking oils, have become one of Dow Chemical's best-selling product lines. The seeds and the oils offer many advantages: The seeds yield more than twice as much oil per hectare as soybeans, making them an attractive crop for farmers. The oils' longer shelf and "fry" lives lower the operating costs of food manufacturers and food service companies. And, last but not least, the oils have lower levels of fat'.*

Pfitzer and his colleagues suggest that corporate leaders are beginning to awake to the reality of this dependent relationship and 'realize that social problems present both daunting constraints to their operations' and yet 'vast opportunities for

---

[3]http://www.tescoplc.com/index.asp?pageid=137&tiletype=news&id=1141#opentile

growth' (Pfitzer et al., 2013:100). However, in a study of 30 companies, it is evident that many are struggling to implement the concept of shared value. The authors point to five mutually reinforcing elements: embedding a social purpose, defining the social need, measuring shared value, creating the optimal innovation structure, and co-creating with external stakeholders.

I now consider the behavioural dimensions in relation to the commitment to outcomes that are in the public interest:

Do leaders proactively develop a public value approach by assessing public confidence and taking action to improve perceptions as assessed through satisfaction, trust, and salience measures?			
Leaders have no regard to public perception as an outcome and take no account of confidence measures.	Leaders publicly acknowledge the importance of perception measures but do not focus activity on the measures.	A public value approach is starting to develop, and meaningful measures are both collected and developed but not routinely used.	Public confidence measures are central to performance and can be traced through to delivery and impact.
1 2 3	4 5 6	7 8 9	10 11 12

Balanced Performance

The example from Dow Chemical illustrates the wider benefit that accrues to society in terms of playing its part in the improvement of health and well-being, rather than focusing solely on the 'easy to measure' profit and loss measures. It is a question of balance. However, even those public service institutions that have a direct role in improving the health and well-being of communities have traditionally focused on similar 'easy to measure' and generally quantitative outcome measures. At a much more specific (and individualized) level, the Department of Health in the UK is making a determined effort to refocus performance assessment towards more qualitative and personalized outcomes. A good example of this is in relation to social care for the disabled. A group of disabled people, family carers, and representatives from eight local authorities worked together to develop a new approach to outcome reviews. The report concluded that:

> These are the things that are important to individuals to achieve. Personal goals may be linked to policy goals, but will be different for every person. Both kinds of outcome need to be measured in order to judge the results being achieved by the social care system as a whole. (DoH, 2009:2)

In this example, a personalized outcome can represent something as individual as 'keeping on top of the garden', or 'keeping in touch with family and friends', and a key mechanism for this (which we will explore in detail in the next chapter) is that of coordinating action across different departments and agencies. This is reflective of Fuller's concept of 'inside-outing' discussed in the preceding chapter.

During my research in relation to local area agreements in the North West of England, both with the policy documentary analysis and, more particularly, during the field studies, it was apparent that the focus was very much on the 'easy to measure' quantifiable outputs rather than qualitative outcomes. The strategic documents were found to be much less focused in relation to the longer-term outcomes with little evidence of analysis other than what could be described as 'fairly routine and standardised' (Brookes and Johnson, 2007:17). During the field studies, specific concerns were expressed in relation to the extent to which the formal agreements were providing 'additionality' – that is, added value. Some participants felt that the agreements 'had merely "brigaded" what already existed rather than encouraging more creative thinking' (ibid:28). Those who expressed this also felt that most of the focus for the agreement concerned the alignment to funding or attempts to capture more funding and serving the process rather than outcomes. In later studies of a metropolitan police force, and health authorities, very similar views were expressed.

Developing balanced performance assessments is not a new approach. Kaplan and Norton inspired the traditional approach to this in 1990 in their formulation of the balanced scorecard (BSC). In 1996, the authors posed the following question:

> Imagine entering the cockpit of a modern jet airplane and seeing only a single instrument there (for example, airspeed). How would you feel about boarding the plane? (Kaplan and Norton, 1996:1)

Following a conversation with the pilot who acknowledges that this is the only instrument that he uses (hypothetically ignoring other issues such as fuel, height, etc.), the authors suggest that we would not board the plane! The analogy to this, of course, is why do we often allow this to happen with our businesses? The BSC (with vision and strategy at its core) has, and continues to be, widely used and comprises four main domains: financial, customer, internal business processes, and learning and growth. There has also been a suggested development in relation to a balanced public value scorecard (PVSC) (Brookes and Wiggan, 2009; Talbot and Wiggan, 2010), in which the service user and service delivery is given prominence.

Let us return to the case study of Tesco PLC. In the previous chapter, I discussed Terry Leahy's focus on the customer, and he was instrumental in the introduction of a form of balanced scorecard that has become known as the 'steering wheel' to support his passion to lead the market through superior customer knowledge. The steering wheel was divided into five sectors: Customer, Community (added more recently), Operations, People, and Finance. The steering wheel no longer appears prominently in either the strategic documents or the corporate website. Whether this is due to the recent change of CEO can only be speculated upon, given that its origin was Leahy. However, the corporate social responsibility report continues to be published, and performance in three social value areas (called big ambitions) continues to be reported on the corporate website in an easy-to-read format. This relates to reducing food waste, improving health, and creating opportunities.[4]

The behavioural dimensions in relation to balanced performance are:

---

[4]Tesco PLC, http://www.tescoplc.com/index.asp?pageid=654.

Is the Performance Management Framework based on Balanced Performance that reflects social values as well as business values?			
The framework reflects only national or business targets with no recognition of social values.	The primary focus is on national/business targets with minimal focus on local social value targets.	There is an increasing commitment to measure and assess local targets based on social values as well as business objectives.	There is an equal commitment to both national/business and local targets and action that support social values.
1 2 3	4 5 6	7 8 9	10 11 12

Evidence-Based Decision Making

For the purposes of collective leadership, being evidence-based concerns the ground for belief, testimony, or facts tending to prove or disprove any conclusion. One could be forgiven for assuming that evidence-based decision making (and evidence-based policy-making) applies only to the not-for-profit sector (and certainly Internet search engines would almost exclusively return results related to the public sector, and the health sector specifically). An understandable response would suggest that the evidence for decisions and outcomes within the public sector would be much more difficult to achieve than it would be in the for-profit sector because, invariably, social problems are far more complex (and 'wicked') for public service institutions than in commercial enterprises where profit and growth would be the main focus.

We would be wrong for making this assumption. As I suggested in earlier chapters, the financial crisis that now affects most of the developed world is due, in no small part, to the use of 'information' that was far from evidence-based but, rather, was motivated (and constructed) by greed and deceit. Moreover, this is not to suggest that similar motivations are not present in the not-for-profit sector, a conclusion that was drawn by Sir Robert Francis in his report in relation to the failings of leadership at the Mid Staffordshire Foundation Trust in 2013.

Enron represented the first of the contemporary corporate scandals in relation to the debt of one of the company's off-balance-sheet vehicles leading to an overstatement of profits by almost $600m over the years 1997–2000. Of relevance to the core argument of this book – leading in the public interest – is the further suggestion that Enron were closely engaged in funding political campaigns (Economist, 2002). The banking crisis followed in 2008 primarily as a result of investment in the sub-prime mortgage market. This crisis involved Bear Stearns, Northern Rock, and the high profile demises of Lehman Brothers and Washington Mutual, as well as the less destructive but almost equally critical situation for the Royal Bank of Scotland Group (RBS). It was perhaps the intervention of the government that prevented it from going the same way as Lehman's and Washington Mutual.

We can also explore the recent crisis with Tesco. Tesco was predicting that it would make £1.1 billion profit for the first half of 2014 and yet a quarter of this was due to a misstatement. As the BBC reported, 'if you cannot trust a business's accounts, then there is not much left to trust' (Ahmed, 2014). We could therefore ask where the evidence was, or, more importantly, what evidence was missing that led to this misstatement? Moreover, as the article continues, 'using a company's legal department to raise concerns rather than going direct to executives or the board – is thought by some to reveal a business where trust is not much evident'. The detail related to a large discrepancy between when profits were accounted for from deals with suppliers and when costs were paid, and there was sufficient doubt on the reasons for this that the share price tumbled. This is indeed support for the fact that a lack of an effective evidence-base is just as dangerous for the for-profits corporates as it is for those that deal in public services.

A key finding of the field research for the North West project was that analytic capability was not being used to its full advantage, nor were there considered sufficient resources to achieve effective development of evidence-based strategies, taking due account of what was known to have worked in other areas or in tackling similar issues. A greater emphasis needed to be placed on the development of 'middle managers' to turn the strategies into evidence-based activity in terms of delivery. The need for tasking, coordination, and commissioning is at the heart of the requirement for evidence-based 'decision-making' and 'co-production'. There were some very encouraging responses in relation to the strengths of tasking and coordination mechanisms, but these tended to relate to areas of community safety, where police tasking and coordination processes had been embedded for some time.

Evidence-based decision-making is thus not just about identifying, applying, and disclosing the evidence, but additionally it is about ensuring that the evidence is grounded in fact. My earlier research suggested that there are four possible levels of adherence to evidence-based decision making:

Are the expressed outcomes evidence-based?			
There is no evidence to support either the identification of outcomes or their assessment.	There is evidence that the outcomes were linked to a strategic assessment but it is mainly quantitative.	Increasing efforts are being made to support both the identification and monitoring of outcomes.	All expressed outcomes are evidence-based in terms of identification and monitoring.
1 2 3	4 5 6	7 8 9	10 11 12

Joint Monitoring and Review

In Chapter 6 we considered the role of cybernetics in taking a whole systems approach, acknowledging that it is about control and communication within organizations. This can be a difficult issue to resolve as a leader within one organization, let alone a network of organizations. This has been a feature of industry since the early days of Taylorism at the turn of the nineteenth to twentieth centuries and is still a key focus of many industries today. A key question to ask is, 'What do we mean by performance'? This was generally described in the opening part of this book, but in tailoring monitoring and review of performance we need to know what performance we are measuring, how, and with what effect. In an industrial setting, comprehensive approaches are required in assessing the effectiveness of control systems including: determining the capability of the control system, development of suitable statistics for monitoring the current system, and diagnosing underlying causes for change and incorporating these within the appropriate industrial setting (Harris et al., 1999), minimum variance control and root cause diagnostics (Qin, 1998), and energy benchmarking (for example, in the construction industry) (Li et al., 2014). These are very much related to the performance of processes and systems as opposed to people and delivery. Performance assessment and review of wider socially desirable objectives can easily become much more nebulous than the assessment of processes, etc.; if you add differing organizations within a network and the consideration of performance in the public interest to this, how can leaders satisfy these more complex requirements?

A good example of a massive multidimensional leadership task was the process of bidding, transitioning, planning, implementing, and conducting legacy review for the London Olympics in 2012. The concept behind the original bid had five key aims: delivering the experience of a lifetime for athletes; leaving a legacy for sport in the UK; benefiting the community through regeneration; supporting the International Olympics Committee and the Olympic Movement; and developing compact, iconic, and well-connected venues (LOCOG, 2013:5). One of the aims in relation to transition planning was that of 'knowledge capture':

> An archive of documents which was a valuable resource to LOCOG staff (as well as to any future bidding cities), as well as a report from each functional area within the bid as to what was done, why they did it and what they could have improved on. The aim of this was to satisfy the reporting requirements of the IOC and stakeholders while effectively creating a 'bidding manual' for future UK bids. (LOCOG, 2012:75)

The London 2012 Olympic Games were revered across the world. In the third volume (post-Games) report, the Chairman, Lord Coe, said that this (success) was a result of intensive planning and preparation by teams that were 'well prepared, enabled and empowered by a leadership whose confidence in the delivery of the Games was the result of strategies and plans that were carefully developed, tested and reviewed' (LOCOG, 2013).

As the Games approached, the testing events proved highly valuable and 'behaviours were adopted and adapted as necessary' (LOCOG, 2013:75). Integrated delivery was identified as a key leadership task, in understanding 'what leadership means in the context of the different phases' (ibid:127), particularly as the team was 'doubling' each year. In terms of the impact across the nation, a Nations and Regions Group was formed, the purpose of which was to pool ideas to form a mechanism for engaging key stakeholders in delivering initiatives, extending beyond just sport and also to education, culture, health, business, and tourism.

One of the key success factors for the integration of delivery through empowered leadership was the inclusion of staff from external partners and other functional areas. They were embedded in the team and this proved to be a very useful method of ensuring mutual understanding of intentions and requirements. In terms of outcomes, lifetime budgeting exercises were undertaken, which was fundamental to ensuring that the financial resources available to LOCOG were directed to the right areas to deliver the desired Games outcomes. At the conclusion of the Games, the venue master plan was reviewed and optimized immediately after the bid to enhance the Olympic Park experience for the athletes and spectators and for legacy (ibid:8).

Tesco has been described as a pioneer in performance management in the retailing sector and yet a quarter of a billion pounds was still misstated. Given that this related to revenues received from suppliers as an incentive for greater promotion and placement of their products, we can further ask to what extent the suppliers were engaged in jointly monitoring this aspect of Tesco performance. Pressure for more supplier income would lead to greater pressure on suppliers by the buyers. The BBC report provided an excellent description of this from a senior retail industry research analyst:

> As a retailer you always have long-term relationships with suppliers – and in any long-term relationship you have give and take, much like a marriage. Clearly while everything was going well, suppliers wanted to work with Tesco and Tesco asked for things back. But because Tesco has been under three or four years of substantial profits pressure it has been pulling the bed cover over to its side a bit more – and it got more and more unbalanced. (BBC, 2015)

Leading in the public interest thus requires an appropriate balance. Let us consider this alongside the behavioural dimensions that emerged from my research:

Do leaders work together in identifying and monitoring outcomes?			
Partners within a network operate within its organizational silos in relation to outcomes with no joint identification or assessment.	Leaders share information in relation to outcomes but do not integrate it with partner organizations processes.	Leaders are strong in sharing outcome data and are increasingly linking it with all organizational performance frameworks.	Performance frameworks are totally integrated in relation to the outcomes supporting the partnerships aims.
1 2 3	4 5 6	7 8 9	10 11 12

OUTCOMES THAT REFLECT THE PUBLIC INTEREST

The focus of the chapter then moved to the desired outcomes of the vision in the creation and demonstration of public value. A critical component of this is to lead in the public interest – to which all else should be subjugated – but within a balanced performance framework that encourages effort across all performance domains in accordance with need. It would be easy, for example, to throw all resources into improving the reputation of the organization and its networks with clients, customers, or the community, but this would be pointless if the levels of leadership, its partnerships networks, action plans, systems and structure and, not least of which, skills and behaviours, are ignored. These behaviours are critical to decision-making, and the third behavioural dimension for the behaviours associated with an outcome focus is the need to be evidence-based. The chapter concluded with looking briefly at the London 2012 Olympic Games as an example of a massive multidimensional leadership task that highlights very clearly the need for joint monitoring and review.

The focus on developing a collective vision, which is outcome-focused, lays a strong foundation for the remaining collective leadership values and behaviours that are explored in the following chapters.

A reflective activity is provided below for this chapter.

Chapter 9 Activity

Write notes below in relation to what you can do to improve your organization or network in these areas.

Do leaders proactively develop a public value approach by assessing public confidence and taking action to improve perceptions as assessed through satisfaction, trust, and salience?

Is the Performance Management Framework based on Balanced Performance that reflects social values as well as business values?

Are the expressed outcomes evidence based?

Do leaders work together in identifying and monitoring outcomes?

10 The Importance of Multi-Level Leadership

'Shared and distributed leadership takes place throughout and across each partner organization or stakeholder group'

Multi-level leadership comprises both the notion of shared (inter-organizational) and distributed (intra- organizational) leadership and thus emphasizes the importance of horizontal, vertical, and diagonal leadership. I described in the earlier chapters that the two terms – shared and distributed leadership – were often, and incorrectly, conflated. Although very similar, the two concepts do represent different forms of leadership, as I describe shortly.

Leaders should acknowledge that there are multiple levels of leadership and determine the extent to which leadership is both shared (between partner organizations or groups) and distributed (between people within its own teams).

Multi-level leadership also focuses on long-term as well as short-term priorities. The success of multi-level leadership rests on the setting of clear goals. Leaders at all levels need to both know and understand what is required of them and why. Within my research in public service institutions and through executive education programmes with public leaders, the extent to which clear goals were being set was a major weakness and was seen to be a major factor inhibiting the development of collective leadership.

SHARED LEADERSHIP

The practice of leadership has traditionally focused on the individual as opposed to the collective. I argue that shared leadership takes place across boundaries, whether this relates to inter- or intra-organizational boundaries, and can be considered at a peer-to-peer level, but also both 'up and down' as well as across. For the reasons that I argued earlier, shared leadership is wider than distributed leadership and concerns the negotiation between leaders in terms of shared priorities and in sharing the practice of leadership specifically.

Shared leadership crosses organizational boundaries. As always, relationships are at the heart of this. In 2013, Tesco's relationships with one of their largest suppliers broke down, allegedly due to the French cosmetics firm L'Oréal threatening legal action after a disputed payment of around £1 million. A Tesco spokesman said that while they value their relationship with such large suppliers, differences do sometimes occur in the course of commercial relationships (Duell, 2015). An agreement was eventually reached on this. However, similar issues sit behind the crisis that is current at the time of writing. In a BBC Panorama programme (BBC, 2015) it was said that a Tesco suppliers survey indicated that a third were unhappy with the way that Tesco treated them, with evidence of aggressive buying, bullying, and an intent to 'hunt around trying to take money from suppliers'. It was further said that it is important for Tesco and their suppliers to think about their businesses together and how they can create new value that they can share together. An important question to ask here is that of the public interest; it is about the wider public as well as the consumers/customers. During the broadcast, its former CEO Terry Leahy said that Tesco needed to address again what really matters to customers, and he pointed to failed leadership at Tesco as the primary cause of the (then) current crisis. A similar report was broadcast on 5 February 2015, when a small-scale chocolate supplier withdrew his partnership with Tesco after he was owed £6,000, which was settled 106 days later and five months after the contract was signed.

There is a clear issue here of inadequate shared leadership between the retailer, the suppliers, and the customers. However, in terms of the language of public value, what about the authorizing environment, that of government? The Groceries Code Adjudicator appeared on both broadcasts and (at the time of writing) is investigating Tesco in relation to bullying and late payments. However, she is unable to levy fines on the retailers because this aspect of the code is still being discussed within government. The Secretary of State for Business, Innovation and Skills also stated on the latter programme that his cabinet colleagues were unable to agree on the right way forward. One could perhaps ask where the public interest features in these deliberations, or is this an example of selfish political leadership that encourages the selfish commercial leadership to exploit the suppliers and ultimately the wider public?

Government thus plays a key role as one of the stakeholders in the public value authorizing environment just as much in the for-profit sector as it does in the not-for-profit sector. There was clear evidence from the public leadership research in the North West of England that government restrictions were a major barrier to increasing shared leadership between public service organizations in working towards shared goals that are in the public interest. This particularly applies in relation to the 'silo-based' performance targets that the different government departments impose on public service organizations. I saw this specifically during my role as a senior civil servant when it proved impossible to get the Department of Health and the Home Office in the UK to agree on shared priorities in tackling problem drug users, with the former favouring clinical interventions whereas the latter favoured criminal justice interventions. There is also a clear link with evidence-based leadership, as research at the time suggested that for every £1 spent on clinical treatment, £7 was saved in the longer term; while this satisfied the Department of Health, the short-term approach to enforcement and incarceration was preferred by the Home Office. At the same time, the Home Office was also at odds with the (then) Office of the Deputy Prime Minister (ODPM) in relation to the partnerships that each department had responsibility for. The ODPM would not support the alignment of 'their' Local Strategic Partnerships (LSPs) – the partnerships that featured in my research – and the Home Office's Community Safety Partnerships (CSPs), as a result of which shared priorities become much more difficult to both agree and achieve.

It is thus interesting to consider how shared leadership takes place within either formal strategic alliances across the for-profit sector or less structured partnering arrangements, such as those between retailers and suppliers as well as those of the not-for-profit sector. Procurement often lies at the heart of these arrangements, within a broad range of relationship contracting models. The terms 'partnering' and 'alliancing' are also conflated (as argued in Chapter 11 later), and yet they represent different forms of relationships. However, shared leadership is common to both and can assist in addressing the barriers that are often presented in terms of sharing both risk and reward. However, there are no easy solutions to this. It is of some concern that a government think tank suggested in the spring of 2014 that the NHS should operate like Tesco and that much of the work the NHS does could be carried out by private or voluntary providers within a decade (Cooper, 2014). The report suggested that the health service should learn from 'supermarket chains such as Tesco, by mirroring its business model of large superstores and smaller local shops, with small-scale community hospitals'. Given the problems associated with other aspects of this business model, such proposals should be treated with extreme caution given the weak association with effective shared leadership.

Behavioural responses in relation to shared leadership range from no dialogue to routine dialogue within networks:

To what extent do leaders share their leadership by negotiating to align their priorities with those of other partners?			
Leaders do not have any dialogue with each other and individual priorities are not aligned.	There is some dialogue between leaders but it is 'as and when' rather than routine.	There is increasing dialogue between leaders but more is needed.	Dialogue between leaders is routine and priorities are aligned.
1 2 3	4 5 6	7 8 9	10 11 12

DISTRIBUTED LEADERSHIP

In my research, there was much less evidence of shared leadership as opposed to distributed, but, even then, the extent to which the distributed leadership was collective and empowered as opposed to hierarchically imposed was not entirely evident.

Generally then, distributed leadership takes place within an organization. This is reflective of a hierarchy but ideally within the context of empowerment. However, the real jewel-in-the-crown is where there is a clear link between the shared and distributed dimensions in which the senior and sharing leaders distribute their leadership in an empowering way, both in terms of leading-up as well as leading-down and where this sharing and distributing is cascaded at the remaining levels of leadership. This starts to define a real compass approach to leadership, in which leadership can take place in any direction (including diagonally).

Within the research, where distributed leadership took place, this was normally supported by what are increasingly termed either 'task-and-finish' or 'tasking-and-coordination' groups (a primarily public service leadership term), although Sir Terry Leahy was keen on an empowerment model of leadership during his Tesco tenure. Tasking and coordination is a consistent approach in policing through a national intelligence model (NIM). There were good examples within my research where these principles worked well across multi-agency partnership networks, for example in tackling what was described as dysfunctional families (in one local government area during the research in the North West of England) or troubled families (in UK government polices from 2011). In 2011, it was estimated that £9 billion was spent annually on troubled families – an average of £75,000 per family each year. Of this, an estimated £8 billion was spent reacting to the problems these families have and cause, with just £1 billion being spent on helping families to solve and prevent problems in the longer term (DCLG, 2014). Policy actions included getting children back into school, reducing youth crime and anti-social behaviour, and putting adults on a path back to work. A further aim is to reduce the high costs these families place on the public sector each year, and local authorities are encouraged to work with families in ways the evidence shows is more effective, such as:

- Joining up local services.
- Dealing with each family's problems as a whole rather than responding to each problem, or person, separately.

- Appointing a single key worker to get to grips with the family's problems and work intensively with them to change their lives for the better for the long term.
- Using a mix of methods that support families and challenge poor behaviour. (ibid)

Distributed leadership behaviours are critical to the alignment between shared and distributed components. The policy aims described above clearly have the potential to achieve this, but it still requires a change in leadership behaviours, to value multi-leadership roles through shared priorities and tasks and empowering those who can deliver the services.

Let us briefly consider the buyers' role in Tesco. Each buyer is subject to strict targets and the extent of aggressive negotiations has been commented upon. An anonymous article published in a reputable management periodical, purporting to be by a graduate trainee buyer in the 'meat' buyers' department, leaves nothing to the imagination in the description of the aggressive, contrived, and often abusive negotiations with suppliers (Anon, 2014) and, it would appear, quite early in the Leahy era. Whether this is a feature of the 'empowerment' that was given to Tesco employees is a matter of opinion, but it is hardly the form of distributed leadership that will encourage integrity and partnership working.

In relation to these behavioural standards we can ask:

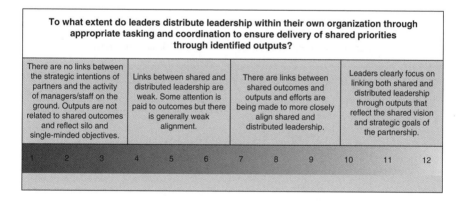

LONG-TERM FOCUS

I see 'time' as one of the key dimensions of leadership (alongside mass and space). Leaders take note of the present situation but envision a future based on the long term. To envision is to see or foresee, as in a vision. It is clearly important to keep track of short-term imperatives, such as the financial and operational aspects of the business or service delivery, but this should not overshadow the longer-term aspirations. However, many leaders do focus on the short term, particularly those in public services and positions of administrative responsibility, such as politicians (where a five-year focus is often the maximum). Leadership involves influencing people within your organization to make day-to-day decisions that lead to long-term sustainability while maintaining short-term financial and human resource capacities and capabilities. The radical turnaround of businesses and public service organizations has often been premised on an appropriate balance between the short and the long term. Conversely, failure often follows from short-term activities without taking account of the 'bigger picture'. I discuss this further in subsequent chapters as part of the adaptive leadership approach; risk taking and rationality are similarly required in both cases.

The London 2012 Games provides a good example of considering the short-term aims of securing the nomination as host city, although long-term legacy goals were also needed. However, long-term goals are much more difficult to measure, and we are unlikely to see the impact of the London 2012 legacy goals for some considerable time. Conversely, focus on short-term priorities can ultimately undermine or destroy long-term goals, as has been seen to be the case at Tesco, with too much reliance on short-term promotions, to the detriment of the company's long-term sustainability (BBC, 2015).

The wider global financial crisis is considered to have been caused by several factors which were exacerbated by 'excessive short-term thinking' (Orsagh, 2012:1). This concerns stewardship in the long term and draws the importance of leadership alongside that of good governance. This is also something that I discuss further in later chapters, but it is important to consider a focus on balancing the short term with the long term as one of the key behaviours of leading in the public interest:

Do leaders at all levels focus on the long term as well as the short term?			
There is no focus at all in relation to long-term goals other than through strategic ambition and all efforts are reactive to day-to-day short-term problems.	There is some focus on long-term issues but it primarily relates to aspiration rather than reality and is not cascaded below executive/ corporate level.	Leaders at most levels focus on long-term issues but there is still a primary focus on short-term.	Leaders at all levels provide an appropriate balance between short-term and long-term issues.
1 2 3	4 5 6	7 8 9	10 11 12

SETTING OF CLEAR GOALS

At its deepest roots, goal-directed action also has its origins in biology; 'all living organisms, from plants to animals to people, must engage in goal-directed actions in order to survive' (Locke and Latham, 2013:3). Some of this is automatic as a result of evolution, whereas other actions are the result of consciousness, which clearly separates people from plants, as those who benefit from experience through learning.

The setting of clear goals is a critical role for leadership. Some 40 years ago, it was suggested that 'hard' goals lead to better performance than soft goals, but only if the goals are consciously accepted by individuals (Locke, 1968, quoted in Latham and

Yukl, 1975). Latham and Yukl reviewed research on the application of goal setting in organizations, particularly in industry, as well as reviewing Locke's original work. They looked at three aspects of Locke's research:

i. The effects of specific goals versus generalized goals or no goals.
ii. The effects of goal difficulty on performance.
iii. Goals as mediators of performance feedback, monetary incentives, and time limits. (Latham and Yukl, 1975:827)

Specific goals were more likely to lead to improved performance, although it proved difficult to isolate the impact of the setting of the goal from other factors. In relation to the second aspect of Locke's research, most of the studies reviewed supported Locke's contention that 'harder goals' lead to better performance. Factors that affected goal difficulty also influenced goal acceptance, particularly where the perception of the employee was that the goal was reasonable and attainable and the outcome desirable. Latham and Yukl could not find any studies that directly addressed the impact of goals as mediators of performance, but they were able to consider work that focused on feedback and its different forms. This appeared to be less consistent, although there was some evidence that employees were motivated by financial incentives.

It is interesting that this review of the research in 1975 conducted as 'Management by Objectives' (MBO) was being implemented by a range of industries and which I referred to in the introductory chapter as being the precursor of New Public Management (NPM) in the public sector.

The authors provide a useful description of MBO:

> Management by objectives is an approach to planning and performance appraisal that attempts to clarify employee role requirements, and relate employee performance to organization goals, improve manager-subordinate communication, facilitate objective evaluation of employee performance, and stimulate employee motivation. An essential feature of the MBO approach is the setting of specific performance goals and, in many cases, goals for personal development of the employee. (ibid:830)

In the 40 years since this review, the setting of goals remains a key element of management both in the for-profit and not-for-profit sector. Locke and Latham have continued to study the issue and developed the approach to goal setting theory, which they describe as a theory of motivation. They published their first book in 1990 (Locke and Latham, 1990) and a further edited book in 2013 (Locke and Latham, 2013). In their latest book, the authors maintain that goal setting theory is still relevant in 2013 and, based on many studies over the 40 years, point to a process of theory building which – while not creating timeless certainty – 'does bring contextual certainty' because additional discoveries widen a theory's context, a point fully acknowledged and supported within the research underpinning this book. This process of theory building includes the following (ibid:623):

i. Formulating clear concepts and definitions.
ii. Collecting data, including making systematic observations across a range of conditions.
iii. Taking measurements.
iv. Identifying causal relationships including causal mechanisms.
v. Looking for limiting conditions.
vi. Looking for and resolving contradictory findings.
vii. Making inductive generalizations that go beyond previous observations.

As is often the case, there is also a dark side to goal setting, which the Enron case illustrated starkly. In this case, it is argued that the beneficial effects of goal setting were overstated and that systematic harm caused by goal setting was largely ignored (Ordóñez et al., 2009:4). Specific side effects associated with goal setting include 'a narrow focus that neglects non-goal areas, a rise in unethical behavior, distorted risk preferences, corrosion of organizational culture, and reduced intrinsic motivation'. The authors recall that:

> Even during Enron's final days, Enron executives were rewarded with large bonuses for meeting specific revenue goals. In sum, Enron executives were meeting their goals, but they were the wrong goals, according to employee compensation expert Solange Charas. By focusing on revenue rather than profit, Enron executives drove the company into the ground. (ibid:4)

Are there some chilling similarities between Enron and Tesco? Returning to our Tesco case study, there is no doubt that the fortunes of the company have been very strong, having reached a position where the company was the second largest retail company in the world, with only Wal-Mart ahead of it (and which, coincidentally, is the second largest organization in the world). Setting clear goals has been a strong feature throughout the rise of Tesco. Performance management in Tesco is paramount and, on the face of it, ethical and transparent (as commented upon in the earlier chapter on outcome focus), as argued by Smith (Smith and Sparks, 2009). There is much more recent evidence of the dark side of setting clear goals, but the principle is still sound; just make sure that they are the right goals!

The National Health Service in the UK is the fifth largest organization in the world (and the largest in Europe), with 1.4 million employees representing 2.5 percent of the country's working population. The most significant crisis in its 60-year history emerged in 2009, when it became apparent that, between 2005 and 2008, conditions of appalling care were able to flourish in the main hospital serving the people of Stafford and its surrounding area. During this period this hospital was managed by a Board, which succeeded in leading its Trust (the Mid Staffordshire General Hospital NHS Trust) to foundation trust (FT) status[1] (Francis, 2013:7). Sir Robert Francis QC was appointed to undertake a public inquiry in relation to these

---

[1] NHS foundation trusts were created to devolve decision making from central government to local organisations and communities. FTs are not directed by government and thus have greater freedom to decide their own strategies and the way services are run.

failings. The Board had been scrutinized by several regulatory bodies and yet none had found systemic failings. The issues nevertheless emerged in part by attention that was drawn to the true implications of its mortality rates, but mainly because of the persistent complaints made by a group of patients and those close to them. In the aftermath of the inquiry, it became clear that it was a failure of leadership as well as systemic failures. In particular, a culture of fear was prevalent in which staff did not feel able to report concerns. The trust board wrapped itself in a culture of secrecy and ignored its patients. A culture of bullying was also present which prevented people from doing their jobs properly (ibid:10).

If one is to consider a collective vision for the NHS, its Constitution provides the foundation for this. Referring to the Constitution and in support of common values, Francis said that patients 'must be the first priority in all of what the NHS does by ensuring that, within available resources, they receive effective care from caring, compassionate and committed staff, working within a common culture, and protected from avoidable harm and any deprivation of their basic rights' (Francis, 2013:67). He made a key recommendation that commissioners and providers determine developmental standards that set longer-term goals and, further, that the set of fundamental standards are easily understood and accepted by patients, the public, and healthcare staff, and that breach should not be tolerated.

In considering the setting of clear goals, we can ask the following question in determining the behavioural standards:

Do leaders set clear goals for their team that are fully aligned to the collective vision with integrity?			
Leaders do not communicate their strategic intentions, and implementation is driven from the top and is directive.	There are some attempts to set clear goals but there is no emphasis on giving distributed and empowered responsibility.	Leaders make real efforts to set clear goals but it remains difficult to cascade these vertically	Clear goals are set for all and individuals know what they are expected to achieve.
1 2 3	4 5 6	7 8 9	10 11 12

A reflective activity is provided below for this chapter.

Chapter 10 Activity

Write notes below in relation to what you can do to improve your
organization or network in these areas.

Do leaders share their leadership by negotiating to align their priorities with those of other
partners?

To what extent do leaders distribute leadership within their own organization through tasking
and coordination to ensure delivery of shared priorities through identified outputs?

Do leaders at all levels focus on the long term as well as the short term?

Do leaders set clear goals for their team that are fully aligned to the collective vision
with integrity?

11 Partnership Working

'Shared and distributed leadership takes place throughout and across each partner organization or stakeholder group'

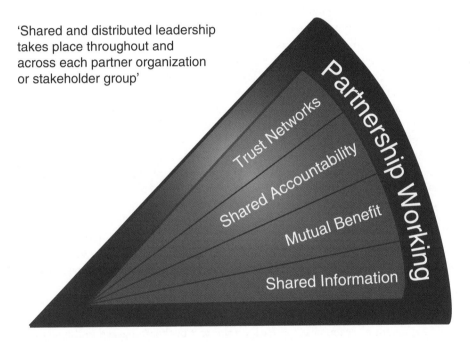

Partnership is viewed as a key to improvement in identifying and responding to shared priorities and performance and in ensuring that all organizations and corporations have a deep understanding of what really matters to users and customers, the public, and those who deliver the services.

Partnership working is a relatively new term in relation to business and institutional working (Segil et al., 2003) and yet the concept has been around from time immemorial. Sun Tzu (in *The Art of War* from the sixth century BC) said, 'If you do not seek out allies and helpers, then you will be isolated and weak' (Sun and Giles, 1910). Partnership has also been important to first nation inhabitants:

First nations people have a long history of seeking out allies and help. We've done this from time immemorial among ourselves as we made our lives on the land. This spirit of partnership guided our efforts in treaty relations with newcomers to this territory now called Canada. Without us, they might have perished. Today it remains as important as ever to seek allies and helpers – among ourselves and with others – as we seek greater economic participation for our communities. (Bellegarde, 2013:4)

The actual term partnership first appeared in the English language in 1647 when Nathaniel Bacon referred to a partnership between the English rulers and the Normans in their ancient right of government, referring also to the need for the English King 'to win and maintain the good opinion of the people by consorting with them under one law' (Bacon and Selden, 1647:122).

As argued earlier, building collaborative advantage is also a means of achieving competitive advantage, but what are the critical factors in enabling this? I further argued that partnership is an association of two or more people as partners for the running of a business, with shared expenses, profit, and loss as a collective, whereas a strategic alliance is an agreement for cooperation among two or more independent firms to work together towards common objectives. Working in partnership is a popular phrase, but the reality is that it is extremely difficult to achieve relying upon trust, shared accountability, and shared information in the achievement of mutual benefit.

All businesses will encounter gaps: gaps in knowledge, technology, financial and human resources, market presence, and supply chains, not to mention the expertise and experience that is required. Collaboration through partnership working can help in bridging those gaps. However, it is not an easy process and can be quite chaotic, particularly in the set-up phase. Some will step carefully while others will seek to take big strides; selfish behaviour will often predominate over selfless behaviour, and working to a sense of shared values and shared purpose can be very difficult. Working in partnership can bridge these gaps but it is one of the hardest tasks to fall to leaders.

Relationship contracting within the for-profit sector (which can be equated to 'tasking and coordination' in the not-for-profit sector) equally requires the adoption of a different philosophical approach on the part of those engaged in the relationship. It requires mutual trust, open and honest communication, and free sharing of information. Inter-organization collaboration has become an important phenomenon in recent decades, and one of the most important characteristics is that each firm contributes what other firms do not have, such as collaborations between a software company and a hardware or cellular phone company; an example of this is the merger between Nokia and Microsoft. The two organizations had previously collaborated but each had different development processes, resources, and cultures. By bringing the two together, each can work to its strengths and gain competitive advantage.

This is what can be described as achieving network advantage. A number of principles have been identified, including: transferring information, cooperation, and power; acknowledging that this is not always evenly distributed within the network; success comes to firms that actively manage their alliance portfolios; recognizing the different mechanisms that are at play, that network advantage accrues to those firms which are best positioned in their alliance networks; and that maximum advantage is realized when an organization coordinates its alliance activities internally (Greve et al., 2013:33).

TRUST NETWORKS

I have described the benefits of partnership working, but it is worth bearing in mind the advice contained in Niccolo Machiavelli's *The Prince*:

> The forces of a powerful ally can be useful and good to those who have recourse to them ... but are perilous to those who become dependent on them.

Trust is a prerequisite of partnership working and is a measure of belief in the honesty, fairness, or benevolence of another. It is a two-way process that requires both a truster, one who trusts, confides, or relies on another and who is willing to rely on the actions of another party, and the trustee, one who is trusted, or to whom something is entrusted. Confidence binds the truster and the trustee. It is thus about mutual trust. Newton suggests that trust is 'the belief that others will not deliberately or knowingly do us harm, if they can avoid it, and will look after our interests, if this is possible' (Newton, 2007:343).

Trust and confidence are often associated with legitimacy, but what is the nature of the relationship between those in government and public services and the public? (Llewellyn et al., 2013). Does trust confer legitimacy on government and public services? How does trust and confidence differ for business corporations? These are important questions to consider within the context of leading in the public interest. Strategic alliances are voluntary collaborations of legally independent enterprises that work together in order to gain competitive advantages. The aim of the alliance is to create common value; in this, they often face a social dilemma. Mutual coopera-tion, although desirable, is not automatic, because the selfish actions of each alliance company may not lead to socially desirable outcomes and trust is very difficult to establish. This is what some describe as a social dilemma, and there has been some interest in applying this concept to the dynamics within alliance networks.

Social dilemmas are situations in which collective interests are at odds with private interests (Kerr, 1983). We can think of this in terms of the relationships between a retailer's buyers and suppliers, such as that of Tesco. As we have learned, short-term selfish interests often conflict with selfless long-term interests, and these conflicts are often at the heart of social dilemmas. These can affect the dynamics between public partnerships or strategic alliances between corporate organizations.

There are two forms of trust that can be considered. The first is 'thin' trust, often maintained in selfish contexts through control and threat of sanction. This may work in relation to command-and-control and technical contexts under some cir-cumstances (Lewicki and Bunker, 1995), but is unlikely to work in more complex leadership situations. In this regard, 'thick' trust develops within relationships between different public and alliance partners based on more selfless, long-term behaviour, through voluntary accepted roles (Hosmer, 1995).

Trust building is an important component of partnership working and the actions of the truster are critical in influencing the motivations of the trustee (Tyler and Degoey, 1996), whether as individuals or as a collective. Based on my research, I sug-gest that a trust cycle can assist in building trust. It is important to first distinguish between 'trust' and 'trustworthiness' which, this chapter argues, is a prerequisite for both confidence and legitimacy. It is what I describe as the trust cycle.

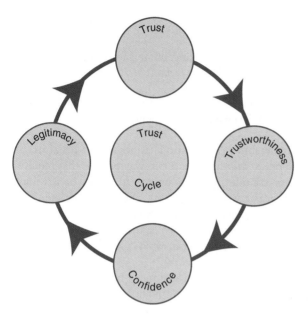

Figure 11.1 *Trust cycle*

This is illustrated in Figure 11.1.

The first stage in the cycle suggests that 'trust' is valued for itself. It is about individuals, people, and relationships. Trust is something that we can feel, sense, or discern.

Trustworthiness is the second dimension of the trust cycle. Hardin (Hardin, 1998:10) tells us that 'a claim that one trusts governments is not closely analogous to a claim that one trusts another person'. I argue that 'trustworthiness' is a higher level plane and is something that others feel about 'us', either as 'us' as 'another' or even an institution as a collection of 'others'. It can thus be viewed as the reflection of trust. The *Oxford English Dictionary* (OED) refers back to Gretton's description from 1889 in which he stated (of an acquaintance) 'Because he trusted them, they proved themselves trustworthy.' The third stage of the cycle is confidence, which I perceive as an institutional outcome. It is susceptible in the longer term to the vulnerability of trust and the fact that trustworthiness can disappear almost immediately, such as the impact on trust in politicians and confidence in the political system amidst political scandals and similar perceptions in relation to the banking sector and some elements of the retail sector. 'Confidence' is about what a person or, more importantly, what a group of people do and is often based on collective transactions. The fourth and final dimension considers legitimacy as an instrumental form of trust. Seligman argues that the very 'legitimation' of modern societies is founded on the 'trust of authority and of governments as generalizations of trust on the primary, interpersonal level' (Seligman, 1997:14). We can view trust at the macro level as that of legitimacy in the purpose of the institution, or enterprise, which supports its very existence. The collective vision is the value that leaders should work towards.

The emphasis in modern societies on consensus, the ideology of pragmatism, problem-solving, and technocratic expertise are all founded on an image of society based on interconnected networks of trust – among citizens, families, voluntary organizations, and the like (Llewellyn et al., 2013). We can thus consider the following behavioural dimensions:

Are wider partnership networks known and built on trust (i.e. beyond the immediate membership of its own partnership)?			
Networks are not known and generally mistrusted.	There is some emphasis on networks but there is little discernible trust.	Networks are increasingly known and used by partners and trust is growing.	Extensive networks are both known and used and built on trust.
1　　2　　3	4　　5　　6	7　　8　　9	10　　11　　12

SHARED ACCOUNTABILITY

Trust is closely aligned to the sharing of accountability. In relation to partnerships and strategic alliances, the absence of a higher authority to ensure compliance in the achievement of mutual goals has to rely on decentralized accountability mechanisms in encouraging commitment.

Accountability is often conceptualized as a mechanism for enforcing control over organizations and programmes, but it is also a means of guiding improvement. This applies at both the organizational and cross-organizational levels. Accountability should also be aligned in relation to obligations, responsibilities, and transparency. Kuglin argues that networked value chain participants must be supported by accountability which 'needs to be matrixed, with accountability to their own company and accountability to the extended enterprise anchored by the ultimate customer' (Kuglin et al., 2002:155) and further makes the point that this will only succeed with board-level sponsorship.

Accountability as a mechanism for enforcing control over organizations and programmes is likely to be more common than its use as a means of improvement. This often accompanies attempts to assess performance rather than manage performance through control mechanisms. I refer to one prominent case study to highlight this.

CompStat (Complaint Statistics) is the accountability process that was used initially by the New York City Police Department's accountability process, but then was replicated in many other policing areas both in the US and elsewhere. CompStat is a performance management process that integrates data analysis on crime and disorder, which is then used for strategic problem-solving. It has been described as a much touted, although largely undocumented, promise as a crime prevention tool. In describing this process, it is of note that its apparent features as a management style have come to be characterized as 'strategic leadership' and 'strategic choice' (Weisburd et al., 2002). The authors Weisburd et al. suggest that elements of strategic leadership date back to Selznick (1957), which we will recall was comprehensively described in Part I of this book. However, the analysis of the rapid uptake of CompStat forms of accountability across a range of US police departments has suggested that what characterizes and distinguishes these reforms from others is the development of the control element. This led researchers to consider whether this can be interpreted more as an effort 'to maintain and reinforce the "bureaucratic" or "paramilitary" model of police organization ... than as an attempt to truly reform models of American policing' (Weisburd et al., 2002:422).

Although Weisburd and his colleagues can be congratulated on undertaking an objective review of CompStat, I differ somewhat in my interpretation of Selznick's concept of strategic leadership (which he actually referred to as institutional leadership). The authors seem to imply that these elements of Selznick's work led to the much wider reforms in the 1980s in influencing progressive management in the private sector, which then led to some of the elements being introduced to government agencies in general. I referred to this in Part I as the drive to introduce new public management (NPL) which been strongly criticized as leading to the aggressive accountability measures introduced in both sectors. This includes, for example, the recent alleged aggressive role played by buyers at Tesco in their relationships with their suppliers, which is akin to the description of CompStat approaches in influencing competitiveness between Police Commanders. I also take issue, for the reasons stated earlier, with its description as 'strategic problem-solving'; sure, there is a strong focus on data-driven analysis, but this alone does not define it as a strategic tool if it concentrates its efforts on individuals achieving competitive advantage rather than genuine partnerships aspiring to achieve collaborative advantage.

Zero tolerance policing has been consistently linked to the abuse of force, allegation of infringements of civil rights, and increase in police brutality (Cunneen, 1999). The term 'zero tolerance' is often used derisively to describe NYPD policy in this regard, and then used synonymously with other terms such as 'quality of life' enforcement and 'broken windows' policing. There is a myth around the provenance of zero tolerance in that it developed as part of the Broken Windows approach. This is not the case. However, one of the most senior police chief constables in the UK at this time made this assertion (Pollard, 1997):

> While 'Zero Tolerance' is presented by the media as a new idea invented in New York, it actually stems from the American academic theory of 'Broken Windows' developed by George Kelling and James Q Wilson back in 1982.

In 1996, I was involved in the planning and implementation of a national debate on zero tolerance policing at the Police Superintendents' Association of England and Wales Annual Conference of that year in Bristol, England, following my implementation of a community-based style of policing in my police division. One representative of the Association had tabled a motion for the England and Wales police service to formally adopt what was described as a 'zero tolerance' policing strategy, and called former NYPD Commissioner Bill Bratton to speak in support of this only a month after his surprise resignation as Commissioner. Being aware of Kelling's view on the use of this term, this motion was opposed in favour of partnership and problem-solving oriented policing, with the attendance and support of Kelling. During the conference, I made a note of what he said:

> I have never used the term 'Zero Tolerance', I do not like the term 'Zero Tolerance' and, as far as I am concerned, the term 'Zero Tolerance' can be assigned to the waste bin. (Brookes, 1996)

Although the motion was defeated overwhelmingly, in May of the following year, the Labour government was elected under the law and order mantra of 'tough on crime; tough on the causes of crime', and zero tolerance became a term that was often used (and replicated in many other policy areas) with political enthusiasm. Critical debate continued. Although Kelling reinforced the positive aspects of a strategic approach to problem-solving, such enforcement tactics were to be employed only when their incidence impacted the critical masses. In his classic work of 1996 – at the height of this debate – and true to his word at the conference of the same year, he did not use the term 'zero tolerance' (Kelling and Coles, 1996). In the postscript to this work, he also referred to the resignation of Commissioner Bratton following what had clearly been tension with Mayor Giuliani. He described how the media 'spin' focused on who would get the credit for the decline in crime – Bratton or Giuliani? Kelling referred to the media focus on personalities, describing this as reflecting the 'great men' view of politics and history. He pointed out that this ignores the true meaning of what occurred in New York City, referring to the much earlier actions of other key people. In particular, while acknowledging the clear and creative leadership of Bratton and Giuliani, he said, 'New York City's story is bigger than this ... It is the tale of an entire community reclaiming its public spaces' (Kelling and Coles, 1996:260). In a much more detailed later study, Kelling provided empirical evidence that showed how this wider 'broken-windows' policing explained recent crime trends in New York City (Kelling and Souza, 2001:3).

Compstat was thus just one aspect of this much wider approach to tackling crime and disorder, and yet zero tolerance remained much more prominent in both government thinking and media attention as opposed to the 'less sexy' elements of problem oriented policing. In 2006, the UK government still used this performance management process as 'good practice' when it argued that the 'reform of New York's police was, for example driven by monthly comparisons and learning between police force areas' (PMSU, 2006:10). Sir Michael Barber, an influential advisor to the then Prime Minister, referring to a model that he described as 'devolution and transparency', supported this the following year. Barber argued (Barber, 2007: 4):

> [T]he government can devolve responsibility to the frontline units delivering the relevant service and then use transparency – making public the results of differing units in a way that allows comparisons to be made – to drive performance.

Barber offered the strong view that units that succeed can be rewarded and potentially expanded, failing units can be made subject to interventions and ultimately shut down, and pointed to the NYPD CompStat system as a good example of this:

The model can operate in a fully public system – the most famous example being the New York City Police Department, where the CompStat process generated competition between precinct commanders – or within a service in which a mix of public and private providers compete on equal terms. This can be done by separating payor and provider and encouraging competition for large contracts offered by the government or its agencies (known as 'contestability' in the U.K.). This approach has been widely adopted, with significant success. Examples include the use of private prisons in California and the contracting of local education services in the U.K. (ibid)

This begins to draw into focus the interactive nature of the collective leadership values. While accountability to shareholders and stakeholders alike is a key requirement of leaders, this – in isolation – is indeed a dangerous tactic (and yes, I prefer to describe this as a tactic rather than a strategy). To become a strategic mechanism, it should be defined through a collective vision, focus on publicly valued outcomes (that are truly in the public interest), cascaded through both shared and distributed leadership at all levels and, most of all, be evidenced-based. What Barber was supporting here is a root-and-branch acceptance of competition, as opposed to collaboration, which favours selfish rather than selfless behaviour. Interestingly, at no point did Barber use the term 'leadership', although the paper was replete with references to 'management' (including rigorous performance management by government).

Almost 20 years later, the principles appear to remain. In 2013, controversy accompanied the release of a CompStat audit, which confirmed that data manipulation took place through such examples as the misclassification of reports (Morganteen, 2013). This report tends to confirm the claims made by a number of retired NYPD officers in relation to CompStat abuses (Eterno, 2003) and secret recordings made of roll call briefings by one NYPD officer who subsequently personally suffered as a whistle-blower (Rayman, 2010).

In concluding on accountability, it is worth quoting Eterno and Silverman's conceptual background for their recent study in relation to the 'Crime Numbers Game: Management by Manipulation', referring to the methodologist Campbell (Eterno and Silverman, 2012) and its similar reference concerning the practice of social research (Babbie, 2013:383):

> The more any quantitative social indicator is used for social decision-making, the more subject it will be to corruption pressures and the more apt it will be to distort and corrupt the social processes it is intended to monitor. (Campbell, 1976:49)

Personal accountability for performance is a key element of a safe system and enhances trust whereas institutional accountability reinforces quality and builds confidence.[1] Most of all, it is important to ensure that accountability is shared, to avoid the types of abuses that can so easily manifest themselves when top-level pressure is brought to bear on numerical targets.

---

[1]See Part III for more discussion in relation to accountability, governance, and personal responsibility.

In relation to behaviours, we can ask:

Are leaders fully open to and do they embrace shared accountability for shared aims?			
Individual leaders do not accept their own accountability and remain focused on the control of individual organizational objectives.	Some attempts are made to take responsibility at different levels but it remains primarily internally focused on control rather than horizontally focused on improvement.	Clear efforts are being made to link accountability between partners and the organizations that compose the partnership with an emphasis on improvement.	Leaders are fully committed to taking responsibility at all levels and across all organizations and to being jointly accountable for improvement.
1　2　3	4　5　6	7　8　9	10　11　12

MUTUAL BENEFIT

If trust is important in networks that seek to jointly task and coordinate their efforts, or in managing their contract relationships and supply chains, achieving mutual benefit stands not too far behind. But what do we mean by mutual benefit? Does it mean that all partners achieve equal benefits at the same time in all activities, or does it concern the extent to which this benefit is shared and distributed at different times, in different measures, and with different outcomes? Mutual benefit has been referred to as 'informal insurance'. It has been argued that the true strength of informal insurance is the 'level of risk-sharing achieved within the network of equilibrium employment relationships which emerges in the absence of formal insurance and credit institutions' (Wang, 2012:1). When we include the public interest within this equation, how does this play out?

I have talked much about the importance of values and behaviours and this is relevant to the achievement of mutual benefit, because these values and behaviours will often be competing before they collaborate. The first step is in building trust, as argued previously; the second step is in acknowledging that there will be competing values but understanding also that the conflict that often arises from this can be beneficial in striving for mutuality! Let me explain further.

When studying the effectiveness of organizations 30 years ago, Quinn, Rohrbaugh, and Cameron, in various studies, noticed that some organizations were effective if they demonstrated flexibility and adaptability. However, other organizations were effective if they demonstrated stability and control. These characteristics could be regarded as different extremes of the same dimension. Similarly, they discovered that some organizations were effective if they maintained efficient internal processes whereas others were effective if they maintained competitive external positioning relative to customers and clients (Cameron, 1986; Quinn and Rohrbaugh, 1981; Quinn and Cameron, 1983). These characteristics can also be regarded as different extremes of the same dimension. They are represented in the Competing Values Framework (CVF) where organizations' cultures are classified as to which quadrant they fall into, such as Clan, Adhocracy, Hierarchy, and Market.

In a later work, it has been said that one or more of the culture types identified by the framework has characterized more than 80 percent of the several thousand organizations that they studied (Cameron and Quinn, 2006). Understanding why values compete is thus important before aligning the differing values to achieve mutual benefit.

A good example of mutual benefit is that of an old folk story that has been used in different cultures, sometimes with different 'actors' but representing the same moral. It is the Stone Soup Story. I first came across this in the early 1990s when I attended one of the first Problem Oriented Policing conferences in San Diego, US. This was at the time that I was involved in the design of a new community-based policing model in my divisional command area in Leicester. A team of community officers who worked in a run-down estate in California explained how they had used the principles in devising a collaborative community safety project which built improved social capital.

The premise of the folk tale is that three travellers (variously described as monks, soldiers, or more general travellers) came to a village, cold and hungry. They possessed an empty cooking pot but nothing else. The villagers were unwilling to share of their own food. The travellers went to a stream, filled the pot with water and dropped stones into it, before placing it on a fire. One of the villagers curiously asks what they are doing. The travellers say that they are making 'Stone Soup', which tastes good but requires more ingredients. One by one, villagers bring out different ingredients: carrots, parsnips, sage, etc. Eventually, a wholesome and very generous soup – which started with a stone – is available to all, the moral of the folk tale being that wonderful things can happen if people work together. Muth (2003), in his excellent portrayal of the story with his art and words, described the original community as a selfish community but one that can eventually be viewed as selfless. This, for me, encapsulates mutual benefit and demonstrates the power of story-telling.

> **Reflection:** Can you think of a story (or a leadership example that can be told as a story) in which mutual benefit emerged from what initially appeared to be a selfish context?

In considering whether mutual benefit is being achieved we can ask:

Do leaders actively seek to achieve mutual benefits between partners in serving the public good?			
Individual leaders are focused entirely on their own agenda and only seek to reach consensus when it benefits themselves or their organization.	There is some attempt to achieve mutual benefit but it tends to be where individual aims still take precedence.	Leaders seek to achieve mutual benefit for the public good but with occasional tensions that reflect individual aims.	Leaders routinely make efforts to achieve mutual benefit within the wider context of the public good and manage competing values.
1 2 3	4 5 6	7 8 9	10 11 12

SHARED INFORMATION

In partnerships and alliances, data will originate from multiple partners and multiple sources. The purpose of this data and information is to utilize it to drive decision-support activities that focus on improving service levels or product manufacture and reducing costs (Kuglin et al., 2002:157).

Information is generally an intangible asset. This is also true of relationships and knowledge, which should be managed by partnership alliances with the same care as more tangible assets (Connell and Voola, 2007). Information sharing is vital to collective leadership across its multiple stakeholders. It is viewed as an important element of an alliance's relationship capital (Chen et al., 2009) and is applied to areas such as supply chain management where information sharing 'describes the extent to which one party in the chain communicates critical and proprietary information to another party in the chain' (Premus and Sanders, 2008:177), new product development (Chou, 2008), and inter-organizational learning (Love and Ellis, 2009).

Information on its own is not sufficient, because often this information should be transformed into intelligence. The difficulties and barriers in relation to information and intelligence sharing have been well documented, and this was also evident within my own research and across all projects. There is a reluctance to share information, even within existing multi-agency partnerships. Barriers to information sharing represented one of the key weaknesses in all research projects ranging from my doctoral study of community-based policing to the shared and distributed leadership required for the Local Area Agreements in the North West. Much of this was due to espoused 'data protection' issues, but the reality was more related to organizational 'silo' thinking or the 'too hard to do' mentality.

An early example of this emerged in the problems associated with the sharing of information that was required when the Crime and Disorder Act 1998 created statutory partnerships to tackle crime and disorder. When those who organize crime reduction efforts come together, four facts become evident (Brookes et al., 2003). First, data-protection officers vary massively in the presumptions they bring to their work; second, some officers interpret data protection so restrictively that the community safety enterprise is compromised; third, and relevant to this collective leadership behaviour, senior officers do not take an active leadership role in shaping agreements on data sharing; and, finally, community safety organizers are often unclear about the action implications of shared data, which feeds the presumption against data exchange. The paper by Brookes et al. says that a common understanding of appropriate data sharing is vital in tackling the limitations of data sharing. Based on a data-sharing partnership for the 40 Crime and Disorder partnerships in the East Midlands region of England, and in encouraging a sense of mutual benefit across all 40, a number of steps were suggested. This included the establishment of a partnership and funding, agreed objectives based on real-time data and an agreement to share data and analysis on outcomes across partners. It further required an analytic capability, the installation of appropriate technology, and top-level support for data-sharing protocols. An evaluation of this data-sharing project established that common problematic themes from the research related to issues of focus, communication, and leadership. Most efforts were focused on collecting data rather than aligning it to need and analysis; in terms of communication, more effort was needed to raise awareness of data protection and how data can be shared to the mutual benefit of all partners without contravening legislation, and, finally, leadership was lacking in most cases.

Leadership has continued to emerge as a problematic area in more recent studies. An example of this is in relation to tackling areas such as cybercrime. Studies were carried out in 2011 and 2012 in relation to public–private, public–public and private–private policing interfaces in the policing of cybercrimes in the UK. It was found that divisions existed between 'the High Policing rhetoric of the UK's Cyber Security Strategy and the (relatively) Low Policing cooperation outcomes in "on the ground" cyber-policing' where there is 'high public concern about indentity theft and public facing consumer cybercrime' (Levi and Williams, 2013:421). Low levels of network capital were part of the problem. Similar difficulties are experienced with strategic alliances, for example in protecting what has been described as the black box protection of core competencies (Milgate, 2000).

The London 2012 case provides a good example of responding to the challenges of sharing information in a complex environment. In its preparation for the bid, London 2012 needed strong backing from a very wide range of stakeholders ranging from getting top-level government Cabinet support and securing the support of businesses to achieving local community engagement. London 2012 and stakeholders wanted to engage directly, share information regularly, and respond to concerns of the local communities about where the Games would take place (LOCOG, 2012:15). This was achieved through a series of activities including a bid forum with a wide constituency of interested bodies at local level, ranging from local authorities to community-based groups and sporting associations. The overall aim of the forum was to achieve a sense of mutual benefit (such as that described in the earlier section of this chapter). The integration of the shared information into shared intelligence was an important step in developing a transition plan for moving from a bid company to a full OCOG (Organising Committee of the Olympic Games) and, of necessity, had to take into account both a 'win' and a 'lose' scenario. Working to a 'win' scenario, part of the transition plan was to allow the smooth transfer of knowledge from a bidding company to a full organizing committee. As a final requirement of the bidding process, LOCOG produced an archive of documents which proved to be a valuable resource of information and intelligence and, in the event of either 'win' or 'lose' effectively creating a 'bidding manual' for future UK bids.

In determining the collective behaviours that will assist in the sharing of information, we can ask the following questions:

Do leaders share information and intelligence in support of turning the partnership strategy into delivery?			
Leaders do not share information or intelligence with other partners.	Information is exchanged on a 'when needed' basis rather than routinely and there is no evidence of shared intelligence.	Leaders have formal procedures for sharing information and are moving towards joint use of intelligence.	Information sharing and the use of joint intelligence is routinely applied.
1　　2　　3	4　　5　　6	7　　8　　9	10　　11　　12

A reflective activity is provided below for this chapter.

Chapter 11 Activity

Write notes below in relation to what you can do to improve your
organization or network in these areas.

Are wider partnership networks known and built on trust (i.e. beyond the immediate
membership of its own partnership)?

Are leaders fully open to and do they embrace shared accountability for shared aims?

Do leaders actively seek to achieve mutual benefits between partners in serving the
public good?

Do leaders share information and intelligence in support of turning the partnership
strategy into delivery?

12 Action Oriented

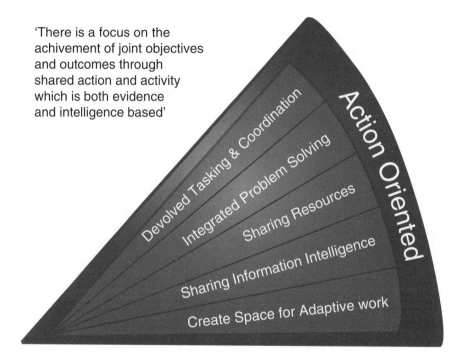

'There is a focus on the achivement of joint objectives and outcomes through shared action and activity which is both evidence and intelligence based'

Action Oriented

Devolved Tasking & Coordination

Integrated Problem Solving

Sharing Resources

Sharing Information Intelligence

Create Space for Adaptive work

This value suggests that leaders should engage in routine action-focused approaches in turning strategic intentions into delivery and in identifying and responding to gaps in delivery. I argue that this is the most important value and sits at the heart of the collective leadership framework.

In relation to leaders' active engagement with other partners, you are encouraged to ask:

- To what extent do leaders engage in activity that is transformational (in encouraging innovative change) as well as transactional (in managing the day-to-day work of the partnership and enterprise or institution)?
- Do leaders actively engage stakeholders in activity through coproduction?
- Do leaders within the partnership or alliance exchange data and information and turn information into intelligence, knowledge, and action through integrated problem-solving approaches?

An action focus goes hand-in-hand with behavioural characteristics that are adaptive. This latter aspect is heavily influenced by the work of Heifetz in relation to his adaptive leadership framework (Heifetz, 1994).

DEVOLVED TASKING, COORDINATION, AND COOPERATION

One of the major characteristics of ineffective collective leadership relates to a gap between the espoused values and strategies of organizations and their networks and actual delivery. Insufficient attention is often given to devolving both responsibility and action throughout the organization and its networks. Similarly, where responsibility is given to others, invariably it amounts to delegation rather than devolution, with fairly loose governance and accountability arrangements.

> **Reflection**: What do you see as the difference between devolution and delegation?

Before exploring the differences, it is useful to consider the similarities. Both delegation and devolution are forms of decentralization, the transfer of authority and responsibility from one agency to another. It is generally considered as the transfer of power and authority from central government to subordinate or quasi-independent organizations. However, it can also apply to the private sector. It is at this point, however, that the similarities end; both are two major forms of decentralization (and, arguably, the two most important) but with different characteristics, policy imperatives, and measures of achievement. In summary, decentralization differs across countries, within countries, and within sectors.[1]

Delegation involves the transfer of authority and functions to semi-autonomous organizations that are now totally controlled by government and are accountable to the government, but with wide-ranging flexibility for decision-making. Examples of this include housing, transport, and school authorities as well as economic development companies. Devolution is more comprehensive and the transfer is made to local governments with corporate status, often presided over by a mayor.[2]

Decentralization, in any form, has both advantages and disadvantages. Major disadvantages are that it can make coordination of policies more complex, can allow functions to be delivered by local entrepreneurs, and can sometimes undermine trust between the public and private sector. Devolution of public services is not too dissimilar from the granting of a franchise in the private sector, in which a franchisor grants permission to sell a product and trade under a certain name in a particular area. The franchisee puts down a certain amount of capital and agrees to buy the franchisor's goods, although the former has complete day-to-day responsibility for the running of the business, with the latter sharing in some of the

---

[1]World Bank: Overview of Decentralisation in India Vol I P 3 World Bank, 2000.

[2]At the time of writing, comprehensive proposals have just been made to devolve power and authority to an elected mayor in the City of Manchester, England, which will have significant implications for both the not-for-profit and for-profit sectors.

profits but without the management responsibility. Such franchisees trade behind the corporate identities and working methods licensed to them by the franchisor but without the command-and-control power that is often associated with large enterprises. This carries with it a risk to corporate brand and reputation. It has been suggested that such enterprises should engage in reputation risk management, which may increase its control over the franchises, something that the franchisees may resent (Burns, 2007) but which itself may carry some legal risks relating to tort and the enterprise's vicarious liability.

Regardless as to whether one is leading in the context of public service delivery or within a franchised or significantly decentralized corporate enterprise (and I would argue that there has been a significant blurring of the boundaries between sectors), the need for both coordination and cooperation is paramount, particularly in relation to the operational delivery of the business, a concept that I refer to as 'tasking', which is the allocation of an essential piece of work that serves as one identifiable component of an overall project. In the sense of collective leadership, it should not be equated with traditional management, in terms of a command-and-control process, but, as with all-things collective, a shared responsibility. For this reason, tasking relies very much upon both shared coordination and cooperation (which, by definition, must be shared?). As argued in the previous chapter, there is a danger that devolution (such as the government model proposed by Barber) can be accompanied by draconian performance management processes that can stifle innovation.

The concept of tasking and coordination originates from the National Intelligence Model (NIM), which is a fundamental element that police forces in England and Wales are legally obligated, by a code of practice, to adhere to. An important component of collective leadership is the intelligent leadership process, which I discuss in the final chapter within the context of what I describe as the social economy, based on the blurring of sectorial boundaries that I hinted at above. Tasking and coordination is the principal means by which leadership maintains intelligence processes. It enables understanding of the reality of the problem profiles, allowing businesses and institutions to pursue strategic, operational, and tactical responses. Tasking and coordination aligns the strategic aspirations with deliberate strategies and provides the foundation for intelligence in pursuing both business and institutional goals. As part of the decision-making process, it provides support in identifying more immediate priorities and the resources (both human and technical) that are needed in responding to them and to commission activity in operational and technical terms. The overall aim of tasking and coordination is to maximize the use of intelligence in achieving the impact sought. In other examples, the term 'task and finish' is used. This was evident during the research in relation to the public service organizations in the North West of England.

In the world of strategic alliances within the for-profit sector, the closest that tasking and coordination can be equated with is in relation to the concepts of cooperation and coordination. Inter-organizational cooperation is considered as the 'joint pursuit of agreed-on goal(s) in a manner corresponding to a shared understanding about contributions and payoffs' (Gulati et al., 2012:533) whereas coordination is defined as 'the deliberate and orderly alignment or adjustment of partners' actions to achieve jointly determined goals' (ibid:537). The importance of coordination and the factors that it is influenced by has been identified in a range of industries. This includes biotechnology, in which the characteristics and contextual factors influence the alliance and its governance (Phene and Tallman, 2012), and within inter-firms research and development where publicly funded programmes focus more on exploratory and peripheral competences than non-funded spontaneous collaborations (Matt et al., 2012). Contract research is moving away from a narrow focus on contract structure, and its safeguarding function towards a broader focus that highlights adaptation and coordination (Schepker et al., 2014). In all cases, for reasons that I have argued, it must also rely upon cooperation.

Having considered examples from both the not-for-profit and the for-profit sectors, I suggest that the three terms tasking, coordination, and cooperation are important and mutually supportive. Devolution is critical but with the safeguard that the corporate and shared vision, goals, and objectives are being given sufficient focus.

Behavioural questions to ask could be:

Is **tasking and coordination** devolved to the appropriate level while ensuring good links with the overall vision through effective cooperation?			
There are no formal tasking and coordination processes.	Tasking and coordination is ad hoc and not aligned with the vision/strategy with minimal evidence of active cooperation.	Tasking and coordination is devolved but it is not routinely linked with other partners' activity with some evidence of cooperation.	Tasking and coordination is devolved and aligned fully with the strategy and that of other partners who cooperate fully.
1 2 3	4 5 6	7 8 9	10 11 12

INTEGRATED PROBLEM-SOLVING

Integrated problem-solving concerns the synthesizing and integration of problem-solving efforts. It helps leaders to improve their substantive and integrative knowledge of problems and to consider appropriate responses. Through intelligent leadership, responses to wicked problems will be applied by means of a comprehensive assessment of progressive problem situations. It requires a collaborative approach supported by the tasking, coordination, and cooperation described in the preceding section.

A problem is described as 'wicked' not because it is evil but rather to denote its characteristics as being difficult or impossible to solve because of its complex nature and its interdependencies. Wicked problems often emerge from circumstances of uncertainty, risk, and the complex nature of people and society. Such problems do not have clear solutions or, indeed, a clear definition of the problem situation. They cannot be solved by traditional analytical approaches.

The term was first used in social planning (Rittel and Webber, 1973), defining its ten characteristics (see Table 12.1). It is essential to frame the problem in the right way at the outset. The opposite of a wicked problem is a tame problem. In these cases, the problem is clearly stated, has a well-defined goal, and often, once solved,

Table 12.1 *Characteristics of 'wicked problems'*

1	There is no definitive formulation of a wicked problem. It's not possible to write a well-defined statement of the problem, as can be done with an ordinary problem.
2	Wicked problems have no stopping rule. You can tell when you've reached a solution with an ordinary problem. With a wicked problem, the search for solutions never stops.
3	Solutions to wicked problems are not true or false, but good or bad. Ordinary problems have solutions that can be objectively evaluated as right or wrong. Choosing a solution to a wicked problem is largely a matter of judgement.
4	There is no immediate and no ultimate test of a solution to a wicked problem. It's possible to determine right away if a solution to an ordinary problem is working. But solutions to wicked problems generate unexpected consequences over time, making it difficult to measure their effectiveness.
5	Every solution to a wicked problem is a 'one-shot' operation; because there is no opportunity to learn by trial and error, every attempt counts significantly. Solutions to ordinary problems can be easily tried and abandoned. With wicked problems, every implemented solution has consequences that cannot be undone.
6	Wicked problems do not have an exhaustively describable set of potential solutions, nor is there a well-described set of permissible operations that may be incorporated into the plan. Ordinary problems come with a limited set of potential solutions, by contrast.
7	Every wicked problem is essentially unique. An ordinary problem belongs to a class of similar problems that are all solved in the same way. A wicked problem is substantially without precedent; experience does not help you address it.
8	Every wicked problem can be considered to be a symptom of another problem. While an ordinary problem is self-contained, a wicked problem is entwined with other problems. However, those problems don't have one root cause.
9	The existence of a discrepancy representing a wicked problem can be explained in numerous ways. A wicked problem involves many stakeholders, who all will have different ideas about what the problem really is and what its causes are.
10	The planner has no right to be wrong. Problem solvers dealing with a wicked issue are held liable for the consequences of any actions they take, because those actions will have such a large impact and are hard to justify.

Source: Based on Rittel and Webber (1973).

stays solved. Indeed, some commentators would argue (Grint included) that if it is a tame problem, it is about management, and if it is a wicked problem, it concerns leadership, whereas a critical problem (which can be either tame or wicked) requires command-and-control.

One of the key challenges for leaders is to first frame the problem correctly. Invariably, leaders will provide a tame response to a wicked problem. A previously tried-and-tested 'solution' will be taken off-the-shelf and applied to a wicked problem and the leaders will subsequently wonder why it did not work. Leaders need to be open to the identification of adaptive challenges and be prepared to work with others and across time by the creation of a problem-solving space. At the heart of this space is the need to apply intelligent leadership in considering a range of responses to achieve a socially desirable outcome in relation to the presenting wicked problem.

> **Reflection**: Having considered the characteristics of a wicked problem in Table 12.1 above, can you think of any wicked leadership challenge that you have been either directly or indirectly involved in? What made it a wicked problem, based on Rittel and Weber's typology? Moreover, how did the leaders respond to this? Did they offer a wicked or a tame response? If it was the latter, which is not unusual, in what ways do you think that the leadership would have been more effective in taking an appropriate 'wicked' response? Make a note of your responses in relation to the characteristics of Rittel and Webber's framework and how you would respond given this approach. We will return to this activity at the conclusion of the chapter.

I want to conclude this section by making a connection between problem-solving, decision-making, risk, and innovation.

First, let me address the distinction between problem-solving and decision-making, two other terms that are often and erroneously conflated. Decision-making and problem-solving are distinct from each other but complementary. From an organizational perspective, problems represent gaps between the results actually achieved compared to what they should be. A decision is the act of deciding between different courses of action. Decision-making is thus a cognitive process that leads to a course of action based on a series of options informed, as described in the previous section, by collective intelligence. In turn, cognition is the action or faculty of 'knowing' in its widest sense, including sensation, perception, conception, etc. It is thus about thinking within the context of decision-making. Decision-making is a complex process and decisions are made in a number of ways. Decisions are not always rational and are liable to several biases, including one that I really like in terms of its description as the 'Sunflower syndrome': 'The tendency (like sunflowers following the sun) to follow the lead of the most senior person in the decision-making process, or to try to anticipate their view even before they have expressed it' (Johnson et al., 2011:512).

Problem-solving is the action of finding solutions to difficult or complex issues. We can thus describe problem-solving as a process through which activities focus on the systematic analysis of a particular situation with a view to generating a range of possible solutions, which are then implemented and evaluated. Decision-making is the means by which choices are made during the problem-solving process. Decision-making is thus part of, and occurs during, the process of problem-solving. Both have similar but also distinctive characteristics within these processes. We can apply a well-known problem-solving framework (known affectionately as 'PAT' (problem analysis triangle)) based on that of its crime reduction foundation (victim-location-offender). It has been translated – for the purposes of collective leadership – as person-place-problem, supported by 'SARA' (scanning, analysis, response, assessment). This is illustrated in Figure 12.1:

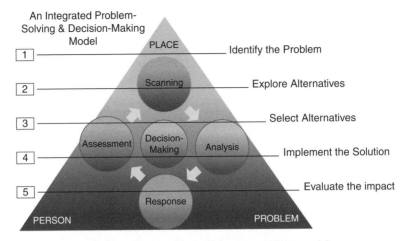

Figure 12.1 *Integrated problem-solving and decision-making model*

In determining the behaviours associated with integrated problem-solving we can ask:

Do leaders engage in integrated problem-solving approaches that tackle wicked problems as well as routine (tame) problems in a way that encourages innovation?			
Individual leaders engage in reactive approaches to routine problems and tend to adopt off-the-shelf solutions and are risk averse.	Basic problem-solving approaches are used when the need arises but they still tend to err on the side of the routine rather than the innovative.	Leaders recognize the importance of tackling wicked problems and encourage innovative approaches where appropriate.	An IPS approach is the routine way of working for leaders and risk is both allowed and properly assessed.
1 2 3	4 5 6	7 8 9	10 11 12

SHARED RESOURCES

It would seem somewhat axiomatic to say that in any collaboration, resources need to be shared in delivering action plans. The sharing of resources is most often associated with computer networks, for example the sharing of peripherals on a network between various terminals. However, the term can also be applied to the sharing of resources across organizational networks. In a survey of more than 1000 start-up businesses in the UK, 55 percent of early-stage companies identified shared resources as essential to business survival, including such shared infrastructure resources as technology, office space, and vehicles and shared human services as accounting, administration, and HR. It is of interest to note that the move towards the sharing of costs was not found to be a reaction to the recession, however, with 65 percent of respondents declaring that it was part of a long-term measure, and 50 percent stating it was part of their original business plan (Zipcar, 2013).

It is not just for new start-ups or small medium enterprises (SMEs). It has been recognized that an increasing number of large and multinational organizations (MNCs) are moving towards a shared services model, particularly in relation to the human resource function (Cooke, 2006). Benefits of shared HR systems – as one example – include the introduction of professional services, a greater degree of structural flexibility to respond to business change and to improve organizational learning across organizational boundaries. Such shared services can operate through merged common functions performed by multiple entities into a single service delivery organization whether by recentralizing within one organization or through an outsourced service delivery organization (Ning et al., 2009). This shifting trend is evident in both the private and public sectors and can be either transactional (based on routine, high volume activities) or transformational (where activities require extensive expertise and strategic approaches). Su Ning et al. suggest that shared services has the potential to bring significant value to the firm, although they also point to a number risks, including unbalanced power concentration, increased complexity, and unclear service accountability. A further example is in relation to supply chain management, relevant also to the earlier discussion on Tesco PLC. One major concern for supply chain management is that an organization's sharing behaviours may initially mean a pre-expectation of common resources available and a perceived fairness between participants for the willingness to participate in the partnership, thus shared resources represent a form of social capital (Chiu et al., 2013). The most recent crisis to effect Tesco illustrates quite clearly that this form of social capital was not present and the relationship was directed through a one-way route, from retailer to supplier.

The sharing of resources is likely to be directed towards a joint action plan, based on shared objectives, that seeks to achieve socially desirable outcomes through a range of agreed goals, objectives, and tasks and which is coordinated through the tasking, cooperative, and coordination processes. Sharing of resources is only likely to take place effectively if the partners to this sharing agreement perceive a sense of mutual benefit. We learned earlier that mutual sharing concerns the extent to which this benefit is shared and distributed at different times, in different measures, and with different outcomes. This is reflective of what is becoming increasingly described as a 'sharing economy'. This is helpfully defined by Matofska as a:

> [S]ocio-economic ecosystem built around the sharing of human and physical resources. It includes the shared creation, production, distribution, trade and consumption of goods and services by different people and organizations. (Matofska, 2014)

The shared economy is an excellent concept to consider within the context of this book, particularly as it has emerged from the notion of the 'tragedy of the commons' that puts forward the view that when we all act solely in our self-interest, we deplete the shared resources we need for our own quality of life (Hardin, 1968) and, further implied, that the public interest should be a key component in mediating this. 'Commons' is a term that has been around since medieval times, such as common land, representing land that is owned by all and its use permitted by all;

as a term it is increasingly being applied to open source resources available through the Internet but also appearing in other media and resource manifestations. We can thus contrast knowledge commons (collectively owned material and goods in the digital age) with the example of commons being applied to sustainability issues in the sense of our wider environment (and aligned, as earlier described, as a measure of social value). In Chapter II, I made reference to the concept of crowdsourcing and crowdfunding. As I describe in Part III, in the notion of sharing resources through a shared economy, within the context of a new social economy, there is a much greater chance that the determination of the public interest will emerge much stronger as an overall public value outcome.

The questions in relation to behavioural standards are:

Do leaders share resources in delivering action plans?			
Individual leaders are focused entirely on their own resources and do not consider the use of shared resources.	There is some attempt to share resources but it tends to be motivated by self-interest.	Leaders are realizing the benefit of sharing resources but still have more to do in doing this routinely.	Leaders routinely share resources in pursuit of common aims and objectives that reflect the public interest.
1 2 3	4 5 6	7 8 9	10 11 12

USING COLLECTIVE INTELLIGENCE IN DELIVERING ACTION PLANS

When earlier describing the value of partnership working, one of the collective leadership behaviours related to the willingness to share information across networks. This behaviour, in support of the value of action-oriented approaches, relates to the actual application and use of collective intelligence in taking forward actions within the context of a collective delivery plan. In the earlier section, I also described the importance of tasking, cooperation, and coordination in the work of partnerships/strategic alliances. Effective cooperation and coordination also requires the application of collective intelligence to the joint objectives of the partners through evidence-based tasking. This presents significant challenges for management accounting systems (MAS) because information and communication systems supplement MAS in support of decision-making; the attainment of inter-organizational exchange of partner performance objectives is important and integrated information systems are necessary (Nicolaou, 2011). The suggestion in terms of collective leadership is to develop an approach to leadership application systems (LAS) rather than MAS to highlight the importance of leadership and its application rather than the potentially misleading focus on management and accounting. Both of these two elements are important, but within a wider governance system that I discuss in the next chapter.

Using collective intelligence is thus simply described as applying the right information, in the right form, from and to the right people, for the right purposes, and in the right sequence. In an interesting study related to a wicked problem in healthcare, collective intelligence was adopted as a central means of identifying children's behaviour in relation to obesity. In this context, collective intelligence is defined as 'the capability of a series of unsophisticated agents to collaboratively solve significant and complex problems that would otherwise remain unsolved by a single agent'. The use of the term 'unsophisticated agents' is useful as the role of intelligence gathering and application is not just for intelligence analysts; we need to engage in the widest possible collation of information in transforming data into intelligence, namely our stakeholders. In this healthcare context, collective intelligence was described as the combination of behaviour, preferences, or notions of clusters of people to create innovative insights. 'To enable collective intelligence, a number of things have to fall in place including: continuous user interaction with the solution, suitable models to amass the learning's of the system and the ability to draw from the aggregated knowledge' (Addo et al., 2013:691).

The use of shared information and collective intelligence emerged as a key challenge for the partnerships in the North West of England, and the critical factor of 'information management' was the least positive attribute referred to by respondents (no one individual respondent referred to this as a 'strength'). The research report suggested that a focused means of information sharing, data analysis, and intelligence-led approaches to tasking and commissioning was required. This could be achieved by securing the buy-in across all organizations and within organizations through improved shared and distributed leadership. This requires a commitment to better understand and work within inter-relational networks (Brookes and Johnson, 2007) and the application of intelligence to the identified problem profiles.

We can thus again appreciate the dynamic relationships between the seven collective leadership values and the appropriate behaviours. I suggest that collective intelligence lies at the heart of this whole process. It is an emergent property from the synergies that I described in some detail in the earlier chapters and is analogous to similar descriptions of collective intelligence in terms of computing technologies. The biggest 'bang for the buck' can be achieved by aligning both forms of intelligence (cognitive and artificial intelligence) through social collectives that share a social identity.

In summary, collective intelligence supports coordination and cooperation across networks based on improved and shared cognitive and artificial intelligence analytic capabilities and capacity. Cognition relates to the thinking and reasoning that is used as part of the problem-solving process but within the wide decision-making 'space' (which I discuss in the next section), based on networks of trust. Artificial intelligence was defined as early as 1955 as the science and engineering of making intelligent machines, with the helpful analogy in that the artificial intelligence problem is taken to be that of making a machine behave in ways that would be called intelligent if a human were so behaving (McCarthy et al., 1955).

Analysis is thus focused on both cognitive and artificial intelligence but driven by a clear sense of collective vision, based on public value outcomes and engaging at multiple levels of the organization and its networks through partnership working. Representing the heart of the collective leadership process, it requires appropriate systems and structures to support it and a commitment to build the skills and behaviours of those who will use the collective intelligence. These latter two values will be considered in the following two chapters, but, before moving on to these, I want to finish this chapter by considering the need for adaptive leadership through time, space, and mass.

In assessing the extent to which leaders use collective intelligence, we can consider the following behavioural questions:

Do leaders use collective intelligence in the actioning of delivery plans?			
Leaders do not use shared information or intelligence with other partners.	Leaders use shared information and intelligence when required but not routinely.	Leaders routinely use information and intelligence in supporting delivery plans and are moving towards joint use of intelligence.	Shared information and intelligence is routinely applied in delivery plans and actions.
1 2 3	4 5 6	7 8 9	10 11 12

CREATING SPACE FOR ADAPTIVE APPROACHES

This collective leadership behaviour, together with the collective intelligence behaviour described above, is also one of the most important in terms of turning vision into strategy and ultimate action. I therefore spend a little longer on this section before moving on to discuss systems and structures and skills and behaviours in support of collective leadership. Most of us have a few works (that we could count on both hands) that have had a significant impact on the way in which we think and practise our work and beliefs. I certainly have and one of those – quite high up in my top ten – is that of Ron Heifetz in his work *Leading without Easy Answers* (Heifetz, 1994). Without doubt, this is one of the classics in relation to the contemporary challenges presented to leaders. His approach to adaptive leadership has been instrumental in shaping this chapter just as much as it was in shaping my practice as a senior leader in a high-profile policing and civil service context. I first remember this work shortly after its publication when, in 1994/5 I took command of a very challenging policing area where I introduced a new model of community policing. I referred to this earlier in my introductory chapter and in the last chapter in my discussion on shared accountability. 'Broken Windows' (Kelling and Wilson, 1982) and the later *Fixing Broken Windows* (Kelling and Coles, 1996) (also in my top ten), were to shape much of my leadership practice in the development of this model.

In relation to 'broken windows', Kelling and Wilson's argument is that the perception of social order in the environment can influence human behaviour in either socially desirable or undesirable ways. In simple terms, if broken windows are evident in a community (and not fixed) this leads to negative perceptions of order more generally and both crime and antisocial behaviour flourish; coactive environmental approaches to crime reduction (often long-term, multi-agency approaches) have a much greater chance of reducing these perceptions and actual occurrences than short-term reactive responses and thus lead to socially desirable outcomes that are in the public interest.

The strategies adopted in tackling environmental order are very much reflective of what Heifetz terms an 'adaptive' problem or challenge:

> Adaptive work consists of the learning required to address conflicts in the values people hold, or to diminish the gap between the values people stand for and the reality they face. (Heifetz, 1994:22)

We can look at the differences between adaptive work and technical work by briefly returning to our primal ancestors whom I discussed in Chapter 1.

We are going to use a business bestiary[3] – using the silverback gorilla as an example – to illustrate the differences between technical and adaptive challenges. Heifetz referred to the silverback gorilla to explain how authority relationships today reflect the dominance and deference of our primate ancestors. He argued that the silverback 'serves a control function, mediating aggression within the group and maintaining stability' (ibid:51). At a later stage of his work, Heifetz also uses the example of the Founding Fathers of the USA as a way of illustrating how there was a need to move away from the 'Silverback':

> In a sense, the presidency as an institution embodied a revolutionary conception of executive leadership. And no wonder; it emerged from the antiauthoritarian sentiment of the new and rebellious nation. No longer were people to look up to the solitary silverback – the Monarch – for decisive answers to the problems of direction, protection, orientation, conflict, and the care of norms. The colonists had grown tired of being misled by rulers whose visions came from within. They wanted public officials whose visions were derived or shaped from without. Presidential perspectives had to be reality-tested against a multiplicity of views. Presidential action would require collaboration. (Heifetz: 177)

The silverback is excellent at practising leadership when facing technical problems (food gathering, protection, direction, mediating conflict) but is useless when faced with a challenge that requires innovation, such as dealing with rifled poachers (or the creation of a New World!). Finley (2000) provides a subtle distinction between technical and adaptive work:

Technical work	Adaptive work
Technical work is problem-solving. Finding berries and breaking up fights is technical work. Once you know how to do it, you simply repeat the process.	Adaptive work, by contrast, is an open-ended challenge. It creates a new environment in which you cannot survive by relying on the wisdom of the old environment.

---

[3]'A medieval collection of stories providing physical and allegorical descriptions of real or imaginary animals along with an interpretation of the moral significance each animal was thought to embody': 'bestiary, n.' OED Online. Oxford University Press, June 2015. Web. 29 July 2015.

It can be argued that the difference between technical versus adaptive work is that the former concerns routine problem-solving whereas adaptive work is about exercising wisdom through intelligence. Let us now consider this in relation to the practice of leadership in achieving public interest outcomes. There are seven principles for leading adaptive work (Figure 12.2):

Figure 12.2 *Seven principles for leading adaptive work*

As a practical form of leadership, adaptive work focuses on the achievement of socially desirable outcomes, such as social, environmental, and economic well-being, based on the work of Heifetz, and later work with his colleague Linsky (Heifetz and Linsky, 2002).

In Chapter 7, when I introduced the Leadership Values Tree, I talked about the three sources of energy for transformational leadership that apply to the concept of collective leadership. I discuss these further below (with Heifetz and Linsky's terms in parenthesis):

- **Time and Perspective (Get on the Balcony):** Leaders need to achieve a balance between both the long term and the short term in understanding how both the strategic direction and operational implementation align. This is what Heifetz calls 'getting on to the balcony'. This is a place from which to observe the wider environment as well as what is over the horizon, but it also about getting 'onto the dance floor' every now and then and to move back and forth. It helps in distinguishing between a technical and an adaptive problem.
- **Mass (Protect the Voices of Leadership from Below):** It is important to ensure that everyone's voice is heard in encouraging willingness to experiment

and learn. Leaders need to support staff that point to the internal contradictions of the organization and empower staff to come up with solutions.

- **Space (Create the Holding Environment):** The first two dimensions help in identifying the adaptive challenge, which is then supported by the creation of a holding environment. This could be either a physical or virtual space in which adaptive work can be done through relationships or wider social spaces.

This further leads to the three forms of response that I discussed in Chapter 7, dependent upon the leadership stance that is adopted:

- **Reactive:** Responding to the incidents as they emerge without giving much thought to issues that leaders can control and those that they can influence. This represents a tame response.
- **Proactive:** Taking the initiative and the responsibility to make things happen. This represents a wicked response.
- **Coactive:** A strategy based on working cooperatively with other organizations and networks to identify and address the conditions needed for improved social and economic well-being.

We will now explore adaptive approaches by giving consideration to a further range of collective behaviours.

We can thus ask:

Do leaders create space for adaptive work?			
Leaders rely on traditional reactive approaches to tacking leadership problems.	Leaders generally adopt a proactive approach but only create the space for this as-and-when needed.	Leaders are proactive in creating space for adaptive work in cases where adaptive challenges are present.	Leaders routinely create space for adaptive approaches and encourage a coactive approach in identifying adaptive challenges.
1 2 3	4 5 6	7 8 9	10 11 12

A reflective activity is provided below for this chapter.

Chapter 12 Activity

Write notes below in relation to what you can do to improve your
organization or network in these areas.

Is tasking and coordination devolved to the appropriate level while ensuring good links with the overall vision through effective cooperation?

Do leaders engage in integrated problem-solving approaches that tackle wicked problems as well as routine (tame) problems in a way that encourages innovation?

Do leaders share resources in delivering action plans?

Do leaders use collective intelligence in the actioning of delivery plans?

Do leaders create space for adaptive work?

13 Systems and Structures

'Systems and structures are in place to support the vision and action plans in delivering tranformational change'

Reflect for Improvement

Stakeholder Legitimacy

Innovation Encouraged

Good Governance

Systems & Structures

'Computer say "No!"' refers to the comical (but a rather cleverly articulated reality) in the BBC television production *Little Britain*[1] in which the 'system' (a computer) says 'No' in a variety of settings. The reality of this was recently highlighted. Many sectors, particularly the financial sector, rely almost exclusively on centralized databases that are worth billions of pounds (for example, to Experian, a FTSE 100 firm based in Dublin, and to Equifax, based in Georgia in the US). Even given these technologies, we are told of many people who are hit by computer-says-no-style rejections. 'Many have perfect credit histories but find that small errors have crept on to their file, often through no fault of their own. It could be that your address clashes with the electoral roll after a house move, or even someone else's card is mistakenly linked to your name' (Hyde, 2013). Often, such customers are made to pay for the organization to unravel the mystery! Hyde asks whether it is fair (and, I

---
[1]Little Britain Television Productions, London.

would add to this, in the public interest) that 'these computer algorithms, which you must pay to uncover and understand, could lead to a mortgage application rejection or a higher loan rate'. He concludes that it is not! The same could apply to many different systems, and, given that systems are generally human constructions, it is important to understand the role of leadership.

Organizational systems and structures are terms that are often conflated and yet both have distinctive characteristics. A system is an organized or connected group of objects, so as to form a complex unity, whereas a structure is the arrangement or organization of mutually connected and dependent elements in a system or construct. The system is therefore the objects (i.e. the actual computer software and algorithms or the different forms of organizational systems that make up the whole) whereas the structure defines how such objects are to be used and organized. Although closely related – and aligned as such, as a combined collective leadership value – it is important to understand this difference.

In the previous chapters we explored the concept of leadership practice and its role in making a difference. The final section of the preceding chapter explored the close connection between the final behavioural dimension of action-oriented behavioural approaches, namely creating the space for adaptive work, and the relevance of this behaviour in terms of the next collective leadership value, developing effective systems and structures.

In considering the collective leadership values in creating appropriate systems and structures that are consistent with the underpinning values and vision, I return briefly to the notion of synergy and cybernetics discussed in detail in Chapter 6; synergy focuses on the overall behaviour of (social or conceptual) systems whereas cybernetics is concerned with communication and control systems.

It is just as important to consider systems and structures as part of the collective leadership framework, because organizational systems and structures are created by humans and are thus fallible! Recall the chilling account of Zimbardo, who created a 'prison system' created as a laboratory experiment with students, which had to be terminated after a week due to the increasingly inhumane behaviours that the 'system' appeared to nurture, when he quite rightly asked the question: 'why do good people turn evil?' (Zimbardo, 2008).

REFLECT FOR IMPROVEMENT

To reflect is to consider or mediate the thoughts or attention on something, especially a past event or experience. Reflection is not just a passive or reactive endeavour and, in terms of a systematic behaviour, is viewed collectively. It should extend beyond just the technical features and play a key role in the identification and development of proactive and coactive responses to improvement within an adaptive learning environment; organizations learn collectively.

A key first step in this is pattern recognition. Patterns offer clues as to what is going on in relation to the problem under review and in identifying the contextual conditions that either help or hinder efforts to deal with the problem. This could be undertaken by means of a formal hypothesis representing a tentative explanation accounting for an observed pattern, which can then be tested by scientific means. Conversely, the patterns can be considered by virtue of a real-world interpretation based on experience and knowledge with a view to building more detailed wisdom. In either case, we must take note of the qualification of '*observe* the patterns'. Too often decisions are made on the whim of an individual, and while initiative can be good (and should be encouraged), heuristics can be experiential, empirical, experimental, investigative, or exploratory. The patterns should therefore be observed within the particular context/s of the problem. This is critical in the case of an adaptive/wicked problem.

Business Patterns are used as a means of analysing the number of business establishments and employment data at both national and sub-national levels and in assisting government agencies in relation to administration, planning, and service improvement. This assists in analysing economic changes over time. Businesses also benefit through an analysis of market potential, measuring the effectiveness of sales and advertising programmes, setting sales quotas, and developing budgets.[2] Similar benefits can emerge in relation to the not-for-profit sector. Observing patterns is a critical component of collective intelligence, which I discussed in the previous chapter.

> Collective intelligence is any intelligence that arises from – or is a capacity or characteristic of – groups and other collective living systems. (Atlee and Por, 2000:1)

Observing business patterns can assist in a wide range of contexts that assist both the businesses and the public interest. This includes examples in relation to assessing the impact that environmental management systems (EMSs) can have in improving the business value for organizations that adopt them (Feng et al., 2014) and how Corporate Social Responsibility (CSR) leads to competitive advantage and organizational transformation (Martinuzzi and Krumay, 2013).

Pattern recognition has been described as an innovative approach to identifying risk (Morrison and Quella, 2000). Business trends are shaped by patterns. Morrison and Quella say that 'Pattern thinking represents a new sense-and-respond approach that's more effective in both characterizing risk and identifying and exploiting new profit opportunities' and, further that 'Business is like a chess game. Once you can recognize the underlying patterns, you can counter strategic risks' (ibid:36). A number of different forms of patterns are suggested, such as customer patterns, knowledge patterns, and organizational patterns. An example of knowledge patterns is the partnership between Wal-Mart and Proctor & Gamble. The two companies decided to share information about customer habits, which allowed both firms to reap economic benefits based on reflection of current and past trends.

In relation to the public domain, let us briefly return to the health inequalities case study introduced in Chapter 9. As a background to this, the Commission on Social Determinants of Health (CSDH), through the World Health Organization

---

[2] See, for example, http://www.census.gov/econ/cbp/ (USA) and http://www.ons.gov.uk/ons/taxonomy/index.html?nscl=Business+and+Energy (UK).

(WHO), identified a range of patterns that underpin inequalities in health, including patterns focused on historical spending (on health), feeding, alcohol consumption, utilization, policy and investment, gender, social disease, and poverty 'together with broader patterns of social exclusion and lack of access to social services' (CSDH, 2008:178). There is a clear association between business patterns and social health patterns (in identifying the determinants of inequality). The Commission noted, 'Alongside trade liberalization, patterns of economic growth, and divergence in health conditions, globalization has seen the rise of other acute risks to health equity' (CSDH:168).

Patterns can also be focused on people. In the UK case study (Marmot, 2010), Marmot argued that the conceptualization of health inequalities (underpinning the then current UK target) did not capture the social gradient in health or the more complex patterning of health associated with other groups (for example, ethnic groups).

In relation to the behavioural dimensions of reflection, we can ask:

Is there sufficient focus on reflection as a means of continuous improvement?			
There is no formal process for encouraging reflection.	Some efforts are made to consider the improvements needed but these tend to be reactive and technical.	Significant efforts are being made although more effort is needed in terms of shared and/or critical reflection.	Reflection and continuous improvement is routinely applied and actioned.
1 2 3	4 5 6	7 8 9	10 11 12

GOOD GOVERNANCE

In Chapter 6, I introduced Bucky Fuller's hierarchy of generalized principle, which he interpreted as possibly governing all of the physical universe's intertransforming transactions (see Fuller and Dil, 1983:94), and I noted that most of our human interventions do not follow these principles (for example, money is a man-made invention). I also drew a distinction between systemic and non-systemic (human) interventions but later acknowledged that humans construct most non-systemic actions. In relation to good governance, I suggest that this is a good starting point in that good governance concerns governing all of the organization's (or network's) intertransforming transactions, thus aligning transformation and transaction, but against a background of shared and distributed leadership. It is likely to be within systems and structures that the mechanisms (both human and non-human) for good governance are likely to be found through both policy and practice. Governors could therefore focus on the synergies, described by Fuller as the behaviour of the whole system unpredicted by the behaviour or integral characteristics of any parts of the system when the parts are considered only separately. In this sense, having 'isolated the system', governance is again related to the whole and its various synergies, rather than its individual parts, returning to what Fuller described as the universal truth at the level of the whole.

Many of the board meetings that I have attended followed a fairly rigid agenda in which the focus is on 'the parts' (i.e. management information, human resources – most often from a budgetary position – and, of course, the budget itself). Rarely will a board focus on the whole system perspective, using what Fuller also described as 'inside-outing', which, from a board's perspective, would be about putting the customer first. In some of the worst scenarios, boards have manipulated data to persuade shareholders and stakeholders that the enterprise or institution is in better shape than it really is. This is not just a phenomenon of the twenty-first century. The Financial Reporting Council, the London Stock Exchange, and the accountancy profession established the Committee on the Financial Aspects of Corporate Governance, known thereafter as the Cadbury Committee, in May 1991. The reason for this creation was an increasing lack of investor confidence in the honesty and accountability of listed companies, occasioned in particular by the sudden financial collapse of two companies. Neither of these sudden failures was predicted due to their apparently healthy published accounts. Codes were subsequently published in relation to corporate governance (Cadbury, 1992).

A similar code was published for public governance. The Good Governance Standard for Public Services is a guide to help those concerned with the governance of public services not only to understand and apply common principles of good governance, but also to assess the strengths and weaknesses of current governance practice and improve it (OPM and CIPFA, 2004).

In practical terms, the role of governance is to assess and understand the impact of either transformation or transactional interventions, whether through leadership or management, respectively, and thus the impact on local processes and relationships and the synergy (or lack of synergies) between action (mechanisms) and its results (outcomes) within its wider contexts. Governance draws these together by exploring how the right things are done by the right people doing things right (mediated through leadership and management), in the right way for the right people and in the right places. This is illustrated in Figure 13.1.

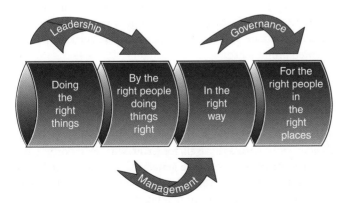

Figure 13.1 Leadership, management, and governance cycle

In Fuller's terms, what governors should be seeking to identify is the precessional effect. This represents the greatest challenge for governance as part of determining if leadership purpose represents the public interest. Putting the 'greatest number' ahead of personal/organizational motivations but also accepting that there may be a positive side effect for you as an individual (person/organization) is the practical description of Fuller's 'precession effect' (PE). In Fuller's terms, it means 'the effect of bodies in motion on other bodies in motion'. We can recall that all motion follows the universal generalized principles (as represented by the 12 degrees of freedom; axial, orbital, inside-outing; expansion and contraction, etc.). Precession does not necessarily follow the universal generalized principles, and can thus have an effect on what nature intended. As with the other degrees of freedom, the precession effect can be both positive and negative (think of global warming as one rather controversial subject as a negative precessional effect on the environment). These 12 degrees of freedom can act as a useful governance portfolio.

The first important point is to understand that these 12 degrees of freedom always exist in any motion or effects on motion. In terms of leading in the public interest, physical motion can be considered to represent both physical and intellectual action within a collective leadership model, and it helps us to take account of how different mechanisms are fired in differing contexts to produce patterns of outcomes.

It is also important to create a governance space. We can draw initially from Stafford Beer's cybernetics and then consider this as a governance space of more than three dimensions, which I have devised and illustrated in Figure 13.2: the dimensions of public interest (as the foundation), levels of governance, the relationships, and the forms of governance. As Beer points out, this will not always be accepted as a role of governance, but to govern is to learn and to ensure continuous improvement through innovation.

A further suggestion is to think about the role of governance in relation to what Grint (1997:5) proposes as a 'constitutive' approach through linguistic reconstructions of others' accounts of leadership. Grint tells us that this approach suggests that:

> What the situation and the leader actually are is a consequence of various accounts and interpretations, all of which vie for domination. Thus we know what a leader or situation is actually like only because some particular version of him, her, or it has secured prominence.

A role for governors, then, is to ensure that what leaders 'say' represents the reality of what they are (or should be) seeking to achieve. We thus begin to move into non-human aspects of leadership, such as the processes by which these phenomena of leadership 'are constituted into successes or failures, crises or periods of calm, and so on' (ibid:5–6). Bolden summarizes this well; for Grint, what is important are the processes by which accounts of leadership are generated, communicated, and consumed within groups and societies and the manner in which issues of power, authority, and experience influence these sense-making processes (Grint, 1997, summarized by Bolden, 2010:70). The space for good governance, as illustrated in Figure 13.2 can assist in these interpretations and evaluation.

The public leadership mechanisms of policy and practice represent a lens through which governors can assess the effectiveness of leaders as well as the effectiveness of the leadership outcomes. I discussed the importance of praxis in Part I of this book, and agree with the wider definition afforded to the term by Bolden (ibid:254) that it 'should be considered not just as "what people do" but, perhaps more importantly, the cognitive processes that inform decisions about practice and the processes by which these are converted into action'. I would also add to this the extent to which the leaders claim 'success'.

The tetrahedron of governance draws these elements together. The overall outcome of leading in the public interest is to develop a sense of trust, leading to confidence and, ultimately, legitimacy, within a framework of quality assurance that considers individual and collective responsibility and accountability. In taking account of the wider contextual conditions, governors can consider leadership from micro to meso and macro levels and evaluate the extent to which relationships are supporting the overall values and purpose through both transactional and transformational relationships. This will be further explored in Part III of the book in terms of applying these principles to leadership development in relation to good governance (Figure 13.2).

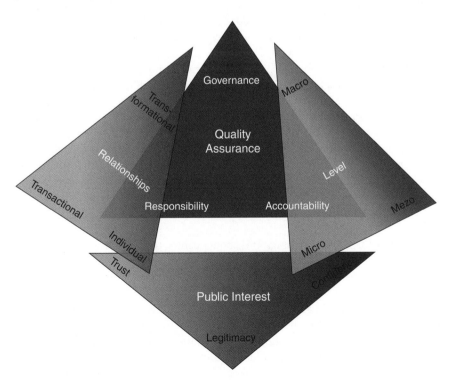

Figure 13.2 Tetrahedron of governance

In keeping with what you will now recognize as a familiar form, I introduce the behavioural dimensions for governance:

Do leaders share accountability through governance arrangements that are open and transparent across partner organizations and then distribute accountability within each organization – for both local and national/corporate priorities?			
Leaders do not communicate and implementation is driven from the top. It is directive and not integrated vertically or horizontally. Decision-making is closed.	Attempts are made to align strategic intention in a vertical manner but there is no emphasis given to shared accountability. Decision-making remains 'closed' in the majority of cases.	Leaders are held accountable vertically and – where appropriate – horizontally and decision-making is open.	There is a full commitment to both shared and distributed governance arrangements and decision-making is open.
1 2 3	4 5 6	7 8 9	10 11 12

INNOVATION ENCOURAGED

I have made mention of the importance of innovation at several points throughout this book. I now want to discuss this directly within the context of systems and structures and make a connection with integrated problem solving as both innovation and risk are closely connected to this. A further question that I pose is that of determining whether innovation is synonymous with risk or whether risk is the antonym of innovation. What do you think?

In keeping with the popular phrase, 'there can be no gain without pain', it has also been said that there can be 'no innovation without risk' (Brands and Kleinman, 2010). A significant problem, particularly within the public sector, is that the form of performance regimes (a term that I favour in this instance over performance management) leads to a single-minded focus on quantitative targets that can stifle innovation in those areas in which the public interest can be improved qualitatively. The same applies equally in the for-profit sector in relation to the focus on the financial 'bottom line' for the benefit of shareholders rather than the investments needed in research and development in the achievement of longer term goals.

A broad definition of innovation is that it is about:

> Changing the way we do things. It is about pushing the frontier of what we know in the hope of generating new and useful ideas, and then putting them into practice. (GOS, 2014:14)

However, it is further argued that the risk of failure is an intrinsic aspect of innovation and it is not without detrimental impacts in other parts of the 'system'. A good example is used in relation to the invention of the electric light bulb that had a significant and detrimental impact on the candle makers of the day (GOS, ibid). The revolutionary nature of this particular innovation far outweighed the impact elsewhere, but the point to note is that leading innovation also requires a close attention to the leadership of change, particularly in cases of revolutionary innovation. Ensuring that a good risk assessment is part of the innovative and transformational change process will most certainly help in confronting the brutal facts of the impact of change.

Within the context of public leadership, innovation can be defined as a means of 'drawing together leadership, management and governance networks within a virtuous circle of collective leadership' (Brookes and Grint, 2010:345), such as that outlined in the previous section on governance. Within industry, innovation is often the difference between survival or demise. The acquisition of knowledge is critical to good innovation.

Knowledge-based approaches are critical to innovative policies and practice, and the ability to manage knowledge assets is increasingly recognized as a core competence, supported by the cognitive capabilities of companies (Scarso and Bolisani, 2010).

In reviewing academic articles submitted up to and including August 2014 using the search terms 'knowledge based approaches', a total of 112,226 articles were returned.[3] These were then analysed by discipline, with the results illustrated in Table 13.1. It will be noted that almost three-quarters relate to computer science, engineering, and mathematics, with just over 14 percent for medicine and 11 percent for social sciences.

Table 13.1 Academic articles focused on knowledge

Discipline	Total no. of articles	%
Computer Science	40,837	36.4
Engineering	31,186	27.8
Medicine	15,783	14.1
Social Sciences	12,512	11.1
Mathematics	11,908	10.6
TOTAL	**112,226**	**100**

Given that leadership is classified within social sciences, further exploration was undertaken. Business, management, and accounting (within social sciences) accounted for just 1188 articles, representing just 1 percent of the total and, of these, a total of 266 articles were returned when adding the search term 'leadership'. An analysis of this is illustrated in Figure 13.3. The interest in the topic appears to have emerged from 2004.

Innovation must be integral to the decision-making process in seeking to explore the alternatives (in addressing the needs of the problem profile), but it carries with it some risk. Fostering innovation is more likely when leaders listen to the voices of all key stakeholders rather than relying on the traditional notion of 'the leader

---

[3]http://www.Scopus.com, accessed August 2014.

knows best'. Recent developments of online technologies have been shown to significantly increase effective stakeholder engagement in securing a greater sense of collective intelligence (discussed in the previous chapter). It is thus a personal capacity of a leader to create a climate of discovery and emergence (Hurley and Brown, 2010).

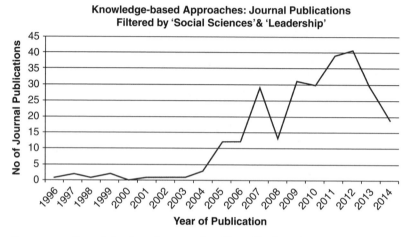

Figure 13.3 *Knowledge-based approaches filtered by 'social sciences' and 'leadership'*

In summary, management of risk is an important determinant of innovation. Where organizations or companies are risk averse, innovation is less likely. As always, a balance is required and an undisciplined approach to managing risk will result in an over-reliance of less well thought through activities. Scientific and technological advances can drive economic growth and lead to significant social benefits; the challenge for society is to channel evidence about innovative technologies and their risks to improve decision-making (GOS, 2014).

The behavioural dimensions are described as:

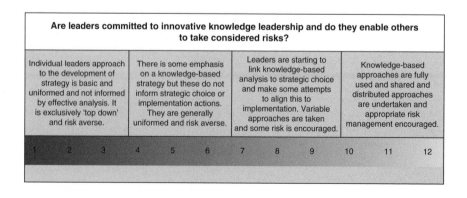

Are leaders committed to innovative knowledge leadership and do they enable others to take considered risks?			
Individual leaders approach to the development of strategy is basic and uniformed and not informed by effective analysis. It is exclusively 'top down' and risk averse.	There is some emphasis on a knowledge-based strategy but these do not inform strategic choice or implementation actions. They are generally uniformed and risk averse.	Leaders are starting to link knowledge-based analysis to strategic choice and make some attempts to align this to implementation. Variable approaches are taken and some risk is encouraged.	Knowledge-based approaches are fully used and shared and distributed approaches are undertaken and appropriate risk management encouraged.
1 2 3	4 5 6	7 8 9	10 11 12

STAKEHOLDER LEGITIMACY

The term 'stakeholder' is preferred to that of 'shareholder' because the former includes the latter but describes a significantly broader group. Stakeholders are identified as:

> Those persons and organizations that have an interest in the strategy of the organization. Stakeholders normally include shareholders, customers, staff, and the local community. (Eaton, 2005:53)

Leaders need to be legitimate (in the use of their power and influence), as argued in the prologue to this book, and organizational legitimacy, as we also noted earlier, is an important component of trust at the level of the organization. It is just as important to further acknowledge that stakeholder legitimacy – the belief that the actions of stakeholders are appropriate to values and goals of the organization and the public interest – is given as much consideration as that of both leader and organizational legitimacy.

There is a close link between stakeholder legitimacy and innovation, given the need to engage with stakeholders widely as part of the innovation process. It is not just about competitiveness (in the for-profit sector) or reputation (in the not-for-profit sector). It has been recently said that 'Each direction for innovation is a social choice involving issues of uncertainty, legitimacy and accountability' (GOS, 2014:47). This comes back to the main argument of this book: leading in the public interest.

The interrelationships between the different values and behaviours of the collective leadership framework emerge once more, in which we can consider stakeholder legitimacy and innovation (systems) as part of an adaptive approach to collective leadership (action oriented). In an interesting study that looked at adaptation to the impacts of climate change, a dynamic process was suggested that is shaped by institutional, cultural, and socio-economic contexts (Amaru and Chhetri, 2013). The authors identified four distinct types of adaptation through which the roles of institutions (and other stakeholders) can be explored in relation to innovation. There was a need for widespread participation, flexibility, and integration of stakeholders for a quick and effective response, and the need to transfer leadership and responsibility from institutionally led adaptation measures to community-based measures so that adaptation is sustained into the future (ibid:128). Tackling climate change is a classic 'wicked problem' and an adaptive leadership challenge and, therefore, the principles of identifying and engaging stakeholders should be perceived as legitimate when leading in the public interest.

A first important step is in understanding who your stakeholders are. A second is to recognize that some will have a greater degree of interest, and influence, than others. A third is to ensure that the decision-making processes include this public interest legitimacy test when engaging with an increasingly wider and social media aware network of stakeholders. Naivety may suggest that we try and achieve consensus across all groups, but the realist approach acknowledges that this is unworkable. In ensuring legitimacy, leaders should be able to provide confidence that an appropriate and ethical approach has been adopted. A range of techniques for analysing stakeholders suggests that understanding this level of interest and influence (or power) is important in determining the priorities for stakeholder engagement (Johnson et al., 2011). While this has some practical significance, we must not ignore the need for equity and ethics. A 'principle of fairness' has been suggested as a means of identifying and adjudicating among stakeholders (and their interests) (Phillips, 1997b). It is argued that within the acceptance of a mutually beneficial scheme of cooperation, obligations of fairness are created in proportion to the benefits received. Building on Phillips, we can say that, 'fairness' is an emotive term and can be applied in a variety of settings, often to seek buy-in for whatever is being proposed. However, a narrow view on stakeholder analysis is likely to exclude those without power or influence, according to Van Buren III (1999), who tells us that:

> 'No one wants to be called unfair; everyone wants to couch their ideas and ideals in terms of fairness'. (ibid:1)

In developing a stakeholder-oriented system of business ethics, Phillips tells us 'those powerless stakeholders who have legitimate and/or urgent claims are of greatest concern' (ibid:3). Legitimacy is thus a property that is valued by all stakeholders. The notion of legitimacy can be given a fairly narrow interpretation, in terms of establishing the legitimacy of a person by an authoritative declaration or decree, or to authorize by legal enactment. Closer to the notion of legitimacy in leadership is its meaning as genuine or real, as opposed to spurious and justifiable, or reasonable. In terms of stakeholders, legitimacy concerns the relationship in terms of its desirability or appropriateness (Mitchell et al., 1997), which is a useful maxim to follow.

In a partnership setting, partnership networks have been branded as a new form of global governance with the potential to bridge multilateral norms and local action by drawing on a diverse number of actors in civil society, government, and business (Bäckstrand, 2006). Bäckstrand, in this respect, views legitimacy as the acceptance and justification of shared rule by a community and adopted a twofold interpretation: input and output. The former determines whether processes conform to procedural demands, such as representation of relevant stakeholders, transparency, and accountability whereas the latter revolves around effectiveness and 'problem solving capacity' (ibid:292). Within the commercial sector, a good definition of legitimacy is that which views the legitimacy of business as 'its ability to command some sort of moral authority' (Moran, 2013:11). In either case, the importance of engaging the right stakeholders, in the right way, and for the right reasons, is critical to ultimate legitimacy, assessed in terms of trust at individual, organizational, and institutional levels. We can consider the following behavioural dimensions:

Do leaders ensure that the shared vision is implemented in a way that is equitable and ethical and can thus be perceived of as legitimate and trustworthy by other stakeholders?			
The delivery of the strategy is not focused equally and supports a single aim rather than the collective good. It is not perceived as legitimate or trusted by stakeholders.	Equity and ethics are acknowledged but there is no demonstrable commitment and perceptions of legitimacy and trust are mixed.	Leaders approach the vision/strategy in an equitable and ethical way. Perceptions of legitimacy and trust are generally positive but it is not yet routine.	Strategy and Delivery is both equitable and ethical and this secures a strong sense of legitimacy and trust with other stakeholders.

1	2	3	4	5	6	7	8	9	10	11	12

A reflective activity is provided below for this chapter.

Chapter 13 Activity
Write notes below in relation to what you can do to improve your organization or network in these areas.

Is there sufficient focus on reflection as a means of continuous improvement?

Do leaders share accountability through governance arrangements that are open and transparent across partner organizations and then distribute accountability within each organization?

Are leaders committed to innovative knowledge leadership and do they enable others to take considered risks?

Do leaders ensure that the shared vision is implemented in a way that is equitable and ethical and can thus be perceived of as legitimate and trustworthy by other stakeholders?

14 Skills and Behaviours

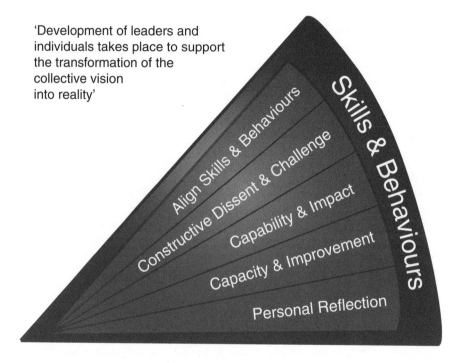

'Development of leaders and individuals takes place to support the transformation of the collective vision into reality'

Align Skills & Behaviours

Constructive Dissent & Challenge

Capability & Impact

Capacity & Improvement

Personal Reflection

Skills & Behaviours

Skill describes discrimination or knowledge in a specified matter. It is thus the capability of accomplishing something with precision and certainty, practical knowledge in combination with ability represented by cleverness or expertness. Behaviour is the manner of conducting oneself in the external relations of life, represented by such characteristics as demeanour, deportment, bearing, or manners. I have argued throughout the book that skills and behaviours support the collective values that leaders aspire to.

ALIGN SKILLS AND BEHAVIOURS

The values of the organization often reflect its culture and long-term condition whereas behaviours define the shorter (and more immediate) term climate. The organizational climate is a key driver of performance within a business or public service organization. It is characterized by the atmosphere of working relationships within and beyond the organization, and reflects how those who work within the organization and, within its teams, feel about their working conditions and relationships. A positive culture is of vital importance to the values in much the same way as demonstrated behaviours are to the prevailing climate. In a positive climate people are more likely to have a sense of clear purpose and what their role is within this purpose.

The alignment of skills with behaviours is a means of bridging the gap between the long and the short term. It is at this point that I return to the importance of the individual within a collective leadership framework. Skills and behaviours are the demonstrable manifestation of values and standards at the level of the individual as well as the organization.

There is a need to gain greater insight in relation to the interplay between people skills and associated behaviours. There has been a tendency to conflate the two terms; for example, Honey suggested in the 1980s that interpersonal skills are face-to-face behaviours (Honey, 1988). However, taking a very brief theoretical stance, we can consider behaviourism – the theory that both animal and human behaviour is explained without appeal to feeling or thought – as opposed to existentialism, a theory that emphasizes the existence of a person as a free agent developing through acts of the will.

Skills involve the enhancement of capability as an individual whereas behaviours determine the outcomes of interaction with other people either within the organization or beyond it. Skills alone do not bring about leadership whereas behaviour can be a much stronger determinant of leadership. From a systemic view, knowledge management develops skills but behaviours are more inherent. Alignment of the two is thus critical.

How do we align skills and behaviours? It first requires a clear understanding of the strategy for the delivery of the organization's or network's vision based on its values. By adopting the intelligent leadership approach, the particular problem profiles will be evident, gaps identified, and proposals for change agreed through goals, objectives, and, ultimately, actions. It is at this point that the practical association between skills and behaviours can be given a priority. The way in which this is done will depend heavily upon the scale of the problems faced and the proposed means of responding to this profile. The skills required will depend equally on the vision and values as part of defining the overall purpose of the organization and on the outcomes being sought. Purpose and public value are therefore essential in shaping the skills needed to bring these about. The second stage is to identify the skills that are either available or missing, in much the same way as the gaps for the problem profile were identified. In relation to a shorter-term, less complex set of problems, the skills may well be known. However, in relation to a classic wicked problem, it is unlikely that these will be known, and a skills audit may then be necessary. In effect, the skills represent the technical aspects of the response to the problem, whereas the behaviours will be more wide-ranging and adaptive.

Once this process has been undertaken, the alignment of the skills with the vision and strategy can then result in a clear statement of the knowledge and capability that is required, with the behaviours defined in terms of outcomes based on standards (which reflect the competencies emerging from the skills audit). Performance of individuals can then be assessed, but within a corporate framework that encompasses strategic priorities alongside public value indicators.

We can thus ask:

Do leaders ensure that individual members of their team are matching the aims of the vision and strategy through their own skills and behaviours?			
There are no mechanisms by which individuals' skills and behaviours are assessed or developed.	Loose arrangements exist to identify alignment between individuals' skills and behaviours to organizational aims.	Formal arrangements exist to assess individual performance against the aims but this is more of a mechanical performance process.	Leaders take full responsibility in ensuring that individuals' skills and behaviours fully reflect the strategic aims.
1　　2　　3	4　　5　　6	7　　8　　9	10　　11　　12

CONSTRUCTIVE DISSENT AND CHALLENGE

In demonstrating and enabling appropriate behaviour, leaders must be prepared to confront the bad news as well as the good, and allow constructive challenge. False hope is not a good strategy. Jim Collins provides a stark example of this in recounting his conversation with Admiral Jim Stockdale, a survivor of eight years as a prisoner of war:

> You must never confuse faith that you will prevail in the end – which you can never afford to lose – with the discipline to confront the most brutal facts of your current reality, whatever they might be. (Collins, 2001:85)

To support pessimism as opposed to optimism may seem intuitively strange, but we come back to my oft-cited call for balance. The following view is insightful:

> As any cynic will tell you, ill-informed optimism deludes people into ignoring reality. Yet doom and gloom pessimism sucks people into depression and inaction. Neither of these mind-sets is helpful in bad situations. (Earle McLeod, 2014)

Catastrophic business results can become their own reality if the true facts are not confronted, whether they are optimistic or pessimistic. This was explicitly evident in some of the illuminating examples recalled by Collins (2001), not only in relation to the optimists in the Stockdale example but also to business practices, such as 'milking cash from profitable arenas, eroding the core business' (ibid:78), which was counter to the emerging evidence that this 'plan was doomed to fail and might take down the rest of the company with it'. As I described in the introduction to the book, the banking industry has been particularly prone to ignoring the brutal facts (often in cases where the evidence was compelling). Collins points also to an early example of this in relation to deregulation when executives at the Bank of America 'failed to confront the one big reality of those regulations' in that banking would become a commodity (ibid:78). For Collins, this requires '"building red flags" and having the discipline to confront the brutal facts' (ibid:128).

The discipline of confronting the facts and encouraging others to do so is a major challenge. I referred to the Zimbardo experiment (Zimbardo, 2008) in both the introductory and previous chapters. Grint (Grint, 2010:182) refers to both Milgram's (1974) (1961) and Zimbardo's (2008) infamous compliance experiments by arguing that 'we have known that most people, most of the time, comply with authority even if that leads to the infliction of pain upon innocent others providing the rationale is accepted by the followers, they are exempt from responsibility, and they engage in harm only incrementally'. In such cases, as Grint argues:

> [S]uch consent is often destructive: subordinates will acquiesce to the enfeebling of their organization rather than challenge their boss through Constructive Dissent. Destructive Consent, then, is the bedfellow of Irresponsible follower-ship and a wholly inadequate frame for addressing Wicked Problems. (Grint, 2010:183)

It is interesting to look at Grint's work within the context of confronting the brutal facts, as it concerns relationships between leaders and followers. This is plotted in a traditional four-quadrant matrix based on two main axes: increasing commitment to the goals of the leaders (the left vertical axis) and increasing independence from the leader (bottom horizontal axis). Moving from bottom left, from what Grint describes as the 'Emperor', through to bottom right the 'Cat Herder' we can observe respectively, minimum and maximum independence from the leader. In both cases, we can then look at the left-hand matrix and note the low commitment to the leadership's goals. At the top left is the 'White Elephant'; this is a metaphorical term for an obvious truth that is either being ignored or going unaddressed, or an obvious problem or risk no one wants to discuss. In terms of leadership, Grint suggests that this refers to a 'leader' – often considered to be divine – but who, in reality, is a false god, misleading rather than leading his or her disciples (Grint, 2005). At the top right, is the Wheelwright, with again, respectively, minimum and maximum independence from the leader. For Grint, this denotes an organization where the leaders recognize their own limitations and where leadership is distributed according to the perceived requirements of space and time.

However, in both of these cases, the White Elephant and the Wheelwright both have high commitment to the leadership's goals. We can interpret this by looking at the Emperor (bottom left) as encouraging 'irresponsible followers', the Cat Herder (bottom right) 'independent individuals', the White Elephant (top left) 'disciplined followers' and the Wheelwright (top right) 'responsible followers' (Figure 14.1).

Grint then introduces two further elements that can be contextualized with the primary axes. I use this as a top horizontal axis ranging from left to right (consent to dissent) and a right-hand vertical axis ranging from bottom to top (destructive to constructive). We thus have the following (Figure 14.2):

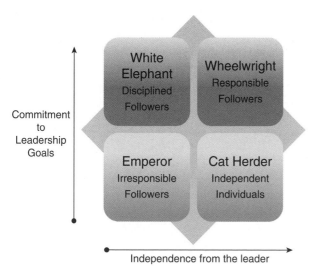

Figure 14.1 Commitment to leadership goals/independence from leader

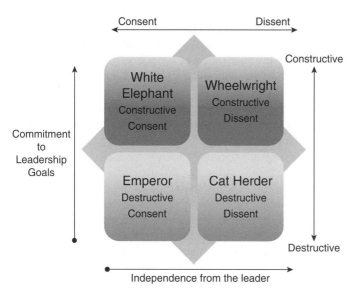

Figure 14.2 Consent and dissent/constructive and destructive

In the final (top right) quadrant, Grint suggests that the Wheelwright (heterarchical leaders) recognizes their own limitations, with leadership switching according to needs (Grint, 2005); he describes this 'rather like a rowing squad (from coach, to captain, to stroke, to cox and back again), or the flexible system of Mission Command employed by the armed services which sets general objectives and allows subordinates latitude in the specific means of achieving them'. In this model, then, Grint tells us that the power of leaders 'is a consequence of the actions of followers rather than the cause of it' (ibid, 2005:38).

To what extent are the following behaviours demonstrated:

Leaders actively invite constructive dissent and challenge			
Leaders do not create a climate for constructive dissent and there is no challenge.	Some efforts are made to encourage constructive dissent but challenge does not does take place.	Constructive dissent and challenge is encouraged where appropriate.	Constructive dissent and challenge is integral to day-to-day working and strategy development.
1 2 3	4 5 6	7 8 9	10 11 12

CAPACITY AND IMPROVEMENT

Capacity can be defined in a number of ways. It originates from the Latin term *capacitatem*, meaning to be able to take in or see. Its primary meaning in contemporary society is the ability to receive or contain, and it describes the abilities or powers of human beings to take in impressions, ideas, or knowledge; in this sense, it relates to mental or intellectual receiving power. At the level of the individual, it concerns mental ability or force of mind and supports the ability for the individual to absorb the knowledge in building skills. Capacity also applies at the institutional level. In literal terms, it is the ability to provide accommodation of a certain amount of volume for the purposes of discharge; simply, a bottle can only carry so much liquid, a theatre or sports stadium only so many people, and an electrical circuit, so much current. This is analogous to an organization creating space for improvement and capability building (or the capacity for transformational change). In industry, it is the ability to produce, such as representing 'full capacity'. Capacity thus enables or renders an individual or an organization capable.

Capacity is closely connected with capabilities or possibilities, but as a quality or condition of admitting or being open to some action or treatment, as opposed to the actual building of capability. I will shortly discuss capability, but capacity is a prerequisite for capability building, both at the individual and organizational level. Individuals and organizations must be 'open' to build capability, both in terms of space and mental ability before the actual capability building takes place. This is important if we consider the importance of creating space for collective leadership activity. If we return to the example of the electrical conductor, or apparatus, the capacity may exist for the absorption of heat, or for the apparatus to store static electricity, but its capability can only be enabled if it is connected to the appropriate supply. Leaders can thus create capacity but can only enable capability.

Trust is an enabler for building capacity, particularly collegial trust between colleagues and collaborators (Cosner, 2009). Trust cannot be guaranteed. For example, trust can be generated by the perceptions of the trustee and the trustor (Llewellyn et al., 2013). This becomes even more difficult when dealing with people within increasingly diverse (and sometimes) global networks. A further example of this is where trust was found to be particularly important in building capacity within the implementation of international reconstruction and development aid projects in a post-conflict environment, namely Afghanistan (Kadirova, 2014). In addition to the conventional 'instrumental' qualities of leadership 'the qualities of "moral" leadership, such as the ability to build trust and respect with national counterparts based on the record of competence, dedication and delivery' were found essential (ibid:887).

In building capacity through trust, the ability of leaders to reflect critically on their leadership practice is a key requirement. Cunliffe's (2009) notion of the 'philosopher leader' suggests a major challenge in relation to the need to think differently about leadership (Cunliffe, 2009). I referred to the importance of Aristotle's practical wisdom in the earlier chapters, a point also raised by Bolden (Bolden, 2010), drawing also on the similar examples used by Cunliffe and Grint (Grint, 2007). Grint asserts that leadership is not just a technical problem that requires more training but, rather, focusing on the problem rather than reskilling; in other words, it is about fixing the problem and not fixing the people. He tells us 'phronesis cannot be taught in any lecture theatre but must be lived through' (Grint, 2007:242).

To enable followers to live through the problem, followers and leaders must be given the opportunity to create the space for this to happen and – just like the analogous electrical circuits – to absorb the energy that is being generated, at a level that can be tolerated. To what extent are the following behaviours evident?

Do leaders pay regard to their own personal impact and development in building capacity as a means of improving the organization and its networks and building trust?			
There is no focus on the assessment of impact or development of individual leadership styles and trust internally is non-existent.	There are some basic efforts to develop individual leaders but there is no evidence of building capacity and trust relationships are minimal.	Opportunities are emerging for individual leadership development based on capacity building and trust is growing.	Leaders are committed to the development of individual leadership styles and capacity building and there is evidence of strong trust between individuals.
1　2　3	4　5　6	7　8　9	10　11　12

CAPABILITY AND IMPACT

Capability is often considered as an individual feature, ability, or competence that can be developed in a person. It could refer to an ability that exists in an individual as distinct from capacity, which is the power to hold, accommodate, or receive something (see above). However, as with capacity, my argument is that an accumulation of individual capability leads to the potential for collective organizational and network capability.

Just as we have distinguished between capability and capacity, we need to do likewise with the term competence in relation to impact. Within the sense of improving organizations, competence refers to a sufficiency of qualification and the ability to deal adequately with a subject. It is a standard of ability that an organization sets for a particular role, task, or combination of roles and tasks. Competence could also act as a bridge between the two former terms. Within the context of this book, capability is thus a collective means through which individual competencies can be channelled and applied to organizational improvement and the assessment of its outcomes. I illustrate these three Cs (capacity, capability, and competence) schematically, superimposed on the three Cs (client, customer, and community) introduced in earlier chapters:

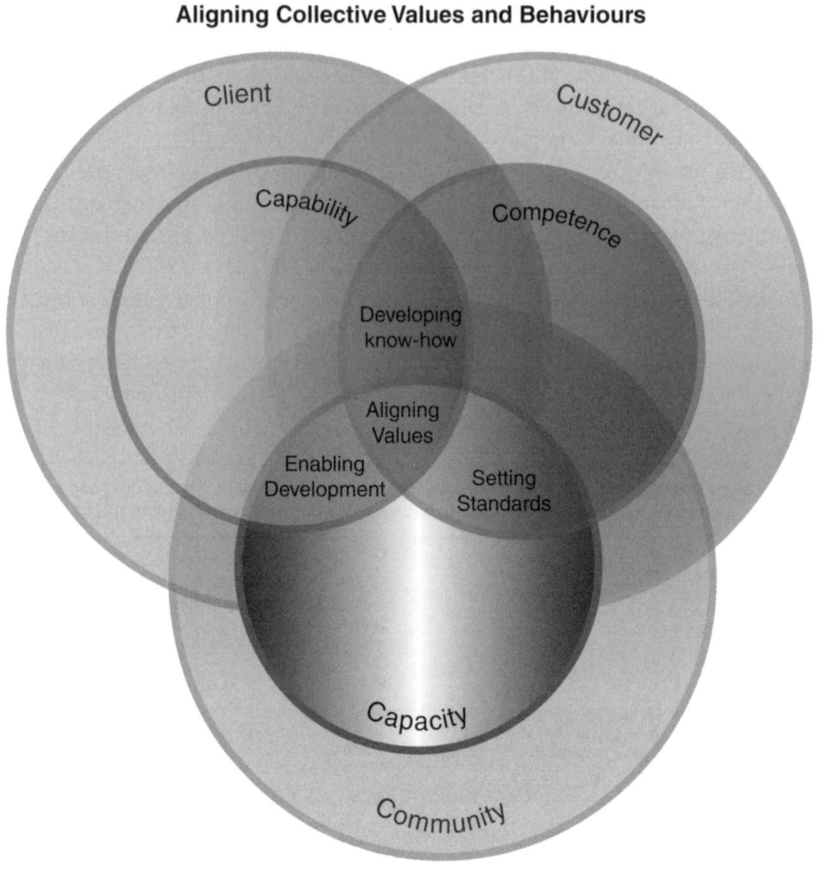

Aligning Collective Values and Behaviours

Figure 14.3 Impact through capability, capacity and competence

Impact is now generally considered to mean the effective action of one thing or person upon another and the effect of such action in terms of its influence or impression. The impact of the joint outcomes of capacity, capability, and competence is illustrated at the heart of Figure 14.3 as developing 'know-how' (capability and competence), 'enabling development' (capability and capacity), and 'setting standards' (capacity and competence). The three properties are dynamic; capability should lead to an impact, grounded on the creation of capacity both at the organizational/network and individual level determined by competences. Ultimately, the collective outcome is the alignment of values (public values) related to these three Cs based on the benefits aimed at, and responsibilities undertaken by, the three Cs of customer, client, and community.

As discussed in the early chapters, evidence of outcome should be collated and analysed. In aligning skills and behaviour, the overall impact should be consistent with the shared values that were developed through the vision (as described in Part I and presented at the heart of the illustration), and then cascaded throughout the institute and its networks, through to the individual level.

There are two main purposes for this: first, to identify the extent to which all individuals are working towards the common goals, and second, and just as important, is to identify the developments needs of all staff and partners and provide the capacity to enable this. A third aim would be to ensure that learning and development is aligned to activity in the workplace in a way that applies learning directly to the values, aims, and goals of the institute or network. This is often overlooked with training and development taking place in a silo, isolated from the real world of practice. This is directly related to one of the Ps of the collective leadership mechanisms, that of pedagogy. As I argue in Part III, although of critical importance, the links between pedagogy and the overall purpose and underpinning practice represent one of the most significant defects in collective leadership. In terms of building collective capability and impact, behavioural dimensions are postured as follows:

Are leaders committed to enabling the collective capability of organizations to transform intentions into evidence-based action and outcomes?			
There is no commitment to enabling collective capability and no space is provided for individual development.	Efforts to enable capability are made within organizations but no space is provided for individual development.	The enablement of collective capability is beginning to emerge based on encouragement for individual development.	Strong efforts are made to enable collective capacity and individuals are routinely encouraged to self-develop.
1 2 3	4 5 6	7 8 9	10 11 12

PERSONAL REFLECTION

This final behaviour brings the discussion fully back to the role of the individual. It is worth reiterating the relevance of reflection in relation to organizational and network improvement. To reflect is to shed light on a subject, question, or issue, or to consider or mediate. Of more relevance to leadership is that of fixing the thoughts or attention (back) on something, especially a past event or experience such as thinking deeply about a past event or response.

Individual reflection makes common sense but it is rare that time is taken to do this. An interesting personal reflection is given on the financial crisis of 2009 and beyond concerning the issue of business ethics. Will Morris claims that there has been something of a vacuum where a strong framework of business ethics should be. It is argued that 'individual employees should be "critical insiders" and that an ethical framework is not an "attack" on business because ethical businesses will be strong businesses, not least because of their ability to recruit and retain employees' (Morris, 2012:5). If leaders are unable to provide the conditions to enable this climate to exist, then employees are less likely to engage in decision-making and thus innovation and improvement will be stifled. As Bolden argues (Bolden, 2010:25), over-idealizing the leader can lead to negative consequences: 'members deskill themselves from their own critical thinking, visions, inspirations, and emotions and unconsciously maintain the status quo.' As I mentioned in the introduction to this book, when I look back over my 40 years of leadership practice, research, and teaching, I have reflected far more on my leadership practice over the last few years (as an academic) than I ever did as a practising leader.

The process of reflection is something that we should routinely practise. I can recall, for example, as a Police Superintendent, when commanding incidents that involved firearms (and where an armed police response was required), and other similar public order related commands, we were trained to reflect in terms of a detailed operational debrief. I was required to reflect on the decisions that I 'did not' make as well as those that I did. It was a good process and one that I could have used more routinely.

Personal reflection is also something that we should practise in terms of our capabilities and competence, discussed earlier. As Part II draws to a close, it is a good point to introduce the notion of reflective practice in learning, something that I discuss in detail in Part III. How often, for example, have we attended training courses, filled out the traditional 'happy sheet' at the end to say how well the session was structured, was taught, and was relevant and, with equal weight, how good the facilities were and, in particular, the catering! Much less do we reflect on how we have transferred this learning to the workplace? This is another critical element. Kolb is probably the best-known proponent of experiential learning (Kolb, 1984), which, simply stated, describes the process of applying meaning from direct experience:

'For the things we have to learn before we can do them, we learn by doing them.'

Our last consideration of the behavioural elements of collective leadership values can thus be stated:

Do leaders create space for individual members to reflect on their competence, skills, and actions to encourage individuals to reflect?			
There is no time available to reflect on either skills or behaviours.	Some efforts are made to reflect on action but no reflection on capability or capacity.	Reflection is encouraged where appropriate in terms of both capacity and capability.	Reflection is integral to day-to-day working and strategy development.
1 2 3	4 5 6	7 8 9	10 11 12

CONCLUSION

This final chapter of Part II has focused on efforts to sustain collective leadership through the improvement of skills of leaders and followers at all levels. An important principle is implicit in this argument. You can be a leader at any point in time and at any level within the organization or its networks. Equally you can be a follower at any point in time and at any level. There is an increasing recognition that the client or customer themselves can be a leader. A good example of this is the notion of the 'patient as leader' within National Health Service reforms in England and Wales. This does not happen per chance; while some individuals have innate characteristics such as confidence, integrity, or such charisma that, to use a common metaphor, they could 'sell snow to the Eskimos', this alone does not guarantee effective leadership.

> As a final reflexive activity for this chapter, identify (1) several competences that you believe leaders must have and (2) competencies that are necessary for managers. In other words, create two lists (you might want to do this in the online reflective journal with the option to upload your reflexive activity, on the companion website at www.palgrave.com/companion/brookes).

By now, we acknowledge that a leader can be a manager (at any point in time or at any level within the organization and its networks) and a manager (in a similar way) can be a leader. While the two terms are often conflated, they are distinct and yet also complementary. In what circumstances would you think that managers' and leaders' competencies would be complementary?

Throughout Parts I and II, the importance of collective leadership has been vigorously argued and the importance of values stated throughout. The third and final part of the book looks in detail at the notion of Leading through 360° Intelligent Networks, Knowledge and Skills (LINKS$^{360°}$).

A reflective activity is provided below for this chapter.

Chapter 14 Activity

Write notes below in relation to what you can do to improve your
organization or network in these areas.

Do leaders ensure that individual members of their team are matching the aims of the vision and strategy through their own skills and behaviours?

Do leaders actively invite constructive dissent and challenge from followers?

Do leaders pay regard to their own personal impact and development in building capacity as a means of improving the organization and its networks and building trust?

Are leaders committed to enabling the collective capability of organizations to transform intentions into evidence-based action and outcomes?

Do leaders create space for individual members to reflect on their competence, skills, and actions to encourage individuals to reflect?

Part III
Making a Difference

15 The Practice and Professionali-zation of Leadership

INTRODUCTION

This first chapter of Part III sets the scene in terms of applying the history, theory, and collective framework and model to practice. Before exploring the concept of leading through 360° Intelligent Networks, Knowledge, and Skills, I first want to consider what we mean by the practice of leadership and its impact on, and by, the increasing professionalization of, leadership.

The practice of leadership is a concept that has been attractive to those who write about leadership. This includes the volume of the same title (sub-titled 'Developing the next generation of leaders') (Conger and Riggio, 2007) and many hundreds of books relating to leadership across such diverse areas as pre-school (Bellamy, 1987) and full-time education (Bush et al., 2010), higher education, and other large organizations (Bolden, 2010) to global aspects of leadership in business, for example in integrating Western best practice with Chinese wisdom (Gallo, 2011).

There has also been an increasing emphasis on the development of professional practice, primarily within the public sector, particularly education (Jameson, 2008; Lewis-Smith, 2013), an early emphasis in health (Fry and McKenzie, 1968), and a building emphasis within policing in the UK, although the recent police reform has been described as 'Macdonaldization' (Heslop, 2011).

There is less written about professionalization in relation to the for-profit sector. However, an early study in 1955 of the chief executives of large corporations over the period from 1900 to 1950 introduced 'specific evidence both to support and explain the thesis, hitherto vaguely entertained by many students of business, that administration of such corporations is rapidly becoming a profession' (Newcomer, 1955:54). In more contemporary times, there is an interesting insight in relation to the need for innovative practices for the twenty-first century executive (Silzer, 2002). Even within this volume, there is a strong tendency to refer to individual traits in illustrating leadership practice rather than the collective approach that is now emerging, and the focus is very much on developing the successful executive leader (often isolated in the form of the singular). If we look at most titles that pertain to the professionalization of practice, there is much more emphasis on organizational development, training, and coaching on the one hand, and data driven analysis, the use of technology, practical applications for organizational development, and performance management on the other.[1]

A search on Amazon using the key words 'professional practice' returned 86,344 titles; when adding the key word 'leadership' to this, it returned 861 (thus representing less than 1 percent of the professional practice titles[2]). A significant number of these related to education (which, coincidentally, is where the term 'professional' originated in the nineteenth century) and, to a slightly lesser, but still substantial extent, health services. A further analysis of the Scopus database identifies similar trends. In searching for the terms 'professionalizing' and 'practice', the search returned 140 journal articles. In adding the term 'leadership', the number reduces to just three and all of them relate to the professionalization and practice of leadership in health services. However, an interesting trend towards the compound concept is shown and supports the view that professionalization of practice is becoming more popular, based on the 140 journal articles since 1980. This is illustrated in Figure 15.1.

First, let us consider the term 'professional'; as an adjective, the *Oxford English Dictionary* (OED) tells us that it concerns the 'senses relating to a profession or vow', or, 'of, or relating to a profession or declaration; that is avowedly (but sometimes falsely) the thing specified; professed'. Of particular relevance is the meaning that is ascribed to 'senses relating to or derived from (the conduct of) a profession or occupation. This is a characteristic of a person or persons that engage in a specified occupation or activity for money or as a means of earning a living, rather than as a pastime; contrasted with amateur' (OED). The OED goes on to say that it is 'sometimes applied disparagingly to a person who makes a trade or profession of something usually associated with higher motives (such as the professional politician)'.

From the mid 1600s through to contemporary usage, the term is considered as being 'preliminary or necessary to the practice of a profession (often requiring a professional examination)'. A professional thus engages 'in a profession, especially one requiring special skill or training; belonging to the professional classes'. 'A professional has or displays the skill, knowledge, experience, standards, or expertise of a professional; competent, efficient.' Such a person has 'knowledge of the theoretical or scientific parts of a trade or occupation, as distinct from its practical or mechanical aspects; that raises a trade to a learned profession', although this meaning is now rare except as merged with senses concerning its interpretation as 'of, belonging to, or proper to a profession' (OED).

---

[1] For example, see:- http://eu.wiley.com/WileyCDA/Section/id-300243.html?sort=DATE&sortDirection=DESC&page=2 (accessed 14 January 2014).

[2] Search conducted on 14 January 2013.

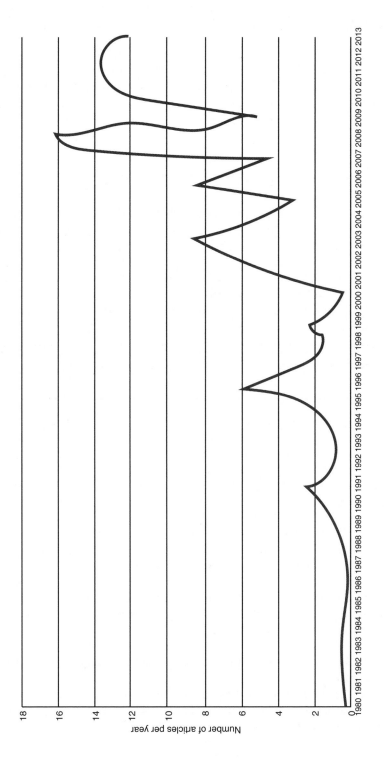

Figure 15.1 *Academic journal articles that include professionalizing practice*

Source: Scopus database (www.scopus.com); search conducted 13th January, 2013.

> **Reflection:** Based on your own experience and learning, identify a number of characteristics that:
>
> 1. You think reflect the notion of professional practice.
> 2. Show how this has manifested itself in practice within an organization or network that you are familiar with.

PROFESSIONAL PRACTICE AND LEADERSHIP

Two compound terms that emerge from the OED's definitions are illuminating and of interest to the reflective questions raised in the last section. The first is that of a *professional class*. This is a body of people engaged in skilled professions, thus professionals as a collective. The second, *professional development*, describes the development of competence or expertise in one's profession. It is the process of acquiring the skills needed to improve performance in a job. There is an implied link, therefore, between a collective profession and its member's development.

> **Reflection:** Does this reinforce or deflect your thoughts in the activity above? In what ways?

If I can be indulged to continue with my purist approach to understanding the language of leadership, in returning to the definition of 'practice': *'the actual application or use of an idea, belief, or method, as opposed to theories relating to it'*. *Does this concur with your earlier reflections, or does it differ?* Another question that we could ask is whether the combination of these two compounds infers that the *collective* professions engage in *collective* professional development. We will return to this point at a later stage of the chapter.

Practice is also described as the 'customary, habitual, or expected procedure or way of doing of something, or the repeated exercise in, or performance of, an activity or skill so as to acquire or maintain proficiency in it'.

The elements within the definition refer primarily to verbs – the 'doing words' – words used to describe an action, state, or occurrence, and forming the main part of the predicate of a sentence (OED), that is, the grounds upon which the sentence is based. Let us explore this a bit further:

i. The *actual application or use* (of an idea, belief, or method, as opposed to theories relating to it).
ii. The *expected procedure or way of doing of something* (such as custom or habit).
iii. The *repeated exercise in or performance of* (an activity or skill so as to acquire or maintain proficiency in it).

We can begin to explore the central importance of practice in aligning context and vision (ideas, beliefs and/or methods) with the outcomes (proficiency in what the leaders are trying to do or bring about). Proficiency is an outcome represented by an improvement in skill or knowledge, thus progress or advancement.

So let us be clear. Practice is about the mechanisms for 'doing', nothing more, nothing less, whereas context and vision concern 'thinking' and outcomes are about 'reflecting on achievement in line with the vision'. I suggest that professionalization encompasses all three, in taking action, but supported by continuous reflexivity and feedback illustrated in Figure 15.2 as follows:

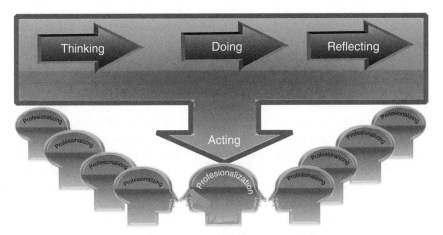

Figure 15.2 *Professionalizing to professionalization*

Transactional versus Transformational Professionalization and Practice

I briefly introduced the difference between transactional and transformational practice in Part I, suggesting that transactional concerns management whereas transformational reflects leadership; both concern the administration of business. It is at this point that I believe we should begin a journey in a different direction to that of our predecessors, but without losing sight of where we (and they) have been. While business administration has played its part in shaping business since the mid 1950s, this has not always been in a positive way. I referred to Hopper and Hopper in the earlier chapters, emphasizing their argument that 'greed' had replaced the 'public good' as the great engine companies of the industrial revolution (primarily under the control of its founder and family) shifted towards what I here describe as the professional classes. The key issue, I suggest, is the extent to which the professional classes reflect a true collective or, given the Hopper brothers' view, does it represent a collection of individuals focused on selfless aims – masquerading as professional – or is a true collective based on selfless motives?

Part of the problem, I suggest, is the continuing use of the term 'administration'. Allow me once more to focus on the language of leadership. The history of language is important in this respect because the term administration has its roots in Anglo-Norman, and Old and Middle French dating back to the twelfth and thirteenth centuries. It was originally defined as the 'action of taking care, looking after (late 12th cent. in Old French), action of managing, management (mid 13th cent)'.[3] In later, frequent use, it denotes the implication of being a supporting or subordinate component of a system (rather than directing or controlling it). This, in particular, suggests a separation from either management or leadership and thus shows more of a support to governance structures (rather than leadership practices) through a form of guardianship. Consider this interesting chronicle from circa 1435:

> Charles Lethbridge Kingsford (St John's College, Oxford) who archived the Chronicles of London in 1905 referred to the pronouncement (Julius B.II) in 1435 *'I Renounce ... to the reule and governance off the same kyngdomes and Lordshipes, and to the admynystracion off hem'*. (Kingsford, 1977)

This early meaning thus subjugates 'administration' as a support to the overarching rule and governance. Yet, business administration – which took root in the mid twentieth century – is still viewed as the 'be-all-and-end-all' of business practice today. We are still producing postgraduates from business schools with Masters in Business Administration (MBA) and Doctors in Business Administration (DBA). Perhaps this has played some part in favouring transactional rather than transformational behaviours, with outcomes focused equally on bottom-line and 'tick the share/stockholders boxes' rather than leading in the public interest? Although my suggestion is unlikely to accord with many of the established academics in this discipline, I firmly believe that we should be looking at moving towards postgraduates in Business (or Public) Leadership (MBL; DBL or MPL/DPL).

Newcomer (1955), referred to earlier, was witnessing the early development of business administration as a means of professionalizing the administration of big business at a time when the founders and family members were gradually being replaced, initially by specialists (for example, engineers and lawyers), but then increasingly by those who were graduates of business administration. Newcomer argued that much of the (then) present prestige of top executives comes from 'financial rewards and power, rather than from the skills required' (ibid:63). Newcomer's final comment in this paper is quite interesting given the current crisis of leadership in the twenty-first century. It is worth quoting in full:

> Nevertheless, it seems quite possible that the professionalization of big business will in the long run make an important contribution towards solving the so-called problem of big business. We have tolerated the giant corporation in this country, even while we have feared it, because mass production is efficient. It is usually given a large part of the credit for our high and rising planes of living. Consequently, we have been half hearted in our enforcement of the antitrust laws. And we have continued to hope that big business could be controlled for the public good, rather than destroyed. Professionalization of leadership in the

---

[3]'administration, n.' OED Online. Oxford University Press, June 2015. Web. 30 July 2015.

big business corporation appears to be one possible route to this end. The critics used to talk about the 'heartless and soulless' corporation. Some of them today are discovering the 'corporate conscience'. (Newcomer, 1955:63)

My argument is that, while the professionalization of practice describes a professional class as a 'collective', it relies on professional development. I prefer to view this as a virtuous cycle in which practice informs development and, conversely, development informs improved practice, and so the cycle continues. I build on my earlier illustration in showing this in Figure 15.3:

This illustration highlights how continuous professional development supports the Professionalization of practice. By including ethics and the public interest, we can perhaps begin to build some increased confidence that the Professionalization

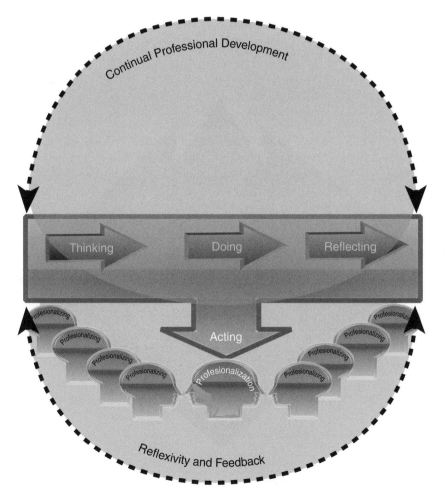

Figure 15.3 *CPD, reflexivity and feedback*

of practice can achieve more selfless goals. A key point to make here is that practice cannot be separated from development hence the mechanism of the 20P model, pedagogy, provides the foundation to achieve this through an appropriate and balanced approach of teaching through to applied practice grounded in action learning and applied leadership challenges.

It has been said that 'Practice is the hardest part of learning, and training is the essence of transformation' (Voskamp, 2010:56). An interesting interpretation of this statement is that while practice can be transactional, it can only be transformational if practice is informed by training and development and vice versa. For example, the role of education in the professionalization of practice, in the evaluation of a nursing degree, identified by its impact on enhancing leadership (Gerrish et al., 2003).

There should be a symbiotic relationship between the triad of teaching, learning, and practice, underpinned by a fourth dimension, research. The pedagogical links therefore between evidence-based teaching, evidence-based learning, and evidence-based practice provide a real opportunity to resolve the perceived pedagogical tensions, supported by evidence-based research. This triad is illustrated in Figure 15.4 in the form of a tetrahedron.

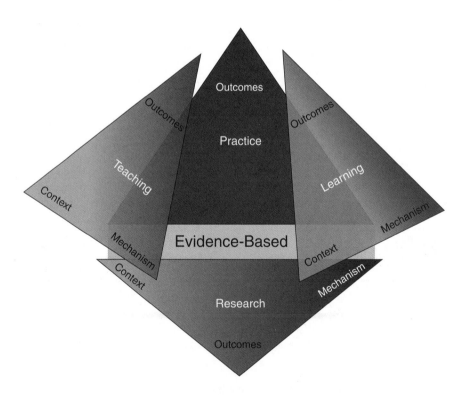

Figure 15.4 *Tetrahedron of evidence-based activity*

An excellent means of aligning these evidence-based activities is through applied leadership. Applied leadership challenges are directly aligned to applied learning and grounded on the principles of Action Learning.

The main idea of Action Learning is a method of reflective learning developed by Reg Revans (Revans, 1980). It can be presented as a learning equation:

$$L = P + Q$$

in which L is Learning, P is Programmed Knowledge and Q is Questioning Insight (Revans, 1998).

Action Learning is certainly increasing in popularity as a pedagogical method and is viewed quite widely as an excellent means of experiential learning between groups of individuals facing organizational problems. An Applied Leadership Challenge (ALC) seeks to take this one stage further and apply the principles of action learning throughout the organization and its networks and directly align the learning to the impact for the organization and its networks in addition to that of the individual learner. In this regard, I build on Revans's formula as follows:

Leadership Transformation =

		Where: P = Programmed Knowledge; Q = Questioning Insight; and
Σ	$\dfrac{(P + Q) * A}{(pi/\varphi)}$	A = Activity
		pi = *Public Interest* φ = *Golden mean (in achieving publicly valued balances)*

In summary, the senior leaders of an organization or partnership would agree to collaborate in the development of a collective vision with a view to delivering outcomes that are in the public interest, based on the presenting problem profile and its integrity. The pedagogical approach would take this further through an initial needs assessment taking due account of wider views and expertise on the wicked problems that organizations and networks face and the skills and behaviours that are required. This could be undertaken through a series of Applied Leadership Challenge Sets (ALCS) also grounded on the principles of Action Learning sets. This is illustrated in Figure 15.5.

In this chapter, I have discussed the practice of leadership and the history of professionalization. In the next and final chapter before a short epilogue, our focus will turn to the extent to which the professionalization of leadership takes place within the context of the dynamic relationships between collaborating leaders across my various research projects. Leadership-in-practice is an interesting approach that explores leadership through a practice-oriented lens. I agree with the view that this aims to penetrate how leaders as actors respond to the work of leadership, 'something which both traditional and mainstream leadership research has shed surprisingly little light on' (Carroll et al., 2008:364).

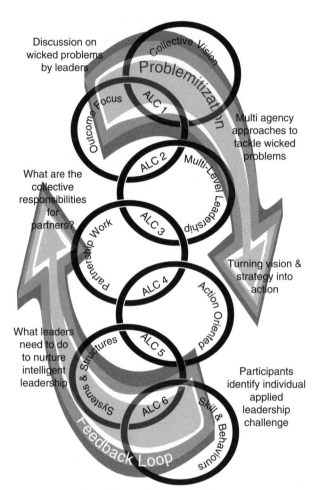

Figure 15.5 *An applied leadership challenge*

In relation to the concept of leadership as practice, we can explore the extent to which a practice perspective on leadership may offer new and valuable insights into how leadership is enacted and developed within organizations (Bolden, 2010:16). In the earlier chapters, I referred to Grint's view that leadership is an essentially contested concept (Grint, 2005), identifying leadership as the property of a person, based on results, considered as a position, or that it may be regarded as a process. Bolden draws attention to the fact Grint did not identify leadership as practice (ibid:38). This is an interesting position to take, although my argument is that practice is implicit within Grint's typology, simply described as the 'who' (person), the 'what' (results), the 'where' (position), and the 'how' (the process). As I commented in an earlier chapter, my only critique of Grint's four contentions is that it neglects the 'why' and the 'when' questions. However, as Grint argues, it is an essentially contested concept, which is why it has proved so difficult to define!

We will now explore these issues in relation to the research. Before doing so, undertake this final reflexive activity in which you can compare the extent to which your organization reflects a professionalized institution.

A reflective activity is provided below for this chapter.

Chapter 15 Activity
Ten Steps for a Professionalization Agenda for Action:

	Ten Steps	Yes	No
1	Standards exist for decision-making, implementation, and delivery.		
2	Synergies are promoted across the organization and its networks with a commitment to shared learning and practice.		
3	There is a clear corporate commitment on professional development at all levels.		
4	Quality assurance processes exist to assess delivery based on standards, with a commitment for testing delivery against the standards.		
5	Openness and transparency exist throughout the organization and the networks in relation to the principles and purpose of the organization and the networks.		
6	Each professional within the organization and its networks has a defined responsibility for their own individual development within the wider framework of corporate continuous development.		
7	A commitment exists to transform professional staff in terms of subject matter expertise, qualification, and skills and in supporting individuals in relation to their own responsibility for professional development.		
8	The talent across the organization and its networks is assessed and developed holistically.		
9	There is a commitment to Knowledge Management with a demonstrable focus on its alignment with evidence-based impact.		
10	Individual and corporate impact is continually assessed in an objective, open, and transparent manner, with full and open dissemination of the analysis, results, and actions taken to continually improve and develop the organization and its networks.		

Given your activity earlier, hightlight which steps of professionalization your organization has achieved.

16 Leading through 360° Intelligent Networks, Knowledge, and Skills (LINKS360®)

This chapter applies the theory of collective leadership to its practice based on the research with the organizations described in earlier chapters. The overall aim of this chapter is to illustrate that collective leadership values and behaviours can be identified and assessed. This helps in developing mechanisms that reflect intelligent leadership practices within a 360° collective leadership context and in achieving the overall goal of creating public value.

COMPASS³⁶⁰ LEADERSHIP

The Context of Collective Leadership Practice

The context of collective leadership has been comprehensively reviewed throughout Part II. This was developed through a qualitative analysis of the various researches undertaken across a range of organizations, informed by the equally comprehensive literature review explored throughout Part I, and both supported by the deliberations of a series of seminars supported by funding from the UK Economic and Social Research Council (ESRC) in seeking to identify the public leadership challenges.

As briefly outlined in the introductory chapter to the book, my research has taken place over a considerable time period and, from a qualitative perspective, has used a mixed-methods, multiple case study approach, including peer-review and discourse analyses of strategic documents (in terms of identifying aspirations), face-to-face interviews, and focus groups in exploring the underlying mechanisms of collective leadership and modelling to determine the potential range of outcomes for collective leadership. A key question throughout this journey has been to consider whether the more collective nature of leadership can be identified and assessed using a realistic evaluation framework and, similarly, to determine the extent to which this can be used to improve collective leadership practice.

The Collective Leadership Inventory

During the course of the research, critical success factors were continuously and cumulatively identified and further explored and modelled as the research progressed. From early 2009, as a means of identifying and assessing collective leadership, I developed a Collective Leadership Inventory (CLI) based on the emerging critical success factors from the qualitative research, informed also by my experience of a similar approach during my doctoral studies from 1997 to 2004 when I undertook research in relation to community policing.

The primary purpose is twofold: first, to develop a realistic framework that can be used to capture the oft 'hidden' virtues and vices that either inhibit or obstruct leading in the public interest, and, second, to create a framework that is both pragmatic and valid in achieving this primary purpose. The first is probably the easiest, but I hope to persuade you at the same time of the validity of this framework in relation to the second aim, without bombarding you with the details of statistical inferences.[1] A secondary purpose is to propose the collective leadership framework as a means of continuously assessing the strengths, weaknesses, opportunities, and threats presented to collective leaders, while taking account of the wider PESTLE external contexts and the internal contexts (suggested by the 20P model), supported by the identification of transformative leadership mechanisms (the four Ps reflecting the mechanisms). Finally, a third purpose is to encourage the accumulation of research in seeking to assess the equally important Ps of socially desirable outcomes reflected by the overall outcome of leading in the public interest, which is that of public value.

The Importance of Transformational Leadership

I suggested much earlier in this book that the concept of leadership is a slippery eel; once you think you have 'got it', something else comes along and it slips out of your grip. Throughout my practice and teaching in the area of leadership, the term 'transformational' leadership has indeed been a very slippery eel! As with a member of a focus group in my very early research who said that the term 'community' is very often 'bandied about' without any real shared meaning, so I argue that the term 'transformational' is often 'bandied about' without fully understanding its meaning. From its earliest uses, transformational has been used in both positive (theatrical) and negative (mutilation at times of war) senses, for example, by William Shakespeare (*Merry Wives of Windsor* (1623) and *Henry IV, Part 1*, i.i. 44).

---

[1]As with my methodology, summarized in Part I, a more comprehensive outline of the research methodology, findings, and statistical interpretations are available elsewhere for those who wish to explore them!

EXPLORING COLLECTIVE LEADERSHIP THROUGH RESEARCH

Some of my later research projects, primarily aligned to executive education programmes, led to a further inventory (in support of the CLI) that sought to identify and assess transformational leadership behaviours based at the level of personal agency. Grounded in the research, and the ongoing analysis of the earlier CLI instrument, a range of such behaviours was identified and tested with members of the cohorts, which were subject of the research.

The aim to introduce a pragmatic framework resulted in the use of two mnemonics to describe them; the first, COMPASS[360,] has been comprehensively described whereas the second, TRANSFORM, will be described shortly as a means of interpreting intelligent leadership practice at the level of the team and the team leader. Lest you may draw the view that I started with the mnemonics and then 'fitted the research' to them, I want to dispel this straight away! Throughout my analysis and modelling, the concepts of compass and transform leadership were uppermost in my mind, and I use these terms to bring some transparency and a form of an aidememoire to support the understanding and use of the inventories in future research and leadership practice.

Before I continue and summarize the key findings and validity of the research, I should point out that the final compass and transform inventories have been slightly amended in line with some of the validation tests that I have undertaken. This will become clear as I outline the key findings and conclusions of my research here.

Measuring the Values of Collective Leadership

The seven values and underpinning behaviours were developed on the basis of the literature review of leadership and the qualitative research undertaken across the various projects. This formed the basis of the Collective Leadership Inventory. The early version was used as described earlier. In total, the CLI was used in the following contexts:

1. Six cohorts of an executive education programme for middle leaders within a Metropolitan Local Authority.
2. Both elected and independent members of a provincial Police Authority.[2]
3. Non-executive directors from a range of different Primary Care Trusts in the North West of England.
4. Executive (and Non-executive) directors from a Primary Care Trust in the South West of England.
5. Seventeen members of a multiple agency partnership, at middle leader level, focused on community safety across a number of different Metropolitan agencies including: police, probation, local authorities, and health authorities.
6. A range of stakeholders who were engaged in supporting a Metropolitan Primary Care Trust, through multi-agency partnership, to tackle inequalities in health.

---

[2]The organization that preceded the introduction and election of Police and Crime Commissioners.

First, I describe the analysis of the CLI that was used across six different cohorts within the Metropolitan Local Authority over a period spanning almost two years. The overall results, per cohort, are illustrated in Figure 16.1.

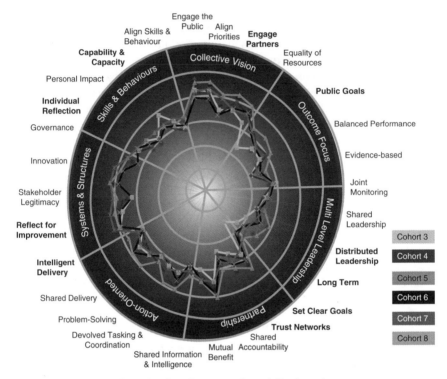

Figure 16.1 *Metropolitan local authority analysis (all cohorts)*

This was comprehensive research over a period of almost two years with a range of middle leaders with varied responsibilities across the large local authority. In exploring Figure 16.1 there are a number of similar trends across all cohorts. Using a Likert scale, perceptions in relation to all seven values and underpinning behaviours were gathered. Perception was explored in relation to the three levels of leadership: team, the organization, and its partnerships. All perceptions have been aggregated in relation to each cohort. Analysis of these trends shows that there is a much stronger relative perception in relation to the development of a collective vision and, to a slightly lesser extent, the focus on outcomes. Conversely, there was much less of a positive response in relation to the alignment of skills and behaviours and supporting systems and structures. Within these results, there was also a stronger response concerning a respondent's own team and, to a lesser degree their own organization, when compared to responses in relation to partners.

These visual representations are illuminating and provide a good initial sense of the strengths and areas for improvement in relation to collective leadership values and underpinning behaviours. Further analysis has been undertaken in relation to both the validity of the research and a more detailed analysis of the associations between the different elements of the Collective Leadership Inventory.

Validity of the Research

The quantitative research (where the qualitative findings were coded and categorized) has been analysed for its internal consistency using the Cronbach Alpha statistical test. The two surveys that were tested were those undertaken with the members of the multi-agency Community Safety Partnership and the members of the various cohorts who undertook an executive education leadership development programme. There were some slight variations to the questions asked, although the construct being assessed was consistent. In total, just fewer than 100 responses were the subject of the analysis.

The questionnaire was used to measure different, underlying constructs of collective leadership. At the values level, all seven value statements sought to measure the broad concept of 'collective leadership' based on a range of collective leadership behaviour statements for each of the seven values. The first analysis tested the aggregate ratings for all (by aggregating the data for the individual leadership behaviours of each value). The scale had a high level of internal consistency, as determined by a Cronbach's alpha of 0.877 (internal consistency can generally be confirmed at the level of 0.300 and above where 0.00 is a nil consistency and 1.00 a perfect consistency). This provides a high level of confidence that the seven values are measuring the same construct, namely collective leadership.

A second analysis sought to measure the associations between the seven collective leadership values, initially by using the same aggregated data at the level of values. In research terms, it is desirable to identify a null hypothesis (and an alternative) and then test it statistically. In this case, the broad null hypothesis is that 'value statements that reflect "collective leadership" will not be associated with each other'. The results of the CLI have been analysed to determine whether the null hypothesis is correct. This was undertaken through a series of statistical correlation tests.[3]

Correlation tells you that as one variable changes, the other seems to change in a predictable way. Correlation does not prove causation but, rather, that two variables are related; in other words, there is an association. It only tells you that as one variable changes, the other seems to change in a predictable way; this can be either *positive*, in which case as one variable goes up or down the other variable tends to go up or down in the same direction also, or *negative*, which suggests that as one variable go up values on the other variable go down.

Analysis

The overall correlation analysis is illustrated in Table 16.1. This provides an immediate visual representation that the vast majority of the values were significantly associated with each other at the highest levels of statistical confidence, and, thus,

---

[3]For the purposes of this research, Spearman's Correlation test was used, considering the data as ordinal rather than interval or relational data. Details of the research and the statistical analysis are available on the companion website resource (www.palgrave.com/companion/brookes).

Responses (N)	Collective vision	Outcome focus	Multi-level leadership	Partnership working	Action-oriented	Systems and structures	Skills and behaviours
	92	93	93	17	93	93	69
Collective vision	1.000						
Outcome focus	.557**	1.000					
Multi-level leadership	.464**	.423**	1.000				
Partnership working[1]	.687**	.842**	.848**	1.000			
Action-oriented	.340**	.500**	.570**	.423	1.000		
Systems and structures	.339**	.547**	.572**	.457	.601**	1.000	
Skills and behaviours	.404**	.434**	.579**	.417	.444**	.447**	1.000

Note:[1] Note that Partnership Working was only included in the Community Safety Partnership and is therefore limited in terms of responses and its comparison with the Local Authority Group

KEY	Not significant	Significant at level of 0.05	Significant at level of 0.001

Table 16.1 Correlation for collective leadership values (collective vision and outcome focus)

the null hypothesis can very confidently be rejected, suggesting that *the seven collective leadership values have a very strong association as evidenced by what is called the correlation coefficients (R).*

This provides some support to the consistency of the questions and ranges applied as well as illustrating that these values are indeed interrelated. They are all *positive* correlations, which mean that as one value either increases or decreases in rating, the other will follow the same direction. There were no *negative* correlations. As these are the total aggregated results, it does, however, tell us little more than this, as important as this resulting analysis is.

It does not tell us if there is any difference between the two groups (the Community Safety Partnership members and the Local Authority group members). To test for this, a Mann-Whitney U test has also been applied. This is a nonparametric test of the null hypothesis that two populations' (in this case, the Community Safety Partnership and the group of Local Authority Middle Leaders) responses are similar against an alternative hypothesis, that one of the particular populations (the Community Safety Partnership members) are likely to have lower (more negative) values than the other group (Local Authority members).

The test was undertaken in relation to all seven collective leadership values to determine if there were differences in assessment grading between Community Safety Partnership (CSP) members and Local Authority (LA) members (Table 16.2). Distributions of the assessment grades relating to the *seven collective leadership values* were not similar, as assessed by visual inspection. For example, in relation to the first value 'collective vision', assessment grades for LA members (mean rank = 53.14) were statistically significantly higher than for CSP members (mean rank = 14.97), $U = 1112.5$, $z = 5.218$, $p = .001$. The descriptive statistics for the data supports this contention that the two groups differ in all respects with regard to mean grades.

Table 16.2 *Community safety partnership and local authority descriptive statistics*

Group and values		Number	Minimum	Maximum	Mean
Community safety[1]	Collective vision	16	2.0	3	2.63
	Outcome focus	17	1.4	3.2	2.44
	Multi-level leadership	17	2.0	3.7	2.81
	Action-oriented	17	2.2	4.0	2.87
	Systems and structures	17	1.7	3.7	2.59
	Skills and behaviours	17	1.9	4.0	2.76
Local authority	Collective vision	76	3.0	4.0	3.42
	Outcome focus	76	1.9	4.0	3.13
	Multi-level leadership	76	2.0	4.0	3.41
	Action oriented	76	2.0	4.0	3.36
	Systems and structures	76	2.0	4.0	3.39
	Skills and behaviours	52	1.7	4.0	3.52

Note: [1]'Partnership working was only assessed with the Community Safety Group and is therefore excluded from this analysis'

Measuring Behaviours as Determinants of Collective Leadership

Analysing the collective leadership values has been useful, but further insight is needed to understand the impact of the differing behavioural statements. First, further Cronbach alpha tests were undertaken. The first construct, 'collective vision', initially consisted of three questions, each asked at the three levels of analysis (team, organization, and partnership) and all nine questions were used for the purposes of testing this validity.

The scale had a high level of internal consistency, as determined by a Cronbach's alpha of 0.800 (as we know, internal consistency can generally be confirmed at the level of 0.300 and above where 0.00 is a nil consistency and 1.00 a perfect consistency). The same statistical process was applied to the remaining six values and underpinning behaviours. All questions had a similar high level of internal consistency ranging from a Cronbach alpha of 0.795 through to 0.913.

Having confidence in the internal validity of the behavioural statements that seek to measure collective leadership values, I then undertook a further analysis of the levels of association between the respective values and behaviours. For example, I looked at the first two collective leadership constructs (values) 'collective vision' and 'outcome focus' and then analysed the levels of association between the respective underpinning behaviours represented by the CLI questions and self-ratings given by both the LA and CSP Groups.

In this case, the broad null hypothesis is that 'collective leadership behaviours that reflect a "collective vision" will not be associated with the collective leadership behaviours reflecting an "outcome focus"'. Table 16.3 shows that this is not the case and that the association between the two constructs is very strong.

Analysis

It is quite clear from the analysis that the null hypotheses can be overwhelmingly rejected in relation to the association between 'collective vision' and 'outcome focus'. Just under a third of all 'R' scores are not significant associations (67 out of 207), and of the 140 significant associations, 105 are highly significant at the level of 0.001, representing just over half of the total.

Although there are strong associations throughout the range of values based on the behavioural statements, the remainder are not as strong as those found between 'collective vision' and 'outcomes'; this is illustrated in Figures 16.2 and 16.3.

These trends have been plotted in the form of a 'hotspot' map, based on the statistical associations (the 'R' score).

The full analysis is not discussed[4] in this section, although the following summary provides the key trends. What is immediately apparent is that, from a start point of 'collective vision' at the upper left position, as one moves from the left to the right (or diagonally from top left to bottom right – *both have the same result*), the levels of association become less evident. This is particularly the case in relation to the values of appropriate 'skills and behaviours' and 'systems and structures'. This tends to suggest that organizations are good at agreeing a 'collective vision' which is

---

[4]Available on the companion website (www.palgrave.com/companion/brookes).

| | | Collective vision | | | | | | | | |
| | | Engage the public | | | Align local and national priorities | | | Shared distribution of resources | | |
		TEAM	ORG	PART	TEAM	ORG	PART	TEAM	ORG	PART
Engage the public	TEAM	1.000	.624**	.301**	.547**	.453**	.308**	.233*	−.033	−.057
	ORG	.624**	1.000	.597**	.372**	.521**	.352**	.283**	.238*	.198
	PART	.301**	.597**	1.000	.124	.229*	.339**	.209	.283**	.270*
Align local and national priorities	TEAM	.547**	.372**	.124	1.000	.549**	.308**	.444**	.162	.204
	ORG	.453**	.521**	.229*	.549**	1.000	.445**	.538**	.401**	.405**
	PART	.308**	.352**	.339**	.308**	.445**	1.000	.224*	.152	.260*
Shared distribution of resources	TEAM	.233*	.283**	.209	.444**	.538**	.224*	1.000	.554**	.452**
	ORG	−.033	.238*	.283**	.162	.401**	.152	.554**	1.000	.732**
	PART	−.057	.198	.270*	.204	.405**	.260*	.452**	.732**	1.000
		OUTCOME FOCUS								
Evidence-based	TEAM	.388**	.378**	.168	.291**	.272**	.274*	.297**	.258*	.163
	ORG	.237*	.481**	.346**	.024	.287**	.301**	.154	.399**	.272*
	PART	.139	.269*	.380**	−.015	.124	.381**	.005	.212	.298**
Shared & distributed accountability	TEAM	.314**	.346**	.201	.497**	.318**	.316**	.471**	.309**	.265*
	ORG	.253*	.459**	.403**	.355**	.403**	.331**	.479**	.563**	.441**
	PART	.150	.317**	.453**	.222*	.209	.374**	.311**	.487**	.533**
Public perception given a focus	TEAM	.284**	.233*	.165	.170	.275**	.124	.283**	.183	.095
	ORG	.240*	.311**	.305**	.241*	.315**	.211	.281**	.293**	.077
	PART	.207	.285**	.375**	.128	.153	.272*	.204	.202	.189
Public have confidence	TEAM	.393**	.349**	.255*	.293**	.181	.241*	.069	.118	.063
	ORG	.215*	.425**	.340**	.023	.163	.205	.106	.315**	.171
	PART	.226*	.338**	.406**	.018	.099	.223*	.076	.236*	.178
Public satisfied with services	TEAM	.442**	.461**	.345**	.256*	.248*	.293**	.224*	.233*	.073
	ORG	.176	.394**	.418**	.044	.151	.259*	.125	.347**	.152
	PART	.238*	.373**	.365**	.158	.232*	.307**	.233*	.406**	.302**
KEY		Not significant			Significant at level of 0.05			Significant at level of 0.001		

Table 16.3 *Statistical associations (collective vision and outcome focus), community safety partnership and local authority*

NS - Not Significant .05 - Significant (95%) .001 Highly Significant (99%) (Spearman's Rank Correlation)	Collective Vision			Outcome Focus			Multi level Leadership			Partnership Working			Action Oriented			Systems & Structures			Skills & Behaviours		
	NS	.05	.001	NS	.05	.001	NS	.05	.001	NS	.05	.001	NS	.05	.001	NS	.05	.001	NS	.05	.001
Collective Vision	16	12	44	45	22	64	33	19	29	44	7	3	66	9	6	65	6	10	56	6	19
Outcome Focus	45	22	64	20	22	168	47	17	71	68	15	9	101	6	28	87	15	33	87	11	37
Multi Level Leadership	33	19	29	47	17	71	40	2	30	32	12	10	58	10	13	64	2	15	59	5	17
Partnership Working	44	7	3	66	15	9	32	12	10	0	6	10	32	6	0	44	6	4	50	4	0
Action Oriented	66	9	6	101	6	28	58	10	13	32	6	0	46	8	18	59	9	13	124	3	17
Systems & Structures	65	6	10	87	15	33	64	2	15	44	6	4	59	9	13	44	10	18	44	10	18
Skills & Behaviours	56	6	19	87	11	37	59	5	17	50	4	0	124	3	17	66	6	9	58	12	0
Totals	325	81	175	453	108	410	333	67	185	268	56	36	486	51	95	429	54	102	478	51	108

	Collective Vision	Outcome Focus	Multi level Leadership	Partnership Working	Action Oriented	Systems & Structures	Skills & Behaviours
Total Significant	256	518	252	92	146	156	159
Value Total	581	971	585	360	632	585	637
% Significant	44.1	53.3	43.1	25.6	23.1	26.7	25.0

Significance Levels for Collective Leadership Values
(based on correlations between underlying behavioural statements)

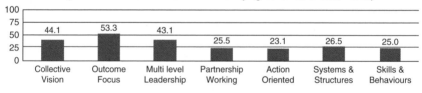

Figure 16.2 Summary of statistical correlations (community safety partnership and local authority)

aligned to 'outcomes' but the reality is that this is more rhetoric than reality. In particular, this adds support to my earlier contention that the development of skills and behaviours takes place in isolation from the commitment to collective leadership. Moreover, the systems and structures (which we recall are human constructions) do not necessarily align with the stated vision for collective leadership and appear to be harder to change.

Health Inequalities Case Study

In Part I of the book, I used the example of health inequalities as a wicked problem. This was explored during a research project with a large Primary Care Trust in a Northern metropolitan area with one of the worst health profiles in

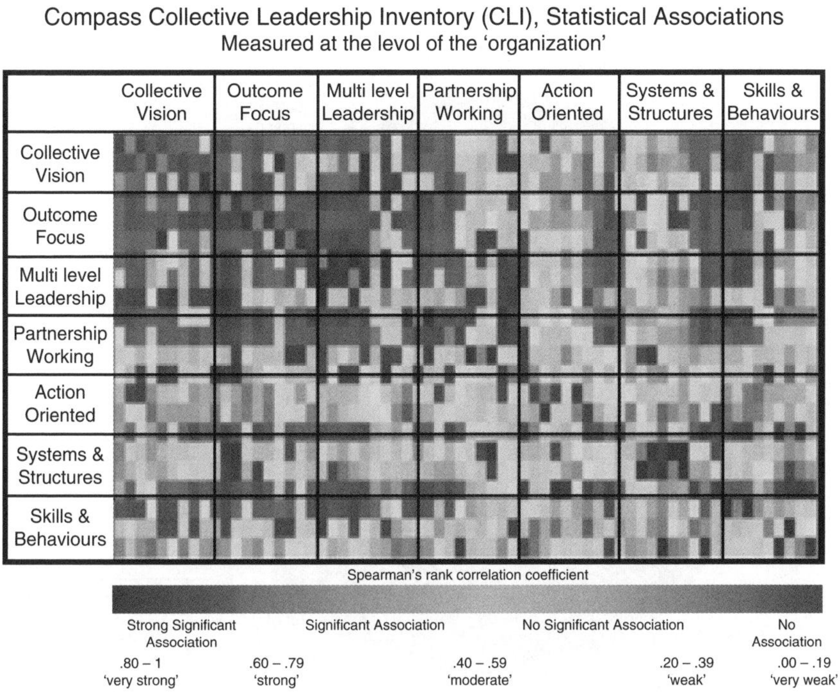

Compass Collective Leadership Inventory (CLI), Statistical Associations
Measured at the levol of the 'organization'

	Collective Vision	Outcome Focus	Multi level Leadership	Partnership Working	Action Oriented	Systems & Structures	Skills & Behaviours
Collective Vision							
Outcome Focus							
Multi level Leadership							
Partnership Working							
Action Oriented							
Systems & Structures							
Skills & Behaviours							

Spearman's rank correlation coefficient

Strong Significant Association	Significant Association	No Significant Association	No Association
.80 – 1 'very strong'	.60 – .79 'strong'	.40 – .59 'moderate'	.20 – .39 'weak'	.00 – .19 'very weak'

Figure 16.3 Hotspot map (community safety partnership and local authority)

England. Using the Collective Leadership Inventory (CLI), the research was able to compare the responses of the partnership executives (from across a range of public agencies) in relation to their perceptions of collective leadership at the level of their own organization, the partnership more widely, and their own executive teams, with those given by non-executive directors (NEDs), elected councillors, and community representatives. The overall findings are illustrated in Figure 16.4.

Respondents at the first level were members of a strategic partnership and/or an executive board and were asked to comment on the strengths of collective leadership in relation to their own organization, the partnership as a whole, or the board. This analysis illustrates the following key points:

- Perceptions of individual organizations appear to be stronger in relation to the setting of a clear vision, its focus on outcomes (particularly balanced performance), although organizations, the partnership, and teams are all relatively strong in this area. Organizations/the partnership and the board are also strong in relation to the championing of partnership working.
- The 'partnerships' do not excel beyond the organization or the board in relation to any dimension.

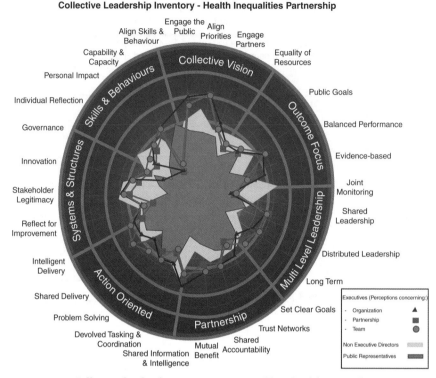

Figure 16.4 *Collective leadership perceptions in tackling health inequalities*

- The board was seen to be marginally better at managing balanced performance, deploying distributed leadership (through effective tasking and coordination), and focusing on the long term.
- Perceptions of individual organizations are less positive (in comparison to the partnership and the board) in relation to multi-level leadership and a focus on the long term, alignment of actions and activity and systems of governance.
- Clear areas for development include equality of resources (the sharing of tasks and resources in line with partnership and organizational priorities), joint identification and monitoring of outcomes, a focus on problem-solving approaches (although individual teams were seen to be stronger in this regard), and the adoption of 'reflection' as a means of continuous improvement. A clear need for development is in relation to the need to align skills and behaviours to the overall vision and strategy.

Respondents at the second level were either NEDs or elected members and were asked to comment on the strengths of collective leadership in relation to their own perceptions on partnership working only. The analysis illustrates the following key points:

- Interestingly, one of the key strengths in relation to NED perception was the focus given to joint identification and monitoring of outcomes – which differed from the perception of executive members. NED respondents seemed to be more positive in relation to the sharing of information and intelligence, shared delivery, and stakeholder legitimacy than the executives.
- Non-executives and elected members were less positive in relation to the extent to which the public and partners were engaged, evidence-based approaches to outcomes, and distributed leadership (in terms of tasking and coordination).

Clear areas for development included the need to 'sell' mutual benefits to partners and stakeholders in serving the public, and (similar to the executives) the focus on problem-solving approaches and the alignment of skills and behaviours.

Respondents at the third level were public or community representatives and were asked to comment on the strengths of collective leadership in relation to their own perceptions on partnership working only. This analysis illustrates the following key points:

- In some respects, some of the perceptions of community representatives seemed to be the reverse of those suggested by the executives or non-executives and elected members. In particular, community or public representatives were of the view that the partnership aligned skills and behaviours of partnership members well to the overall vision and aims of the partnership. In support of this, they also felt that partnership members set clear goals, shared information and intelligence well, and were stronger in the area of intelligence-led delivery and reflection for improvement.
- As with the NEDs/elected members, they were less positive in relation to the engagement of the public and partners and the alignment of priorities. Although these representatives were reasonably positive in relation to the importance of public value goals (satisfaction and confidence measures), they were less positive with regard to balanced performance and joint monitoring. They also felt that distributed leadership was less strong and inferred that more needed to be done in relation to the communication of 'mutual benefits' through partnership working.
- Clear areas for improvement included the focus on problem-solving approaches, stakeholder legitimacy, and, significantly, efforts made in relation to the development of appropriate skills and behaviour. Although respondents were relatively positive in relation to the alignment of skills and behaviours, they were much less positive in relation to individual reflection, personal impact, and the priority given to building capacity and capability.

From a general perspective:

- Most felt that partners were aligning their national and local priorities within the collective vision in tackling inequalities.
- More needs to be done to engage with the public and other partners in aligning efforts to tackle inequalities.

- There was a strong perception that much more is needed to align skills and behaviours to the overall vision and aims of tackling inequalities.
- Sharing of resources, information, and intelligence was considered to be an area for improvement in developing networks and coordinating actions and activity.
- Improvements in evidence-based assessment, joint monitoring, and problem solving are required.
- Governance, innovation, and stakeholder legitimacy were considered relative areas for improvement in addition to both partnership-wide and individual reflection in seeking continuous improvement.

TRANSFORMATIONAL LEADERSHIP BEHAVIOURS

From Aspiration to Achievement?

I argued in Parts I and II that there is a huge difficulty in trying to identify and measure the factors that support or hinder the development of collective leadership. Transformational leadership has become an increasingly topical term in contemporary studies and there is a plethora of suggestions as to which leadership behaviours are transformational. Practice is somewhat different, and it is often the case that many leaders profess that either they or their organizations are transformational without either evidencing this or, indeed, understanding what it really means to be transformational.

Through qualitative research (described in Part I), a number of potential transformational leadership behaviours were considered based on the literature and empirical field studies. This was later refined and structured through an individual transformational leadership inventory (Transform Leadership Inventory (TLI)) in support of the CLI, and used as a means of quantitative research across the executive education programmes undertaken with the Metropolitan Local Authority with seven cohorts. It was later applied within a similar, but cross-organizational leadership development programme, for middle leaders from a range of public service organizations who are members of a strategic Community Safety Partnership (CSP) and a private sector company. The transformational leadership behaviours (again using a mnemonic: TRANSFORM) are illustrated in Figure 16.5.

A total of seven cohorts completed the TLI and, during the course of this period, I also had the opportunity to use the instrument in a similar programme undertaken with leaders from a private sector company in the construction industry. The overall results are illustrated in Figure 16.6, expressed as a relative improvement factor (in which each element is considered in relative 'development' terms to each other).

As with the collective leadership values described earlier, this visual representation illustrates some very similar patterns. There is a strong level of positive responses across all cohorts and with the private sector company in those areas that describe some of the softer, more personal elements of leadership: appreciating and encouraging others, nurturing and coaching, and openness and transparency. Leaders also felt they were strong in relation to maintaining momentum and encouraging freedom for delivery through networks. They were less positive in terms of developing trust by 'telling it how it is', relinquishing control and empowering, and, with one exception, setting clear goals.

Where: '1' is Need for Development, '2' Fair, '3' Good, '4' Strong

	1	2	3	4

T rust (Tell it how it is)

You always push the shared goal/s in a way that shows belief

You give positive messages always

You confront the brutal facts of the reality and do not take things on face value

You practice what you preach

R elinquish Control and Empower

Let go of tasks and responsibilities that will help others to develop

Let go of authority to make decisions about the work

Provide clear understanding of the levels of authority, expectations and constraints

You ask questions not make statements

A ppreciate and Encourage Others

Know what others in the group can do and want to do

Reward and recognise ideas and initiative through compliments, rewards etc

You make a conscious effort not to put down or discount ideas

You know what method of reinforcement works for each individual

N urture and Coach

Build people's skills to take over by involving them in the work

Delegate specifically to challenge and develop your people

Coach before, during and beyond the task/s.

Is coaching a regular part of the job?

S et Clear Goals for All

Encourage the work group to take a lead role in setting goals & assessing their own

Ensure that goals are clear, concise and aligned with the shared vision

Undertake regular performance review and development (i.e. at least quarterly)

People know how its fits with the shared vision

F reedom for Delivery through Networks

Have appropriate controls but which encourage freedom rather than restrict

Allow your team members the freedom to manage their respective agendas

Building positive relationship externally is paramount

Building positive relationship internally is paramount

O pen and Transparent

Let people know how they are doing in meeting goals and support development

Actively seek ideas and suggestions from the work group and external partners

Make sure people have the right information they need to do the job

Encourage the sharing of information

R isk is Allowed

You empower your team members to implement ideas through problem solving

Allow people to run with an idea, even if it is risky

You show empathy in the face of risk

You support people when the 'going gets tough' instead of punishing/taking over

M aintain Momentum

You continuously monitor performance

You acknowledge the need for short term gains

Focus on medium to long term goals is maintained

You recognise when activity needs extra momentum

Figure 16.5 *Transform leadership inventory*

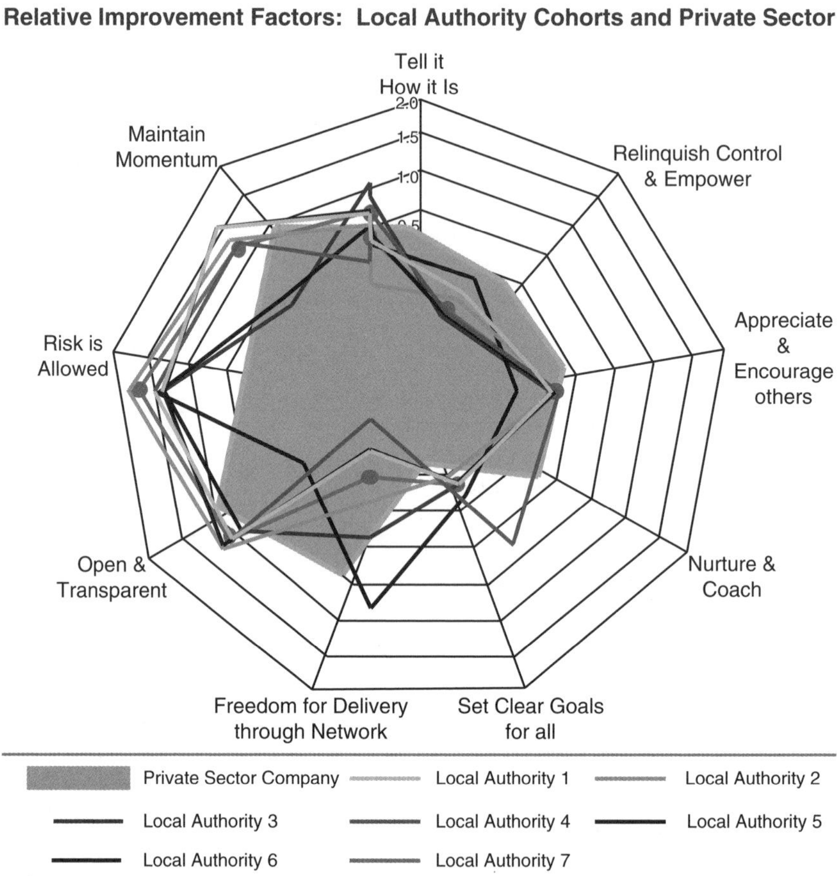

Relative Improvement Factors: Local Authority Cohorts and Private Sector

Figure 16.6 Transformational leadership behaviours (local authority and private sector organization)

Comparison with Multi-Agency Community Safety Partnership

As with the data for the collective leadership values, the transformational behavioural leadership data was standardized and then subjected to a Mann-Whitney U test. This is a nonparametric test of the null hypothesis that two populations (in this case, the Community Safety Partnership and the group of Local Authority Middle Leaders) are the same against an alternative hypothesis, especially that one of the particular population (the Community Safety group members) is likely to have larger (more positive) values than the other (Local Authority members).

The first test was undertaken in relation to the various elements of 'Setting Clear Goals'. Figure 16.6 indicates that a leadership behaviour that requires strong development for local authorities is in the setting of clear goals. In comparing this to the Community Safety Partnership,[5] the same applies, as illustrated in Figure 16.7.

---

[5]Although different grading systems were used, the results have been standardized and expressed as an improvement factor based on 'z scores'.

Relative Improvement Factors: Local Authority Cohorts and Community Safety Partnership

Local Authority Cohorts   **Community Safety Members**

Figure 16.7 *Transform leadership behaviours (community safety partnership)*

I also undertook an analysis of the combined and standardized data from both the local authority and community safety partnership groups, first in relation to the reliability of the behavioural statements underpinning transform leadership and, second, in relation to the similarities and differences between the LA and CSP groups. In relation to the reliability of the TLI instrument, the analysis returned a Cronbach's alpha of .707, which indicates a high level of internal consistency for the scale with this particular instrument.

A Mann-Whitney U test was run to determine if there were differences in assessment grading between CSP members and LA members. Distributions of the assessment grades relating to the *encouragement for setting clear goals* were not similar, as assessed by visual inspection. Assessment grades for CSP members (mean rank = 44.19) were statistically significantly higher than for LA members (mean rank = 32.23), $U = 277, z = -2.472, p = 0.05$.

The second test looked at the individual leadership behaviour reflective of 'setting shared goals'. This resulted in a finding that there were even less similar grades with a wider disparity between the more positive grades given again by CSP members (mean rank = 45.34) which was more highly statistically significant than for LA members (mean rank = 31.88), U = 258.5, z = −2.826, p =.001.

Further similarities and differences were analysed. These are summarized in Table 16.4. There are more similarities than differences. However, where differences are significant, it raises some further interesting questions.

Nurturing and coaching behaviours show the most significant difference in nearly all respects and in relation to trust by 'telling it how it is'. Although there is no statistically significant difference in relation to 'pushing shared goals' and the 'giving of positive messages', significant differences do exist with 'confronting the brutal facts' and 'practising what is preached'.

Significant differences are apparent in 'relinquishing control and empowering' and 'letting go of tasks and authority', respectively. 'Performance monitoring' (as a means of maintaining momentum) and 'letting people know how they are doing' (reflecting openness and transparency) was significantly different between both groups, as was the focus on the 'medium and longer term', in which CSP partnership members were more positive.

The community safety members were also much higher in their self-assessment of 'Empowering team members through problem solving approaches' and in 'building positive relations externally'. Similar trends were thus evident, but there were some clear differences, possibly explained by the very different contexts within which the respondents operated.

Collective Leadership Values and Behaviours and Transformational Leadership Behaviours

The links between these individual, transformational leadership behaviours and those underpinning wider collective leadership represents another focus of analysis. In this case, the broad null hypothesis is that 'individual transformational leadership behaviours will not be associated with leadership at the level of collective'. The results of the TLI have been analysed alongside the CLI to determine whether the null hypothesis is correct. This was undertaken through a series of statistical correlation tests[6] using the local authority cohort group member's responses, given the differences between the two groups, described in the earlier section. A separate comparison with the community safety group members will be described at a later point.

Analysis

Setting and Monitoring Goals

In the early CLI instruments, the importance of goals was not included, and yet this emerged as a key factor within the TLI. An impact of setting clear goals relates to TLI behaviours associated with maintaining momentum. One of the

---

[6]For the purposes of this research, Spearman's Correlation test was used, considering the data as ordinal rather than interval or relational data. Details of the research and the statistical analysis are available on the companion website resource (www.palgrave.com/companion/brookes).

Transformational leadership behaviour	Sig.	Decision regarding the null hypothesis
Appreciate and encourage others		
Know what others in the group can do and want to do	.871	Retain
Reward and recognise ideas and initiative through compliments, rewards etc.	.183	Retain
You make a conscious effort not to put down or discount ideas	.449	Retain
You know what method of reinforcement works for each individual	.133	Retain
Freedom for delivery through networks		
Have appropriate controls but which encourage freedom rather than restrict	.217	Retain
Allow your team members the freedom to manage their respective agendas	.162	Retain
Building positive relationship externally is paramount	.013	Reject
Building positive relationship internally is paramount	.145	Retain
Maintain momentum		
You continuously monitor performance	.002	Reject
You acknowledge the need for short-term gains	.559	Retain
Focus on medium-to long-term goals is maintained	.004	Reject
You recognise when activity needs extra momentum	.310	Retain
Nurture and coach		
Build people's skills to take over by involving them in the work	.062	Retain
Delegate specifically to challenge and develop your people	.007	Reject
Coach before, during and beyond the task/s	.003	Reject
Is coaching a regular part of the job?	.001	Reject

Transformational Leadership behaviour	Sig.	Decision regarding the null hypothesis
Openness and transparency		
Let people know how they are doing in meeting goals and support development	.013	Reject
Actively seek ideas and suggestions from the work group and external partners	.289	Retain
Make sure people have the right information they need to do the job or know where to get it	.289	Retain
Encourage the sharing of information	.261	Retain
Risk and innovation		
You empower your team members to implement ideas through a problem solving approach	.022	Reject
Allow people to run with an idea, even if it is risky	.352	Retain
You listen to people and are encouraging of discussion and show empathy in the face of risk	.311	Retain
You support people when the 'going gets tough' instead of punishing/taking over	.334	Retain
Relinquish control and empower		
Let go of tasks and responsibilities that will help others to develop	.003	Reject
Let go of authority to make decisions about the work	.044	Reject
Provide clear understanding about the levels of authority, your expectations, and constraints	.100	Retain
You ask questions, not make statements	.970	Retain
Trust ('Tell it how it is')		
You always push the shared goal/s in a way that shows belief	.730	Retain
You give positive messages always	.059	Retain
You confront the brutal facts of the Reality and do not take things on face value	.031	Reject
You practice what you preach	.038	Reject

Table 16.4 *Transformational leadership behaviour similarities (community safety partnership and local authority)*

key behaviours associated with maintaining momentum is to tell people how they are doing and in continuously assessing performance. We could conjecture that there is no relationship between the factor of maintaining momentum and telling people how they are doing (referred to as a null hypothesis), and this can be tested statistically. When tested, using the variable representing maintaining momentum of 'continuously monitoring performance', there was a very strong association as evidenced by what is called the correlation coefficient ($r = .164$; $n = 53$), which is statistically significant at the 0.01 level of significance.

The Coefficient of Determination ($r2$) tells you the percent of variance in one variable that is accounted for by the other variable. In the case of these two factors ('continuous monitoring' and 'telling people how they are doing'), this tells us that 37.7 percent of how a person rated maintaining momentum in this sense is directly related to the extent to which they tell people how they are doing. It is therefore not likely to have occurred by chance and suggests that performance monitoring would be more effective by actively engaging with those being assessed. We could probably assume that this would be the case, but it is the manner in which this is done that is also important. As outlined earlier, a single-minded pursuit of performance targets has had a detrimental effect on collective leadership. Targets thus need to be accompanied by other leadership behaviours.

In contrast, there was a strong *negative* association between the 'alignment of priorities' and the 'putting down of people's ideas', where the percent of variance between the two accounted for 15 percent. In this case, we can predict that the extent to which priorities will be aligned will increase dependent on how little other people's ideas are 'rubbished'! This is an important predictor in terms of developing a sense of shared values.

Transformative behaviour was clearly associated with an indicator of 'trust', 'leaders practising what they preach', where the percent of variance between this variable and that of 'encouraging the setting of clear goals' was almost 10 percent. Interestingly, there was a *negative* association between a further indicator of setting clear goals, namely setting goals that are clear, concise, and aligned, with an indicator of 'empowerment' ('letting go of tasks'), thus predicting that the more clear, concise, and aligned goals are set, the less is the tendency to 'let go of tasks'. This suggests that the agreement of shared goals may be more likely through participation.

Active Participation as a Collective Leadership Behaviour

The association between the individual transformational leadership behaviours representing the 'setting of clear goals' from the TLI and the collective leadership behaviours represented by the development of a 'collective vision' from the CLI were explored. As with the *negative* association between 'empowerment' ('letting go of tasks') and the 'setting of clear, concise, and aligned goals' in relation to individual leadership behaviours, there was also a strong *negative* association with the collective leadership behaviour of aligning priorities with team members (supporting the prediction from the association with the corresponding individual behaviour from the individual TLI) but not in relation to the organization and other partners at the collective level. However, at the collective level there was an association and a strong association respectively between leaders 'encouraging the setting of clear goals' and active participation within the organization and other partners. *Active participation at the first point of team leadership, and active encouragement within the organization and with other partners, thus appears to be critical to the development of shared goals.* This is shown in Table 16.5.

Table 16.5 Association between developing a collective vision and the setting of clear goals

Collective leadership Developing a collective vision	Individual leadership Setting clear goals	
	Encourage setting of goals	Clear, concise, and aligned
Active participation		
Your team	.130	−.221
Your organization	.345*	.066
Your partners	.381**	.175
Align local/national priorities		
Your team	−.005	−.397**
Your organization	−.083	−.084
Your partners	.112	−.037
KEY for statistical significance confidence levels	@ 0.05*	@ 0.01**

In terms of individual leadership behaviours, building skills by involving people appears to lead to a strong sense of actively engaging team members, although with partners, as priorities are aligned across boundaries there is a *negative* association with building skills at this level, suggesting two explanations: first, as priorities are increasingly aligned, there is less of a need to build skills at the level of partnerships, or, conversely, that this represents a tendency to align but not to develop at this level. Of interest, 'challenge' – as an indicator of nurturing and coaching – has a strong negative association with the alignment of priorities with partners, suggesting that different behaviours will be needed with partners. It may thus be less about nurturing and coaching and more about influencing and negotiating. To explore this point further, focus returned to the dynamics at the individual leadership level. Where the active participation of partners is encouraged there is a strong propensity to let go of decisions, and at both individual and organizational level, letting go of tasks through empowerment. Nurturing and coaching is also strongly associated with an increase in active participation at the level of the team. Within teams, it is strongly enhanced when leaders recognize a need for more momentum. A further conclusion that can be drawn is that *different individual leadership behaviours need to be called upon in encouraging partners to align priorities through influencing and negotiating whereas nurturing and coaching behaviours are important at the level of the team.*

Trust – as transformational leadership behaviour – was represented by four indicative behaviours, illustrated in Figure 16.8. It is evident that leaders were positive about all trust behaviours, with the exception of 'giving positive messages' always.

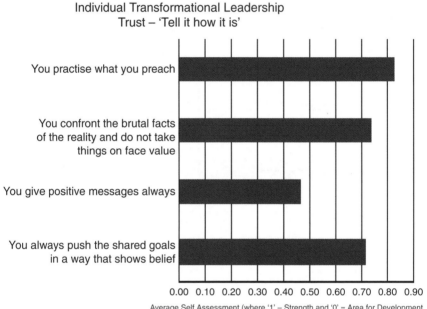

All Cohorts: Metropolitan Local Authority

Figure 16.8 *Transformational leadership behaviour (trust)*

The identification of the need to increase the level of positive messages, from individual leaders, was evident when comparing this individual leadership behaviour with the collective leadership behaviour of developing a 'collective vision' through active participation. There was a significant *negative* association between these two behaviours in relation to the active participation of the team and (highly significant) when engaging with other partners. This is shown in Table 16.6.

Overall, there is a very low level of association with other elements of trust at the individual level and active participation at the collective level. This suggests *leaders need to focus more on trust in encouraging active participation and, in particular, to give more attention to giving positive messages and balancing this with confronting the brutal facts.*

Table 16.6 *Collective vision and trust*

Collective leadership Developing a collective vision	Individual leadership Trust ('Telling it how it is')			
Active participation	Push goals	Give positive messages	Confront brutal facts	Practise what preach
Your team	−.157	−.287*	−.023	−.168
Your organization	.135	−.260	.173	.059
Your partners	.182	−.383**	.098	−.027

From Actions to Outcomes

Trust appears to play a more significant role in tackling problems focused on agreed outcomes. For example, trust at the individual level in terms of 'practising what one preaches' was *positively* associated with collective leadership behaviours that lead to open and transparent accountability at all three levels (team, organizational, and other partners), strongly so at the level of team and partners. Practising what leaders preach was also *positively* associated with the collective leadership behaviours of 'engaging in problem solving' at the level of the team and, strongly so, in working with partners.

Although the encouragement of setting clear goals at the level of the team and reviewing performance with partners correlated with the collective behaviour of devolved resources and planning, the lack of positive messages (in which there was a *negative* association with devolvement at all three levels) seems to be out of balance with the strength associated with confronting the brutal facts. There was further support for this in observing the self-perception of individual leaders' behaviour in terms of freedom for delivery through networks reflected by the behaviour of balancing controls and freedom at the level of the organization. *This appears again to suggest the need for an appropriate balance between confronting the brutal facts and the giving of positive messages when leading teams and other partners.*

Individual leaders 'telling people how they were doing' was *positively* associated with evidence-based activities at the collective leadership level in terms of the organization and other partners, but not so with teams. It is interesting that the more positively leaders rated the collective leadership behaviour of 'evidence-based actions', the less they appear to focus on giving people the right information to do their job, which has a *negative* association at the level of the team and a very low association with the organization or partners. In alignment with both the literature and the qualitative research, encouragement to 'share information' and seek ideas and suggestions from others is particularly low in terms of its association with evidence-based action and outcomes. This is illustrated in Table 16.7. *The need for a greater level of openness and transparency is therefore critical to the practice of intelligent leadership in the encouragement and development of evidence-based actions and outcomes and in sharing information.*

Table 16.7 Outcome and action focus associated with openness and transparency

Collective leadership Outcome and action focused	Individual leadership Open and transparent			
Evidence-based actions and outcomes	Tell people how they are doing	Seek ideas and suggestions	People have right information to do job	Encourage sharing of information
Your team	.167	−.026	−.273*	.128
Your organization	.295*	.058	−.029	.041
Your partners	.362*	.189	−.109	.013

Time as a Currency of Leadership

I have argued consistently throughout Parts I and II that time is a critical component of leadership practice. This was borne out strongly by the analysis, as Table 16.8 shows.

Table 16.8 Multi-level leadership and openness and transparency

Collective leadership Multi-level leadership	Individual leadership Open and transparent			
Focus on long-term as well as short-term problems	Tell people how they are doing	Seek ideas and suggestions	People have right information to do job	Encourage sharing of information
Your team	.073	.070	−.311*	−.092
Your organization	.128	.219	−.155	−.089
Your partners	.241	.313*	.009	−.032

It is apparent that, at the level of the team, there is a *negative* association between the focus on time and the giving of information in much the same manner as its association with an evidence-based approach. This may suggest that the more that individual leaders give their teams information, the less the focus is on the long term as well as the short term. There is a similar tendency, but not significant, for the organization and no association to speak of in either direction with partners, although in seeking ideas and suggestions from partners, there is a *positive* association between this and the focus on the long term with partners. We can draw an inference from this *that leaders need to take more account of the long term, in balance with the short term, across all levels and, in particular, when dealing with action and activities rather than just with ideas and suggestions.*

Building Capacity and Capability

We can recall from earlier chapters that the concept of public value is considered to represent the overall outcome of leading in the public interest and that public value concerns social goals, delivering those goals in a way that secures trust and legitimacy, and developing the organizational capability and capacity to do this. It was also suggested in earlier chapters that the latter aim of public value was often the one that is neglected. This emerged from the analysis as shown in Table 16.9.

Table 16.9 Public value outcomes and openness and transparency

Collective leadership Public value outcomes	Individual leadership Open and transparent			
Public confidence in delivery	Tell people how they are doing	Seek ideas and suggestions	People have right information to do job	Encourage sharing of information
Your team	.191	.232	−.081	−.069
Your organization	.455**	.376**	.027	−.152
Your partners	.441**	.444**	.209	−.126
Public satisfied with delivery				
Your team	.305*	.274	−.136	−.095
Your organization	.397**	.223	−.078	−.051
Your partners	.207	.283	.129	.028

Telling people how they were doing, and seeking ideas and suggestions, in relation to public confidence was strongly and *positively* associated at the level of both the organization and partners, but not so in relation to the team. The relatively low assessments in relation to having the right information and sharing of information perhaps suggest with some confidence that it is more about 'telling than selling'. In terms of satisfaction, there is a *positive* association at the level of the team and the organization in relation to telling people how they are doing (but again, it appears, not in terms of 'selling').

In considering the individual leadership behaviours it is significantly telling that there are no more significant associations at all with the collective leadership behaviours, with one final exception: maintaining momentum.

In exploring Table 16.10, we can note that all associations between the first two individual leadership behaviours concerned with maintaining momentum (continuous monitoring of performance and acknowledging short term gains) are all *negative* associations, but in relation to continuous monitoring at both the level of the team and the organization, these are both significant relationships. In keeping with the earlier table, the more *positive* associations are between focusing on the long term and in recognizing when more momentum is needed at the level of partnership working.

Table 16.10 Public value outcomes and maintaining momentum

Collective leadership Public value outcomes	Individual leadership Maintaining momentum			
Building capacity and capability	Continuous monitoring of performance	Acknowledge short-term gains	Medium to long term	Recognize more momentum
Your team	−.347*	−.048	.131	.149
Your organization	−.274*	−.014	.049	.151
Your partners	−.090	−.203	.322*	.321*

These previous three tables provide some stark and alarming indications that while public confidence and satisfaction appear to be given priority, neither time nor capacity are provided to enable further development to take place, suggesting perhaps that there is strong rhetoric, but very weak commitment, such as that that emerged during the earlier documentary analysis of local authorities in the North West of England in comparison with the qualitative field studies. In particular, there are significant predictions that as continuous monitoring of performance is increasingly applied, there is likely to be an associated decline in the building of capacity and capability and little recognition of achievement. *The need to build both capacity and capability must represent an integrated part of an intelligent leadership approach in tackling shared goals that are in the public interest.*

Summary: Is This the Tipping Point?

I want to refer back briefly to the Collective Leadership Values tree, described earlier in the book, where I posed the question 'What is the Tipping Point in turning values into appropriate behaviours?' I tentatively suggested that the trunk of our metaphorical leadership values tree – which connects its roots to its fruit – represents the transformational leadership behaviours at the level of the individual leader when they are fully aligned with the shared values and collective behaviours. Both the qualitative and the quantitative research tend to provide support to this contention, although evidence of it being applied is not strong.

The last inference drawn from the quantitative research analysis strongly supports the views expressed during the qualitative research, that capacity and capability are not aligned with either aspirations or delivery. What is of particular note is that there is a strong tendency to 'tell' rather than 'sell', and this is apparent when we consider those areas of the Transformational Leadership Inventory that appear to reflect transactional rather than transformational behaviours. This is particularly evident in the encouragement of evidence-based action and outcomes (space and mass) and in terms of time.

Space, time, and mass thus represent the foundation of what I will describe as the Intelligent Leadership approach. This has potential to bridge the gap between aspiration and delivery, telling and selling, and the short and long term.

LEADING THROUGH 360° INTELLIGENT NETWORKS

Six Honest Serving Men Re-visited

I want to return to Rudyard Kipling's six honest serving fellows who served us so well in considering the history and accumulated theories of leadership. I am suggesting that our fellows still serve us very well, and in the order in which they appear. Unlike Eric Morecambe – who, in 1971 'played' Grieg's 'A minor Piano Concerto' in front of André Previn and, much to Previn's distaste, said 'I'm playing all the right notes – but not necessarily in the right order' (McCann, 1999) – my reuse of Kipling's six honest serving men will still make poetic sense, even though it is used in this order to be reflective of the practicalities of leadership!

The key intelligent leadership questions are:

WHAT   is the issue or issues?
WHY   do we need to lead?
WHEN   do we need to act?
HOW   are we going to tackle the issues?
WHERE   can we have the greatest impact?
WHO   is best to lead?

The process is then followed within a virtuous cycle, following leadership action:

WHAT   impact did it have?
WHY   did it have this impact?
WHEN   will we succeed (if at all)?
HOW   did we achieve the impact?
WHERE   can we continue to improve?
WHO   is best to lead?

At no point within this intelligent leadership process do we focus on the 'I' of leadership, but rather the collective 'We', and not in terms of what have 'I' or 'You' achieved (or not achieved) but what have 'We' achieved or not achieved.

> **REFLEXIVE ACTIVITY:** Go back and examine the original activity that you undertook in Part I of the book in relation to the six honest serving fellows. In the light of your reading and learning, now record how you would do things differently.

A reflective activity is provided below for this chapter.

Chapter 16 Activity

Plot your organization and network's achivements between a scale of 1 to 12 and then determine its CLI 360 Profile Grade.

Epilogue

I want to end this book with a short epilogue, rather than a traditional concluding chapter. My purpose for this is two-fold. First, this is a continuing story and I want to look forward rather than backward, while taking account of my maxim that we must always consider what went before, a task that I hope I fulfilled in the main body of my writing. If this book were about a main character or other characters, then the epilogue would tell its readers how the characters have moved on from the journey. In this case, my characters are those metaphorical contexts, mechanisms, and outcomes of leading in the public interest, implicitly acknowledging that its characters are those who are charged with leading in the public interest across the vast array of leadership contexts.

Second, the foundation of this book is based on many hundreds of years of writing and practice of leadership, some, going back 4000 years or more, to our ancient forefathers, and I want to provide some indication as to the future direction for the philosophies and morals that underpin this book, related primarily to the notion of selfless leadership (which is clearly in the public interest).

In achieving both of these purposes, I want to provide a sense of 'where we go next' in terms of a new way of thinking about leadership. During the course of the last ten years, during which time much of the inspiration underpinning, and the activity leading to, this book have been developing, I have had many opportunities to discuss, teach, write about, and practise the notion of selfless leadership in a number of different contexts, with different agencies, and different organizational and international contexts, not least of which was working in a voluntary capacity with a group of like-minded individuals in my local community in putting on a 'free' music festival through fundraising.

As is often the case, the journey is not yet over but is rather more at its beginning. Within the book, most of my examples have derived from past and ongoing practice and research across public leadership within the UK context, from its humble beginning as I grappled with the leadership challenges concerned with community policing, as a senior practitioner, a regulator, a pseudo senior civil servant in the UK Home Office through to my current role as a developing international academic, executive education facilitator, and commentator. During the last two to three years, I have also been able to compare and contrast this with leadership challenges in a number of different regions in the world, including the Middle East, the Far East, the Indian sub-continent as well as European, Scandinavian, and North and South American contexts and across a range of public leadership functions including policing, healthcare, and leading at times of crises. These are all representative of what I have universally described as 'wicked problems'.

Although the context clearly changes, two points have struck me through all of my global considerations, of which both seem intuitively counter to each other.

The first is that all leaders with whom I have engaged have been passionate about what they do whereas the second is that they feel constrained by what they actually can do, referring to what I have described as the 'Them' factor, as opposed to 'Us' and 'I' rather than 'We'. From thereon, one who is engaged with leaders from differing contexts is likely to fail, sometimes in a spectacular way, if they then fail to take note of the contexts that lead to that passion or those which detract from their achievement, and if they do not take time to understand these differing contexts. On a very recent flight following visits to the Far East and the Middle East, I was listening to an inflight podcast on top tips for leading in the Middle East. The author being interviewed referred to an interesting term of what he described as 'leadership colonialism'.[1] Listening to a group at a nearby dinner table in Dubai, he overheard a group of potential consultants to leaders in the Middle East noting a rather naïve comment: 'We are going to show them how to do it.' This is what the author described as basically saying, 'I know better, I am going to do it my way.' We could assume, could we not, that this is more akin to the selfish and ego-driven characteristics of leadership but embodied by those who claim to be supporting the development of leadership.

Throughout the book I have argued that leadership is in crisis and that this applies across all sectors and most nations. There are global as well as regional, national, and sub-national differences. In the commercial sector, it is argued that while American businesses are prepared to contribute generously to defend collective interests, British business has proved adept at defending the interests of individual enterprises (often promoting Weir's notion of colonial leadership) but poor at mobilizing for collective purposes (Moran, 2013). This is another international factor that stands out for further attention and requires a shift away from patriarchal colonialism and more towards global leadership behaviours based on a much greater understanding of contextual differences. Collective leadership mechanisms can only be 'fired' if those who are promoting the collective leadership style both identify and respect the dynamic nature of the external contextual factors of leadership (PESTLE) and the desired public value outcomes before considering both the internal contexts and the strategic choice of mechanisms that may just have a role in promoting collaborative and collegial change.

WHERE DO WE GO IN THE FUTURE?

Throughout this book we have explored the concept of leadership practice and its role in making a difference. We have also examined the importance of aligning practice to the achievement of public interest outcomes through supporting systems and structures and the appropriate skills and behaviours required for collective leadership. It is here that we can look to the future. We have an opportunity to develop the concept of intelligent leadership through 360° networks, knowledge, and skills. Moreover, we can do this through a process that applies learning and development

---

[1]Dr. Tommy Weir, being interviewed on a podcast as part of the Emirates 'inflight' podcasts (see http://www.emirates.com/english/flying/inflight_entertainment/podcasts.aspx).

to work-based practice through applied leadership challenges grounded in action learning but with an added dimension (to action learning) by the inclusion of the public interest and activity. The aim is to display certain types of behaviours (that can be called transformational) in encouraging people to attain a higher level of achievement in a way that transcends their personal interests (Bass, 1985).

How does this translate in practice, and to what extent can leadership have a real impact on socially desirable outcomes at individual, group, organizational, and cross-organizational levels? This is what I refer to as the Leadership Quomodo, the latter term originating from classical Latin, and describing the 'manner, way or means' of doing something (OED, 2015), in this case, leading in the public interest as its overall impact (or, to continue the Latin origins, its *quibus auxillis* (in what way)). Is this as close as we may dare suggest in putting forward a definition of the virtue of leadership in matching leadership's aims to its methods? This, I believe, has real promise for the further promotion of leading in the public interest. Quomodo is an interrogative term that asks (of its subject matter – in this case, leadership): how, and in what way? It is supported also, I suggest, by asking why (*cur*)? These three Latin terms, quomodo (how), quibus auxillis (in what way), and cur (why) represent ablatives of the Latin terms *quis* and *quid* (who or what), as well as *ubi* (where) and *quando* (when). Circumstances (or contexts) will thus differ and Quomodo thus provides a distinct focus on the modus of leadership and brings back Rudyard Kipling's six honest serving fellows that I have referred to extensively throughout this book with its accompanying ablatives. Together, the ablative terms describe the source from which an action proceeds, its cause or ideal source of a leadership event, the instrument or agent of material sources of a leadership action, and the manner in which, and sometimes the place and time at which, anything is done.

There is no natural end to a book and it is often tempting to keep adding to the current manuscript. However, it is time to draw this to a close and it is opportune to acknowledge that – at the time of final editing and submission to the publishers – the United Kingdom has just elected a Conservative government with an overall majority, against all expectations and predictions. After five years of a coalition government, the dominant rule of a single party has been restored. The next surprise was Prime Minister David Cameron's announcement that some of his key cabinet colleagues from the previous coalition administration were to continue in these roles. Political commentators were incredulous, but we could ask, 'Why should this be case?', when so often stability is undermined by constant change of senior leaders.

It will be interesting to consider whether this single rule will have a greater impact than the coalition that preceded it. A week prior to the election, it was argued that while UK politicians may still be getting used to the concept of coalition, businesses have been collaborating for mutual gain for years, a trend – it is argued – that is only going to go one way (Reeves, 2015). Such coalitions still have their place, but the strength of the five laws of coalition commerce make sense: coalitions are contingent; the shared purpose must be clearly defined; in achieving a 'win–win' all members must gain; trust and transparency are critical; and, finally, coalitions should disband when the job is done.

A COLLECTIVE LEADERSHIP MANIFESTO

Just as my research has called upon Pawson's realist evaluation manifesto, so I conclude with a collective leadership manifesto. This is provided as the final 'activity' for this book, representing what I describe as my 'top ten tips for successful collective leadership':

Chapter 17 Activity		
C	ontexts	Do you <u>understand</u> and <u>respect</u> the history of the leadership contexts and mechanisms that the current form of leadership is based upon?
O	bjective	Are you able to take a 'step back' from your own context and cognitive assumptions and take an <u>objective</u> rather than a subjective (and often biased) stance on how you are viewing the current leadership context that you are facing?
L	isten	Can you proactively <u>listen</u> to those who have something to say without prejudice or preconception?
L	egitimate	Can you be perceived as legitimate in what you are trying to say or propose in terms of collaborative rather than competitive behaviour?
E	mpathy	Do you empathize with what is being said and can you apply your own understanding, experience, and views within the context in which your clients or colleagues view the challenges from their perspective?
C	apacity & capability	Are you actively pursuing the alignment of capacity and capability building within the context of the collective vision and desired public value outcomes?
T	rust	Are you proactively and coactively working towards an increased sense of trust with your clients and colleagues in what you are trying to jointly achieve?
I	ntelligence focused	Are you encouraging people to <u>think out of the box</u> through innovation but within an appropriate risk assessment framework in determining an intelligence-led approach?
V	alues-based	What values are you promoting and ask yourself whether you are truly engaging in a process that is aiming to achieve a sense of shared values?
E	thical	Finally, is what you are trying to do ethically based in terms of integrity, openness, selflessness and does this underpin your leadership practice or consulting?

The final question is:

Why are you doing this? Be honest in your reflection!

References

Acton, J. E., Figgis, J. N. & Laurence, R. 1907. *Historical Essays & Studies,* London, Macmillan.

Addo, I. D., Ahamed, S. I. & Chu, W. C. 2013. *Toward Collective Intelligence for Fighting Obesity.* Boston, MA, IEEE Computer Society, 690–695.

Adler, F. H. 1995. *Italian Industrialists from Liberalism to Fascism,* Cambridge, Cambridge University Press.

Ahmed, K. 2014. Tesco, what went wrong? *BBC News Business,* 22 October.

Alimo-Metcalfe, B. & Alban-Metcalfe, J. 2005. The crucial role of leadership in meeting the challenges of change. *Vision: The Journal of Business Perspective,* 9, 27–39.

Allen, K. 2004. *Authenticity,* London, Sage.

Amaru, S. & Chhetri, N. B. 2013. Climate adaptation: Institutional response to environmental constraints, and the need for increased flexibility, participation, and integration of approaches. *Applied Geography,* 39, 128–139.

Anon. 2014. I was a trainee Tesco meat buyer. *Management Today* [Online].

Archer, M. S. 1995. *Realist Social Theory: The Morphogenetic Approach,* Cambridge, Cambridge University Press.

Archer, M. S. 2012. *The Reflexive Imperative in Late Modernity,* Cambridge, Cambridge University Press.

Argyris, C. & Schon, D. A. 1978. *Organizational Learning: A Theory of Action Perspective,* Reading, MA; London, Addison-Wesley.

Aristotle, Ross, W. D., Brown, L. & Dawson, B. 2009. *The Nicomachean Ethics [Electronic Book],* Oxford, Oxford University Press.

Atlee, T. & Por, G. 2000. *Collective Intelligence as a Field of Multi-Disciplinary Study and Practice.* Available from: http://community-intelligence.com/files/Atlee - Por - CI as a Field of multidisciplinary study and practice .pdf [Accessed 1 May 2014].

Avolio, B. J. & Bass, B. M. 1994. *Evaluate the Impact of Transformational Leadership Training at Individual, Group, Organizational and Community Levels.* Final Report. Cited by Bass, 1988, W.K. Kellogg Foundation.

Babbie, E. 2013. *The Practice of Social Research,* Belmont, CA, Wadsworth.

Bäckstrand, K. 2006. Multi-stakeholder partnerships for sustainable development: Rethinking legitimacy, accountability and effectiveness. *European Environment,* 16, 290–306.

Bacon, N. & Selden, J. 1647. *An Historicall Discourse of the Uniformity of the Government of England: The First Part: From the First Times Till the Reigne of Edward the Third,* London, Printed for Matthew Walbancke.

Baldwin, J. 1996. *BuckyWorks: Buckminster Fuller's Ideas for Today,* Chichester, NY, Wiley.

Barber, M. 2007. *Three Paradigms of Public-Sector Reform.* London, McKinsey and Company.

Barker, C. 2012. *Cultural Studies: Theory and Practice,* London, SAGE.

Bass, B. M. 1985. *Leadership and Performance Beyond Expectations,* New York, London, Free Press, Collier Macmillan.

Bass, B. M. & Avolio, B. J. 1994. Transformational leadership and organizational culture. *International Journal of Public Administration,* 1, 541–554.

Bass, B. M. & Bass, R. R. 2008. *The Bass Handbook of Leadership: Theory, Research, and Managerial Applications*, New York, London, Free Press.

Bass, B. M. & Steidlmeier, P. 1999. Ethics, character, and authentic transformational leadership behavior. *Leadership Quarterly,* 10, 181.

Bass, B. M. & Stogdill, R. M. 1990. *Bass & Stogdill's Handbook of Leadership: Theory, Research, and Managerial Applications,* New York, Free Press; London, Collier Macmillan.

BBC. 1960. The Listener and BBC Television review · 1960–1967. London: British Broadcasting Corporation.

BBC. 2015. Trouble at Tesco, Panorama, BBC TV, 19 January 2015.

Beck, U. 1999. *World Risk Society,* Cambridge, Polity.

Beer, S. 1981. *Brain of the Firm: The Managerial Cybernetics of Organization: Companion Volume to the Heart of Enterprise,* Chichester, Wiley.

Bellamy, S. M. 1987. *Parent and Toddler Group Leadership: Philosophy, Practice and Training with Particular Reference to Groups Meeting in a Severely Disadvantaged Urban Area of South Yorkshire.*

Bellegarde, L. 2013. Collaborative relationships: What it takes to work together. *The Journal of Aboriginal Management,* 12, 4.

Benkler, Y. 2011. The unselfish gene. *Harvard Business Review,* 3–11.

Bennett, T., Cattermole, M. & Sanderson, H. 2009. *Outcome-Focused Reviews: A Practical Guide,* London, Department of Health.

Bennis, W. & Nanus, B. 1985. *Leaders,* New York, Harper Collins.

Benton, T. 2004. Critical realism. *In:* Lewis-Beck, M. S., Bryman, A. & Futing Liao, T. (eds.) *The Sage Encyclopedia of Social Science Research Methods.* Thousand Oaks, CA, Sage Publications, Inc.

Bevir M, Rhodes RAW and Weller P (2003) Traditions of governance: Interpreting the changing role of the public sector. Public Administration 81(1): 1–17.

Blake, R. R. & Mouton, J. S. J. A. 1964. *The Managerial Grid: Key Orientations for Achieving Production through People,* Houston, TX, Gulf Pub. Co.

Bolden, I. 2010. *The Elusive Nature of Leadership Practice: An Investigation into the Distribution, Practice and Discursive Processes of Leadership in Universities and Other Large Organisations.* PhD, University of Cardiff.

Bonfante, L. 2011. *Lessons in IT Transformation: Technology Expert to Business Leader,* Hoboken, NJ, Wiley.

Brands, R. F. & Kleinman, M. J. 2010. *Robert's Rules of Innovation: A 10-Step Program for Corporate Survival,* Hoboken, NJ, Wiley; Chichester, John Wiley [distributor].

Brookes, S. 1996. *Debate on 'Zero Tolerance' –v– 'Problem Oriented Policing'.* Police Superintendents Association of England and Wales National Conference, September, 1997, Bristol, England.

Brookes, S. 2004. *Identifying the Conditions that Help or Hinder the Development of Community Based Policing.* PhD, Nottingham Trent University.

Brookes, S. 2006. Community policing in context. *Crime Prevention and Community Safety: An International Journal,* Spring, 2006.

Brookes, S. 2008. *The Public Leadership Challenge: ESRC Research Summary.* Swindon, Economic and Social Research Council (ESRC).

Brookes, S. 2010. Telling the story of place: The role of community leadership. *In:* Brookes, S. & Grint, K. (eds.) *The New Public Leadership Challenge.* Basingstoke, Palgrave Macmillan.

Brookes, S. 2011. Crisis, confidence and collectivity: Responding to the new public leadership challenge. *Leadership,* 7, 175–195.

Brookes, S. & Fahy, P. 2013. Public trust in policing. *In:* Llewellyn, S., Brookes, S. & Mahon, A. (eds.) *Trust and Confidence in Government and Public Services.* London, Routledge.

Brookes, S. & Grint, K. 2010. *The New Public Leadership Challenge*, Basingstoke, Palgrave Macmillan.

Brookes, S. & Johnson, C. 2007. *Leading Places: Research in relation to the delivery of LAAs in the North West*, Manchester, University of Manchester.

Brookes, S., Moss, K. & Pease, K. 2003. Data sharing and crime prevention: The long and winding road. *Crime Prevention and Community Safety*, 5, 7–14.

Brookes, S. & Wiggan, J. 2009. Reflecting the public value of sport: A game of two halves? *Public Management Review*, 11, 401–420.

Browning, G. 2013. The rise of the backstabber. *Management Today*. London, Haymarket Consumer Media.

Burns, J. M. 1978. *Leadership*, New York, London, Harper and Row.

Burns, T. 2007. The legal implications of reputation risk management for franchisors. *Journal of International Commercial Law and Technology*, 2(4), 231–240.

Bush, T., Bell, L., Middlewood, D., Harris, A., Levacic, R. & Allen, T. 2010. *The Principles of Educational Leadership and Management*, Los Angeles, London, Sage.

Bushev, M. 1994. *Synergetics: Chaos, Order, Self-organization*, Singapore, London, World Scientific.

Businessballs. n.d. *Business Networking*. Available from: http://www.businessballs.com/business-networking.htm [2014].

Butler, S. 2015. If Tesco's boss can trim the fat, 2015 could see the retailer rise again. *Guardian*.

Cadbury, A. 1992. *Report of the Committee on the Financial Aspects of Corporate Governance*. London, The Committee on the Financial Aspects of Corporate Governance and Gee and Co. Ltd.

Cameron, K. S. 1986. A study of organizational effectiveness and its predictors. *Management Science*, 32, 87–112.

Cameron, K. S. 2006. *Competing Values Leadership: Creating Value in Organizations*, Cheltenham, Edward Elgar.

Cameron, K. S. & Quinn, R. E. 2006. *Diagnosing and Changing Organizational Culture: Based on the Competing Values Framework*, Beijing, China Renmin University Press.

Cameron, K. S. & Quinn, R. E. 2011. *Diagnosing and Changing Organizational Culture: Based on the Competing Values Framework*, third edition, San Francisco, CA, Jossey-Bass.

Campbell, D. T. 1976. *Assessing the Impact of Planned Social Change. The Public Affairs Center*, Hanover, NH, Dartmouth College.

Carlyle, T. 1852. *On Heroes, Hero-Worship and the Heroic in History: Six Lectures, Reported with Emendations and Additions*, London, Chapman and Hall.

Carroll, B., Levy, L. & Richmond, D. 2008. Leadership as practice: Challenging the competency paradigm. *Leadership*, 4, 363–379.

Cartwright, D. 1965. Influence, leadership, control. *In:* March, J. G. (ed.) *Handbook of Organizations*. Chicago, IL, Rand McNally.

Chen, T. Y., Liu, H. H. & Hsieh, W. L. 2009. The influence of partner characteristics and relationship capital on the performance of international strategic alliances. *Journal of Relationship Marketing*, 8, 231–252.

Chiu, M. L., Fu, C. Y. & Wu, I. L. 2013. *An Analysis of Supply Chain Collaboration and its Impact on Firm Performance: An Integration of Social Capital, Justice, and Technology Use*, 2013 Angers, 5–12.

Chou, A. 2008. The role of knowledge sharing and trust in new product development outsourcing. *International Journal of Information Systems and Change Management*, 3, 301–313.

Chu, H.-Y. & Trujillo, R. G. 2009. *New Views on R. Buckminster Fuller*, Stanford, CA, Stanford General; London, Eurospan [distributor].

Collins, J. C. 2001. *Good to Great: Why Some Companies Make the Leap – and Others Don't*, London, Random House Business.

Collins, J. C. & Porras, J. I. 1994. *Built to Last: Successful Habits of Visionary Companies*, New York, HarperBusiness.

Conger, J. A. 1990. The dark side of leadership. *Organizational Dynamics*, 19, 44–55.

Conger, J. A. & Riggio, R. E. 2007. *The Practice of Leadership [Electronic Resource]: Developing the Next Generation of Leaders*, San Francisco, CA, John Wiley & Sons.

Connell, J. & Voola, R. 2007. Strategic alliances and knowledge sharing: Synergies or silos? *Journal of Knowledge Management*, 11, 52–66.

Connelly, J. B. 2007. Evaluating complex public health interventions: Theory, methods and scope of realist enquiry. *Journal of Evaluation in Clinical Practice*, 13, 935–941.

Cook, T., Cooper, H., Cordray, D., Hartman, H., Hedges, L., Light, R., Louis, T. and Mosteller, F. (1992) Meta-Analysis for Explanation. New York: Russell Sage Foundation.

Cooke, F. L. 2006. Modeling an HR shared services center: Experience of an MNC in the United Kingdom. *Human Resource Management*, 45, 211–227.

Cooper, C. 2014. NHS should be run like Tesco, claims Reform think tank. *The Independent*, 18 June 2014.

Cosner, S. 2009. Building organizational capacity through trust. *Educational Administration Quarterly*, 45, 248–291.

Cotterell, A., Lowe, R. & Shaw, I. 2006. *Leadership: Lessons from the Ancient World*, Hoboken, NJ; Chichester, Wiley.

Covey, S. R. 1989. *The Seven Habits of Highly Effective People: Restoring the Character Ethic*, London, Simon & Schuster.

Crozier, M. 1971. Comparing structures and comparing games. *In:* Pugh, D. S. (ed.) *Organization Theory: Selected Readings*. Harmondsworth, Penguin.

Crumley, C. L. 1995. Heterarchy and the analysis of complex societies. *Archeological Papers of the American Anthropological Association*, 1–5.

CSDH. 2008. *Closing the Gap in a Generation: Health Equity through Action on the Social Determinants of Health*. Final Report of the Commission on Social Determinants of Health. Geneva, World Health Organization.

Cunliffe, A. L. 2009. The philosopher leader: On relationalism, ethics and reflexivity—A critical perspective to teaching leadership. *Management Learning*, 40, 87–101.

Cunneen, C. 1999. Zero tolerance policing: Implications for indigenous people. *Indigenous Law Bulletin*, 4.

DCLG. 2014. *Helping Troubled Families Turn their Lives Around* [Online]. Available from: https://http://www.gov.uk/government/policies/helping-troubled-families-turn-their-lives-around [Accessed 3 September 2014].

Derue, D. S. & Ashford, S. J. 2010. Power to the people: Where has personal agency gone in leadership development? *Industrial and Organizational Psychology*, 3, 24–27.

DFES. 2007. *The National Programme for Specialist Leaders of Behaviour and Attendance*. London, Department for Further Education and Skills.

Donald in Mathmagicland. 1959. Motion Picture. Directed by Walt Disney.

Duell, M. 2015. Tesco has lost the trust of customers and suffered a failure of leadership says former boss Sir Terry Leahy. *Mail Online*, 19 January.

Earle Mcleod, L. 2014. *Optimism v. Pessimism: A Treacherous False Choice*. Available from: http://www.huffingtonpost.com/lisa-earle-mcleod/optimism-v-pessimism-a-tr_b_379349.html [Accessed 1 May 2013].

Eaton, G. 2005. *Management Accounting Official Terminology*, Oxford, Chartered Institute of Management Accountants (CIMA) Publishing.

Economist. 2002. Four committees in search of a scandal. *The Economist* [Online].

Edmondson, A. C. 1992. *A Fuller Explanation: The Synergetic Geometry of R. Buckminster Fuller,* New York, Van Nostrand Reinhold; London, Chapman & Hall.

Einstein, A. 1954. *Ideas and Opinions,* London, The Folio Society by Arrangement with The Crown Publishing Group.

Emerson, J., Wachowicz, J. & Chun, S. 2000. Social return on investment: Exploring aspects of value creation in the nonprofit sector. *In: Social Purpose Enterprises and Venture Philanthropy in the New Millennium.* San Francisco.

Eterno, J. 2003. *Policing within the Law: A Case Study of the New York City Police Department,* Westport, CT; London, Praeger.

Eterno, J. & Silverman, E. 2012. *The Crime Numbers Game: Management by Manipulation,* Boca Raton, FL, Taylor & Francis.

Fayol, H. 1930. *Industrial and General Administration,* [S.l.], Pitman.

Felsted, A. & Oakley, D. 2015. Tesco's plans for new era put it on investors' shopping lists. *Financial Times,* 8 January 2015.

Feng, T., Zhao, G. & Su, K. 2014. The fit between environmental management systems and organisational learning orientation. *International Journal of Production Research,* 52, 2901–2914.

Ferguson, J. 1958. *Moral Values in the Ancient World,* London, Methuen & Co.

Fernie, J. 2009. Relationships in the Supply Chain. *In:* Fernie, J. & Sparks, L. (eds) *Logistics and Retail Management: Emerging Issues and New Challenges in the Retail Supply Chain.* London, Kogan Page.

Fernie, J. & Sparks, L. 2009. *Logistics & Retail Management: Emerging Issues and New Challenges in the Retail Supply Chain,* London, Kogan Page.

Fielder, F. 1964. A theory of leadership effectiveness. *In:* Berkowitz, L. (ed.) *Advances in Experimental Social Psychology.* New York, Academic Press.

Finley, M. 2000. *A Business Bestiary* [Online]. Available from: http://mfinley.com/list-bestiary.htm [Accessed 22 November 2013].

Francis, R. 2013. *Report of the Mid Staffordshire NHS Foundation Trust Public Inquiry: Executive Summary,* DOH (ed.). London, HMSO.

Frede, D. 2013. Plato's ethics: An overview. *The Stanford Encyclopedia of Philosophy* [Online], (Fall 2013 edition). Available from: http://plato.stanford.edu/archives/fall2013/entries/plato-ethics/ [Accessed 15 October 2013].

French, J. R. P. & Raven, B. 1959. The bases of social power. *In:* Cartwright, D. & Zander, A. (eds.) *Group Dynamics.* New York, Harper Row.

Fry, J. & Mckenzie, J. 1968. *The Mood of General Practice and the Need for Professional Leadership,* [s.l., s.n].

Fuller, R. B. 1973. *Nine Chains to the Moon,* London, Cape.

Fuller, R. B. (1975) *Synergetics: Explorations in the Geometry of Thinking,* New York: Macmillan.

Fuller, R. B. (1979) *Synergetics 2: Explorations in the Geometry of Thinking,* New York: Macmillan.

Fuller, R. B. 1998. *Thoughts of Buckminster Fuller. Whole Earth.*

Fuller, R. B. & Dil, A. S. 1983. *Humans in Universe,* New York, Mouton.

Gallo, F. T. 2011. *Business Leadership in China: An Integration of Western Best Practice with Chinese Wisdom,* Singapore, Chichester; Wiley, John Wiley [distributor].

Gerrish, K., Mcmanus, M. & Ashworth, P. 2003. Creating what sort of professional? Master's level nurse education as a professionalising strategy. *Nursing Inquiry,* 10, 103–112.

GOS (ed.). 2014. *Innovation: Managing Risk, Not Avoiding It: Evidence and Case Studies,* London, HMSO.

Greiner, L. E. 1994. Evolution and revolution as organizations grow. *In:* Mainiero, L. & Tromley, C. (eds.) *Developing Managerial Skills in Organizational Behavior: Exercises, Cases, and Readings.* Englewood Cliffs, NJ, Prentice Hall.

Greve, H. R., Rowley, T. J. & Shipilov, A. V. 2014. *Network Advantage: How to Unlock Value from your Alliances and Partnerships*, Chichester, John Wiley.

Grint , K. (1997) *Leadership: Classical, Contemporary, and Critical Approaches*, Oxford, Oxford University Press.

Grint, K. 2000. *The Arts of Leadership*, Oxford, Oxford University Press.

Grint, K. 2005. *Leadership: Limits and Possibilities*, Basingstoke, Palgrave Macmillan.

Grint, K. 2007. Learning to lead: Can aristotle help us find the road to wisdom? *Leadership*, 3, 231–246.

Grint, K. 2008a. *Leadership, Management and Command: Rethinking D-Day*, Basingstoke; New York, Palgrave Macmillan.

Grint, K. 2008b. Wicked problems and clumsy solutions: The role of leadership. *Clinical Leader*, 1(2), 54–68

Grint, K. 2010. Wicked problems and clumsy solutions: The role of leadership. In: Brookes, S. & Grint, K. (eds.) *The New Public Leadership Challenge*. Basingstoke, Palgrave Macmillan.

Grol, R. & Grimshaw, J. 2003. From best evidence to best practice: Effective implementation of change in patients' care. *The Lancet*, 362, 1224–1229.

Gulati, R., Wohlgezogen, F. & Zhelyazkov, P. 2012. The two facets of collaboration: Cooperation and coordination in strategic alliances. *Academy of Management Annals*, 6, 531–583.

Hands, D. W. 2001. *Reflection without Rules: Economic Methodology and Contemporary Science*, Cambridge, Cambridge University Press.

Handy, C. B. 1993. *Understanding Organizations*, London, Penguin Books.

Handy, C. B. 1999. *Understanding Organizations*, Harmondsworth, Penguin.

Hardin, G. 1968. The tragedy of the commons. *Science*, 162(3859), 1243–1248.

Hardin, R. 1998. Trust in government. In: Braithwaite, V. & Levi, M. (eds.) *Trust & Governance*. New York, Russell Sage Foundation.

Harris, T. J., Seppala, C. T. & Desborough, L. D. 1999. A review of performance monitoring and assessment techniques for univariate and multivariate control systems. *Journal of Process Control*, 9, 1–17.

Haywood, S. 2014. Tesco bosses splurge £31MILLION on luxury jet while supermarket's sales plummet. *The Mirror*, 4 October 2014.

Heclo, H. 2002. The statesman: Revisiting leadership in administration. In: Kagan, R. A., Kriegier, M. & Winston, K. I. (eds.) *Legality and Community: On the Intellectual Legacy of Philip Selznick*. Berkeley, CA, Berkeley Public Policy Press.

Heifetz, R. A. 1994. *Leadership without Easy Answers*, Cambridge, MA; London, Belknap Press of Harvard University Press.

Heifetz, R. A., Grashow, A. & Linsky, M. 2009. *The Practice of Adaptive Leadership: Tools and Tactics for Changing your Organization and the World*. Boston, MA, Harvard Business Press.

Heifetz, R. A. & Linsky, M. 2002. *Leadership on the Line: Staying Alive through the Dangers of Leading*, Boston, MA, Harvard Business School Press.

Hersey, P. & Blanchard, K. H. 1969. An introduction to situational leadership. *Training and Development Journal*, 23, 26–34.

Heslop, R. 2011. The British police service: Professionalisation or 'McDonaldization'? *International Journal of Police Science & Management*, 13, 312–321.

HMSO (ed.). 2000. *Calling Time on Crime*, London, HMSO.

Hofstede, G. H. 1980. *Culture's Consequences: International Differences in Work-Related Values*, Beverly Hills; London, Sage.

Hofstede, G., Hosfstede, G. J. & Minkov, M. 2010. *Cultures and Organizations: Software of the Mind*, New York, McGraw-Hill.

Honey, P. 1988. *Face to Face: A Practical Guide to Interactive Skills*, Aldershot, Gower.

Hopper, K. & Hopper, W. J. 2009. *The Puritan Gift: Reclaiming the American Dream Amidst Global Financial Chaos,* London, I.B. Tauris.

Hopper, K., Hopper, W. J. & Ebrary, I. 2007. *The Puritan Gift: Triumph, Collapse and Revival of an American Dream,* London, I.B. Tauris.

Hosmer, L. T. 1995. Trust: The connecting link between organizational theory and philosophical ethics. *Academy of Management Review,* 20(2), 379–403.

Hurley, T. J. & Brown, J. 2010. Conversational leadership: Thinking together for a change. *Oxford Leadership Journal,* 1, 1–9.

Hutton, W. 2012. Now is not the time to turn our backs on Enlightenment values from Hungary to South Africa, the US to the UK, the right no longer embraces progress or tolerance, reason or democratic argument. *The Observer* [Online]. Available from: http://www.theguardian.com/commentisfree/2012/jan/08/will-hutton-lost-enlightenment-values [Accessed 15 October 2013].

Hyde, D. 2013. Who to blame when 'computer says no'. *Telegraph,* 23 September 2013.

Investopedia. 2014. *Synergy* [Online]. Available from: http://www.investopedia.com/terms/s/synergy.asp [Accessed 22 July 2014].

Jameson, J. 2008. *Leadership: Professional Communities of Leadership Practice in Post-Compulsory Education,* Bristol, Higher Education Academy.

Jami, A. A. N. & Walsh, P. R. 2014. The role of public participation in identifying stakeholder synergies in wind power project development: The case study of Ontario, Canada. *Renewable Energy,* 68, 194–202.

Johnson, G., Whittington, R., Scholes, K., & Pyle, S. 2011. *Exploring Strategy: Text & Cases,* Harlow, Financial Times Prentice Hall.

Kadirova, D. 2014. Implementation of post-conflict reconstruction and development aid initiatives: Evidence from Afghanistan. *Journal of International Development,* 26, 887–914.

Kaplan, R. S. & Norton, D. P. 1996. *The Balanced Scorecard: Translating Strategy into Action,* Boston, MA, Harvard Business School Press.

Kechichian, J. A., Dekmejian, R. H. & Ibn, Z. M. A. 2003. *The Just Prince: A Manual of Leadership,* London, Saqi.

Kelling, G. L. & Sousa, W. H. 2001. Do Police Matter? An Analysis of the Impact of New York City's Police Reforms, Civic Report No. 22, New York: Manhattan Institute Center for Civic Innovation.

Kelling, G. L. & Coles, C. M. 1996. *Fixing Broken Windows: Restoring Order and Reducing Crime in our Communities,* New York; London, Free Press.

Kelling, G. L. & Wilson, J. Q. 1982. Broken windows: The police and neighborhood safety. *Atlantic Monthly,* 249, 29–38.

Kellerman, B. 1987. The politics of leadership in America: Implications for higher education in the late 20th century. Invitational Interdisciplinary Colloquium on Leadership in Higher Education. National Center for Postsecondary Governance and Finance, Teachers College, Columbia University: Columbia University, NY.

Kerr, N. L. 1983. Motivation losses in small groups: A social dilemma analysis. *Journal of Personality and Social Psychology,* 45, 819–828.

Kingsford, C. L. 1977. *Chronicles of London,* Dursley, Alan Sutton; Wakefield, Distributed by EP Publishing.

Kipling, R. 1907. *Just So Stories,* London, Macmillan & Co.

Kolb, D. A. 1984. *Experiential Learning: Experience as the Source of Learning and Development,* Englewood Cliffs, NJ; London, Prentice-Hall.

Kotter, J. P. 2012. *Leading Change,* Boston, MA, Harvard Business Review Press.

Krygier, M. 2012. *Philip Selznick: Ideals in the World,* Stanford, CA, Stanford University Press.

Kuglin, F. A., Hook, J. & Ebrary, I. 2002. *Building, Leading, and Managing Strategic Alliances [Electronic Resource]: How to Work Effectively and Profitably with Partner Companies,* New York, Amacom.

Lakatos, I. 1978. The methodology of scientific research programmes. *In:* Worrall, J. & Currie, G. (eds.) *Philosophical Papers.* Cambridge, Cambridge University Press.

Lank, E. 2006. *Collaborative Advantage [Electronic Resource]: How Organisations Win by Working Together,* Basingstoke, Palgrave Macmillan.

Latham, G. P. & Yukl, G. A. 1975. A review of research on the application of goal setting in organizations. *Academy of Management Journal,* 18, 824–845.

Leahy, T. 2012. *Management in 10 Words,* London, Random House Business.

Lee, S., Upneja, A., Özdemir, Ö. & Sun, K. A. 2014. A synergy effect of internationalization and firm size on performance: US hotel industry. *International Journal of Contemporary Hospitality Management,* 26, 35–49.

Levi, M. & Williams, M. L. 2013. Multi-agency partnerships in cybercrime reduction: Mapping the UK information assurance network cooperation space. *Information Management and Computer Security,* 21, 420–443.

Lewicki, R. J. & Bunker, B. B. 1995. *Trust in Relationships: A Model of Development and Decline,* Columbus, OH, Max M. Fisher College of Business, Ohio State University.

Lewin, K. (1951) *Field theory in social science; selected theoretical papers.* D. Cartwright (ed.). New York: Harper & Row, page 169.

Lewin, K., Lippit, R. & White, R. K. 1939. Patterns of aggressive behavior in experimentally created social climates. *Journal of Social Psychology,* 10, 271–301.

Lewis-Smith, A. 2013. *A Community of Practice: A Case Study Exploring Safety and Quality through Professional Leadership,* Great Britain, University of Southampton.

Li, Z., Han, Y. & Xu, P. 2014. Methods for benchmarking building energy consumption against its past or intended performance: An overview. *Applied Energy,* 124, 325–334.

Llewellyn, S., Brookes, S. & Mahon, A. 2013. *Trust and Confidence in Government and Public Services,* London, New York, Routledge.

Locke, E. A. & Latham, G. P. 1990. *A Theory of Goal Setting & Task Performance,* Englewood Cliffs, NJ; London, Prentice-Hall.

Locke, E. A. & Latham, G. P. 2013. *New Developments in Goal Setting and Task Performance [Electronic Resource],* London. New York, Routledge.

LOCOG. 2012. London 2012: *Olympic Games: Official Report,* London, The London Organising Committee of the Olympic Games and Paralympic Games Limited.

LOCOG. 2013. London 2012: *Olympic Games: Official Report.* London, The London Organising Committee of the Olympic Games and Paralympic Games Limited.

Logan, D. C. 2009. Known knowns, known unknowns, unknown unknowns and the propagation of scientific enquiry. *Journal of Experimental Botany,* 60, 712–714.

Love, P. E. D. & Ellis, J. 2009. Knowledge sharing, learning and situated practice: Communities of practice for projects, 6th European and Mediterranean Conference on Information Systems.

Macionis, J. J. & Gerber, L. M. 2011. *Sociology,* Toronto, Pearson Canada.

Marmot, M. 2010. *Fair Society, Healthy Lives [Electronic Resource]: The Marmot Review Executive Summary; Strategic Review of Health Inequalities in England Post-2010,* [S.1.], The Marmot Review.

Martinuzzi, A. & Krumay, B. 2013. The good, the bad, and the successful – How corporate social responsibility leads to competitive advantage and organizational transformation. *Journal of Change Management,* 13, 424–443.

Matofska, B. 2014. *What is the Sharing Economy.* Available from: http://www.virgin.com/entrepreneur/what-is-the-sharing-economy [Accessed March 2015].

Matt, M., Robin, S. & Wolff, S. 2012. The influence of public programs on inter-firm R&D collaboration strategies: Project-level evidence from EU FP5 and FP6. *Journal of Technology Transfer*, 37, 885–916.

Mayo, E. 1933. *The Human Problems of an Industrial Civilization*, [S.l.], London, Macmillan.

McCann, G. 1999. *Morecambe & Wise*, London, Fourth Estate.

McCarthy, J., Minsky, M., Rochester, N. & Shannon, C. 1955. A proposal for the dartmouth summer research project on artificial intelligence. *Dartmouth Sumer Research Project on Artificial Intelligence*. Stanford University.

Mcshane, J. 2007. *Pedagogy – What Does it Mean?* [Online]. Available from: http://www. teachingexpertise.com/articles/pedagogy-what-does-it-mean-2370 [Accessed 12 May 2013].

Medford, W. n.d. Relocation Astrology, Buckminster Fuller, Sacred Geometry, and Arkansas Quartz Crystals. *Selfgrowth.com* [Online, 2014].

Mesharov, M. & Khurana, R. 2013. Leading amidst competing technical and institutional demands: Revisiting Selznick's conception of leadership. *Harvard Business School Working Paper, No. 13-049, November 2012*, Harvard.

Milgate, M. 2000. Black-box protection of core competencies in strategic alliances. *Journal of Management and Organization*, 6, 32–43.

Milgram, S. 1974. *Obedience to Authority: An Experimental View*, London, Pinter and Martin.

Mintzberg, H. 1983. *Power In and Around Organizations*, Englewood Cliffs, NJ, Prentice-Hall.

Mitchell, R. K., Agle, B. R. & Wood, D. J. 1997. Toward a theory of stakeholder identification and salience: Defining the principle of who and what really counts. *The Academy of Management Review*, 22, 853–886.

Moore, M. H. 1995. *Creating Public Value: Strategic Management in Government*, Cambridge, MA; London, Harvard University Press.

Moran, M. 2013. *Schumpeter's Nightmare? Legitimacy, Trust and Business in Britain*. London: The British Academy.

Morganteen, J. 2013. What the CompStat audit reveals about the NYPD. *The New York World* [Online, March 2015].

Morris, W. 2012. *Not Just 'How' But 'Why': A Personal Reflection on Business Ethics and the Crisis*. London: Reform.

Morrison, D. J. & Quella, J. A. 2000. Pinpointing patterns. *Financial Executive*, 16, 36–38.

Muth, J. J. 2003. *Stone Soup*, New York, Scholastic Press.

Nakota, N. 2009. *Beyond Hofstede: Culture Frameworks for Global Marketing and Management*, Basingstoke, Palgrave Macmillan.

Newcomer, M. 1955. Professionalization of leadership in the big business corporation. *The Business History Review*, 29, 54–63.

Newton, K. 2007. Social and political trust. *In:* Dalton, R. J. & Klingerman, H. D. (eds.) *The Oxford Handbook of Political Behaviour*. Oxford, Oxford University Press.

Nicolaou, A. I. 2011. Integrated information systems and interorganizational performance: The role of management accounting systems design. *In:* Arnold, V., Bobek, D., Clinton, B. D., Lillis, A., Roberts, R., Wolfe, C. & Wright, S. (eds.) *Advances in Accounting Behavioral Research*, Volume 14. Bingley, UK, Emerald Group, 117–141

Ning, S., Akkiraju, R., Nayak, N. & Goodwin, R. 2009. Shared services transformation: Conceptualization and valuation from the perspective of real options. *Decision Sciences*, 40(3), 381–402

Northouse, P. G. 2009. *Leadership: Theory and Practice*, London, SAGE.

OED. 2012. *Oxford English Dictionary*, third edition [Online]. Available from: http://www.oed .com [Accessed 15 March 2012].

Oettmeier, T. & Wycoff, M. 1997. *Personnel Performance Evaluation in the Community Policing Context.* Washington, DC, Department of Justice.

Olsen, M. 1965. *The Logic of Collective Action: Public Goods and the Theory of Groups,* Cambridge, MA, Harvard Business Press.

OPM & CIPFA. 2004. *The Good Governance Standard for Public Services, The Independent Commission on Good Governance in Public Services,* London, OPM and the Chartered Institute of Public Finance and Accountancy.

Ordóñez, L., Schweitzer, M. E., Galinsky, A. D. & Bazerman, M. H. 2009. Goals gone wild: The systematic side effects of over-prescribing goal setting. *Harvard Business School Working Paper* [Online]. Available from: http://www.hbs.edu/faculty/Publication Files/09-083.pdf [Accessed 30 May 2014].

Orsagh, M. 2012. *Visionary Board Leadership: Stewardship for the Long Term,* Codes, Standards and Position Papers, Volume 2012, No. 3, Virginia, USA, CFA Institute.

Pagel, M. D. 2012. *Wired for Culture: The Natural History of Human Cooperation,* London, Allen Lane.

Parel, A. 1992. *The Machiavellian Cosmos,* New Haven, CT; London, Yale University Press.

Parsons, T. 1952. *The Social System,* London; printed in the USA, Tavistock Publications.

Partridge, G. E. 1932. Behaviorism by John B. Watson. *American Journal of Psychiatry,* 89, 187–189.

Pawson, R. 2013. *The Science of Evaluation: A Realist Manifesto,* London, SAGE.

Pawson, R., Greenhalgh, T., Harvey, G. & Walshe, K. 2005. Realist review – A new method of systematic review designed for complex policy interventions. *Journal of Health Services Research & Policy,* 10, 21–34.

Pawson, R. & Tilley, N. 1997. *Realistic Evaluation,* Los Angeles; London, Sage.

Pearce, C. L. & Conger, J. A. 2003. *Shared Leadership: Reframing the How's and Why's of Leadership,* Thousand Oaks, CA, Sage Publications.

Pease, K. 2001. *Cracking Crime through Design.* London: Design Council.

Pfitzer, M., Bockstette, V. & Stamp, M. 2013. Innovating for shared value. *Harvard Business Review,* 91, 100–109.

Phene, A. & Tallman, S. 2012. Complexity, context and governance in biotechnology alliances. *Journal of International Business Studies,* 43, 61–83.

Phillips, D. T. 1997a. *The Founding Fathers on Leadership: Classic Teamwork in Changing Times,* New York, NY, Warner Books.

Phillips, R. A. 1997b. Stakeholder theory and a principle of fairness. *Business Ethics Quarterly,* 7, 51–66.

Pishchikova, K. 2014. Greater synergy and improved collaboration: Do complex partnerships deliver on the promise in countries emerging from armed conflict? *Voluntas,* 25, 2–27.

PMSU (ed.). 2006. The UK Government's approach to public service reform, London, HMSO.

Pollard, C. 1997. Zero tolerance: Short-term fix, long term liability. *In:* Bratton, W. J., Mallon, R. & Orr, J. (eds.) *Zero Tolerance: Policing a Free Society.* Institute of Economic Affairs, Health and Welfare Unit.

Pool, D. S. 1959. *Trends in Content Analysis,* Urbana, University of Illinois Press.

Pool, I. D. S. & Etheredge, L. S. 1998. *Politics in Wired Nations: Selected Writings of Ithiel de Sola Pool,* New Brunswick, NJ; London, Transaction Publishers.

Porter, M. E. & Kramer, M. R. 2011. Creating shared value: How to reinvent capitalism and unleash a wave of innovation and growth. *Harvard Business Review,* January–February 2011 Issue, 2–17

Potter, N. N. 2009. *Mapping the edges and the in-between: A critical analysis of borderline personality disorder,* Oxford; New York, Oxford University Press.

Premus, R. & Sanders, N. 2008. Information sharing in global supply chain alliances. *Journal of Asia-Pacific Business,* 9, 174–192.

Qin, S. J. 1998. Control performance monitoring: A review and assessment. *NSF/NIST Measurement and Conrrol Workshop,* New Orleans.

Quinn, R. E. & Cameron, K. S. 1983. Organizational life cycles and shifting criteria of effectiveness: Some preliminary evidence. *Management Science,* 29, 33–51.

Quinn, R. E. & Rohrbaugh, J. 1981. A competing values approach to organizational effectiveness. *Public Productivity Review,* 2, 122–140.

Radder, H. 1997. Philosophy and history of science: Beyond the Kunian paradigm. *Studies in History and Philosophy of Science,* 28, 633–655.

Rayman, G. 2010. *NYPD Tapes 4: The Whistleblower, Adrian Schoolcraft.* Available from: http://www.villagevoice.com/2010-06-15/news/adrian-school-craft-nypd-tapes-whistleblower/ [Accessed March 2015].

Reeves, R. 2015. When enemies become [temporary] friends. *Management Today,* London, Chartered Management Institute (CMI).

Revans, R. W. 1980. *Action Learning: New Techniques for Management,* London, Blond and Briggs.

Revans, R. W. 1998. *ABC of Action Learning,* London, Lemos & Crane.

Rhyne, D. 2014. Public–Private Partnerships: Unholy Unions. *Youshouldbuygold. com* [Online]. Available from: http://www.youshouldbuygold.com/2014/05/public-private-partnerships-unholy-unions/

Rittel, H. W. J. & Webber, M. M. 1973. Dilemmas in a general theory of planning, *Policy Sciences,* 4, 155–169

Rossi, S., Kumar & Cohen, P. R. *Distributive and Collective Readings in Group Protocols.* Nineteenth International Joint Conference on Artificial Intelligence, IJCAI, 2005 Edinburgh, IJCAI, 971–976.

Ruddick, G. 2014. Tesco scandal could spark a long overdue shake-up of the retailer-supplier relationship. *Telegraph,* 26 September.

Rumsfeld, D. 2002. Press Conference, NATO HQ, Brussels, 6 June 2002. Available from: http://www.nato.int/docu/speech/2002/s020606g.htm [Accessed December 2014].

Scarso, E. & Bolisani, E. 2010. Knowledge-based strategies for knowledge intensive business services: A multiple case-study of computer service companies. *Electronic Journal of Knowledge Management,* 8, 151–160.

Schepker, D. J., Oh, W. Y., Martynov, A. & Poppo, L. 2014. The many futures of contracts: Moving beyond structure and safeguarding to coordination and adaptation. *Journal of Management,* 40, 193–225.

Schluter, M. & Lee, D. 2009. *The Relational Manager: Transform your Workplace and your Life,* Oxford, Lion.

Schumpeter, J. 1908. On the concept of social value. *Quarterly Journal of Economics,* 23, 213–232.

Segil, L., Goldsmith, M. & Belasco, J. A. 2003. *Partnering: The New Face of Leadership,* New York, AMACOM.

Seligman, A. 1997. *The Problem of Trust,* Princeton, NJ, Prenceton University Press.

Selznick, P. 1957. *Leadership in Administration: A Sociological Interpretation,* Evanston, IL, Row.

Selznick, P. 1992. *The Moral Commonwealth: Social Theory and the Promise of Community,* Berkeley, University of California Press.

Sherf, E. 2010. *Synergy in Management* [Online]. Available from: http://comparativeadvantage.wordpress.com/2010/05/27/synergy-in-management/ [Accessed 22 July 2014].

Silzer, R. F. 2002. *The 21st Century Executive: Innovative Practices for Building Leadership at the Top,* San Francisco, Chichester; Jossey-Bass, Wiley [distributor].

Simon, Herbert (1957). 'A Behavioral Model of Rational Choice', in Models of Man, Social and Rational: Mathematical Essays on Rational Human Behavior in a Social Setting. New York: Wiley

Simon, H. A. & Newell, A. 1958. Heuristic problem solving: The next advance in operations research. *Operations Research,* 6, 1–10.

Smith, D. & Sparks, L. 2009. Tesco's supply chain management. *In:* Fernie, J. & Sparks, L. (eds.) *Logistics & Retail Management: Emerging Issues and New Challenges in the Retail Supply Chain,* third ed. London, Kogan Page.

Sober, E. & Wilson, D. S. 1998. *Unto Others: The Evolution and Psychology of Unselfish Behavior,* Cambridge, MA; London, Harvard University Press.

Stogdill, R. M. 1974. *Handbook of Leadership. A Survey of Theory and Research,* New York, London, Free Press, Collier Macmillan Publishers.

Strauss, A. L. 1978. *Negotiations: Varieties, Contexts, Processes, and Social Order,* San Francisco; London, Jossey-Bass.

Sun, W. & Giles, L. 1910. *Sun Zi Bing Fa Sun Tzu's on the Art of War. The Oldest Military Treatise in the World.* Translated from the Chinese with Introduction and Critical Notes by Lionel Giles. London, Luzac & Co.

Talbot, C. & Wiggan, J. 2010. The public value of the National Audit Office. *International Journal of Public Sector Management,* 23, 54–70.

Tannenbaum, R. & Schmidt, W. H. 1957. How to choose a leadership pattern. *Harvard Business Review,* March–April 1957, 95–101.

TESCO. 2014. *Annual Report and Financial Statements 2014,* London, TESCO PLC.

Tilley, N. 2010. Can leadership be evaluated? *In:* Brookes, S. & Grint, K. (eds.) *The Public Leadership Challenge.* Basingstoke: Palgrave Macmillan.

Turing, A. M. 1952. The chemical basis of morphogenesis. *Philosophical Transactions of the Royal Society of London. Series B, Biological Sciences,* 237, 37–72.

Tyler, T. R. & Degoey, P. 1996. Collective restraint in social dilemmas: Procedural justice and social identification effects on support for authorities. *Journal of Personality and Social Psychology,* 69, 482–497.

Uhl-Bien, M. 2006. Relational leadership theory: Exploring the social processes of leadership and organizing. *The Leadership Quarterly,* 17, 654–676.

Van Buren III, H. J. 1999. If fairness is the problem, is consent the solution? Integrating ISCT and stakeholder theory. *Academy of Management Proceedings & Membership Directory,* C1–C6.

Vanebo, J. O. & Murdock, A. 2012. Innovation and creative leadership in local government. *In:* Westeren, K. I. (ed.) *Foundations of the Knowledge Economy: Innovation, Learning and Clusters.* Cheltenham, Edward Elgar.

Voskamp, A. 2010. *One Thousand Gifts: A Dare to Live Fully Right Where You Are,* Grand Rapids, MI, Zondervan.

Wang, X. Y. 2012. *Risk, Incentives, and Contracting Relationships.* Available from: http://economics.mit.edu/files/8368 [Accessed 16 January 2014].

Watson, J. B. 1913. Psychology as the behaviorist views it. *Psychological Review,* 20, 158–177.

Watson, J. B. 1930. *Behaviorism,* New York, W.W. Norton and Company, Inc.

Weisburd, D., Mastrofski, S. D., McNally, A. M. & Greenspan, R. 2002. Reforming to preserve: Compstat and strategic problem solving in American policing. *Criminology and Public Policy,* 2, 421–456.

Western, S. 2007. *Leadership: A Critical Text,* Los Angeles; London, SAGE.

Wiener, N. 1948. *Cybernetics, or Control and Communication in the Animal and the Machine,* New York, Chapman & Hall.

Wilkinson, R. G. & Marmot, M. 2006. *Social Determinants of Health,* Oxford, Oxford University Press.

Wilson, T. 1560. *Wilson's Arte of Rhetorique.* Ed. G. H. Mair. Oxford: Clarendon Press, 1909.

Wittgenstein, L. & Russell, B. 1922. *Tractatus Logico-Philosophicus [with translation],* [S.l.], K. Paul.

Wright, C. 2013. Morphogenesis, continuity and change in the international political system. *In:* Archer, M. S. (ed.) *Social Morphogenesis.* New York, Springer Dordrecht Heidelberg.

Yin, R. K. 2009. *Case Study Research: Design and Methods,* London, Sage.

Yukl, G. 2012. Effective leadership behaviors: What we know and what questions need more attention? *The Academy of Management Perspectives*, 26(4), 66–85

Yukl, G. A. 2009. *Leadership in Organizations,* Upper Saddle River, NJ; London, Pearson.

Zimbardo, P. G. 2007. *The Lucifer Effect: Understanding How Good People Turn Evil*, New York, Random House.

Zipcar. 2013. *Majority of UK Start-Ups Say Sharing Costs is Essential for Survival.* London: Zipcar UK.

Index

Please note: Locators in **bold type** indicate figures or illustrations, those in *italics* indicate tables.

12 degrees of freedom *see* twelve degrees of freedom

Abu Ghraib Prison   19
abuses of power   23, 116
accountability
  as mechanism for enforcing control   149
  NYPD CompStat example   149–52
  personal vs institutional   152
  shared   149–52
action focus
  and adaptive characteristics   160
  and adaptivity as leadership challenge   103
  the concept of   159
  creating space for adaptive approaches   169–72
  devolved tasking, coordination and cooperation   160–2
  integrated problem solving   162–5
  shared resources   119, 165–7
  using collective intelligence in delivering action plans   167–9
action learning
  applied leadership and the principles of   211
  learning equation   211
  popularity of as pedagogical method   211
Acton, J. E.   15
adaptive approaches
  action focus and adaptive characteristics   160
  adaptive work vs technical   171
  behavioural dimensions   172
  the challenge for adaptive leadership   185
  climate change as challenge for adaptive leadership   185
  creating space for   169–72
  Heifetz's approach to adaptive leadership   169
  principles for leading adaptive work   171
  Selznick's argument on adaptive institutions   28

administration
  definition   208
  etymological perspective   208
  problems with the term   207
Afghanistan   194
Agincourt   5
Alban-Metcalfe, J.   18
Alimo-Metcalfe, B.   18
altruism
  definition   xiv
  searching for genes that predispose towards   10
  and sharing resources   120
Amazon, number of leadership titles   7
ancient leadership, examples of   5
applied leadership
  an applied leadership challenge   **212**
  as means of aligning evidence-based activities   211
  and the principles of action learning   211
Archer, M. S.   40–1
areas of concern, Covey's description   55, 69
Aristotle   5–6, 21, 37, 61, 64, 92, 95, 195
Arte of Rhetorique (Wilson)   7–8
artificial intelligence, definition   168
augmented trials   42
authenticity of a leader, determining the   15
authoritarian style of leadership   12–13
authority, position and   16
axial rotation   88

Bäckstrand, K.   186
Bacon, N.   146
balanced performance, behavioural dimensions   128
balanced scorecard
  Kaplan and Norton's formulation   128
  Tesco's approach   128
'balcony' and 'dance floor ,' Heifetz's analogy   30, 171
Baldwin, J.   96
banking crisis *see* global financial crisis
Barber, M.   151–2, 161
Barnard, L.   29

Bass, B. M.   9, 13, 18
Beer, S.   76, 84, 93, 96–7, 180
behavioural dimensions
  adaptive approaches   172
  balanced performance   128
  capability and impact   197
  capacity building   195
  constructive dissent and challenge   194
  distributed leadership   139
  goal setting   143
  governance   182
  innovation   184
  integrated problem solving   165
  multi-level leadership   137
  mutual benefit   154
  performance assessment   132
  personal reflection   198
  public interest outcomes   127
  reflection   178
  shared accountability   153
  sharing information   156
  sharing resources   167
  skills and behaviours alignment   191
  stakeholder perceptions of legitimacy   186
  tasking and coordination   162
  trust networks   149
  using collective intelligence   169
behaviourism, definition   190
behaviours
  Collins and Porras's argument   30
  as determinants of collective leadership   222–4
  and the leadership values tree   106
  and the understanding of social processes   30
  values and   105
Bevir, M.   64
BHAG (big hairy audacious goals)   115
biotechnology sector, importance of coordination   162
Blake, R. R.   14
board meetings, traditional focus   179
Bolden, I.   181, 195, 198
books on leadership, numbers of   7
Bratton, Bill   150, 151
Broken Windows (Kelling/Wilson)   169

broken windows approach to policing 150, 169
bullying 136, 143
Burns, J. M. 13, 17
Bushev, M. 82–4
business management, traditional method 118
business patterns, value of observation 177
Businessballs (blog) 85

Cadbury Committee 179
Cameron, David 245
Cameron, K. S. 153
Campbell, D. T. 43, 152
capability and impact, behavioural dimensions 197
capacity
   building capability and 239–40
   capability vs 195
   defining 194
   etymological perspective 194
   institutional application 194
capacity building
   behavioural dimensions 195
   trust as enabler for 194–5
Carlyle, T. 8
catastrophe theory 83, 85
centralized databases, fallibility 175
challenges of leadership
   action focus and adaptivity 103
   exploration of 102–4
   facing the real world 102
   multi-level leadership 103
   outcome-focusing 102
   partnership working 103
   skills and behaviours alignment 104
   systems and structure development 103
circles of influence
   vs areas of concern 55
   the concept of 56
civil war, Hobbes' view 6
climate change
   adaptive approach 185
   as 'wicked problem' 185
CMO configurations xxi, 44–5
   and interventions 45
   Pawson and Tilley's description 44
   reliance of the realistic evaluation framework on xxi
   suggestion of multi-level nature xxi
coactive approach 56, 69, 104, 169, 172, 176
collaborative advantage 25, 70, 98, 102, 117, 125, 146, 150

building through partnership working 146
collaborative working, positioning as optional extra 98
collective
   definition 109
   vs distributed 110
collective intelligence
   behavioural dimensions 169
   definition 168, 177
   enabling conditions 168
   health care context 168
   and pattern observation 177
   using 167
   using in delivering action plans 167–9
collective leadership
   active participation as a behaviour of 234–6
   and the alignment between 'distant' and 'nearby' leadership 18
   benefits 17
   contextual dynamics 67
   creating space for as a holding environment 65
   developing the framework (*see also* collective leadership framework) 46–9
   exploring through research 217
   importance of information sharing 155
   importance of the intelligent leadership process 161
   major characteristic of ineffective 160
   measuring behaviours as determinants of 222–4
   mechanisms of *see* mechanisms of collective leadership
   and personal compasses 41
   public interest aim 72
   and the role of realist inquiry 42
   scope 16
   stakeholder legitimacy and innovation as part of an adaptive approach to 185
   underlying theory **110**
collective leadership framework
   with desired outcomes **76**
   etymological perspective 53
   importance of considering systems and structures as part of 176
   importance of the individual 190
   internal and external contexts **69**

mechanisms (*see also* mechanisms of collective leadership) 69–72
mnemonics 217
outcomes (*see also* outcomes of effective public leadership) 72–5
from values to vision **70**
collective leadership inventory (CLI)
   basis and development 216–17
   development of 216
   four statement scale 114
   health inequalities case study 224–8
   Metropolitan local authority analysis **218**, 219
   purpose 216
   research cohorts 217
   results analysis 219–24
   statistical associations 223
   statistical correlations summary 224
   as visible manifestation of realist evaluation framework 52
collective leadership model, COMPASS360° framework and icosahedron (*see also* COMPASS360°) **97**
collective leadership practice, LINKS360® context (*see also* LINKS360®) 215–16
collective leadership values
   correlation table **220**
   interactive nature 152
   measuring 217–19
   statistical analysis process 222
   and transformational leadership behaviours 232
   tree 104–6
collective values
   adaptation 28
   framework 34–5
   public value (*see also* public value) 33
   public value framework **33**
   pursuing 31–6
   social value (*see also* social value) 31–2
collective vision
   defining the 109–12
   engaging partners 116–18
   engaging with the public 112–14
   equality of resources 119–20
   initial structure 222
   priority alignment 114–16
   setting of clear goals and 235
   and trust 237
   from vision to delivery 120–1

collectivism
  Bevir *et al.*'s description 64
  collectivity vs 64
Collins, J. C. xviii, 27–30, 36, 102,
    114, 191
Commission on Social Determinants
    of Health (CSDH) 177–8
community based policing, research
    project 47
community health, company
    competitiveness and 126
community safety, national review
    47
community safety partnership,
    transformational leadership
    behaviours **231**, *233*
COMPASS 360°
  framework and icosahedron **97**
  geometric representation of values
    96–7
competing values framework 153
competitive advantage, successful
    strategies for achieving 118
complexity, characteristics 81
complexity of leadership,
    understanding the 111
compliance experiments 102, 192
CompStat, NYPD's accountability
    process 149–52
confidence, place in the trust cycle
    148
Conger, J. A. 17
consensus 149, 185
constructive dissent xviii, 64
constructive dissent and challenge
    191–3
  behavioural dimensions 194
  consent and dissent/constructive
    and destructive **193**
context
  etymological perspective xxi, 54
  importance of in leadership
    theory 13
  understanding 54
context, mechanisms and outcomes
    configurations *see* CMO
    configurations
context of leadership
  conceptual analysis 5, 53, 65
  context specificity 4
  contexts, behaviours and values
    68
  differentiating between terms
    56–7
  external contexts of public
    leadership **55**
  food and drink analogies 4–5
  the language of leadership 53
  partnership 63–4
  people 62
  phronesis 64

place 65
power 62–3
primary approaches 13
from principles to public value
    54–6
problem profiles 62
processes 59
purpose 58–9
understanding context 54
values to vision *60*
values to vision, and core purpose
    58
values to vision, questions **60**
contingency theory
  dimensions 14
  focus 13–14
  introduction of 14
  vs situational leadership theory
    13–15
continuous professional
    development
  reflexivity and feedback **209**
  role of in professionalization and
    practice of leadership 209
control
  accountability as mechanism for
    enforcing 149
  role of in synergetics 82
control systems, requirements for
    assessing the effectiveness of
    in an industrial setting
    131
Cook, T, D. xx
cooperation
  coordination and 160–2
  devolved tasking and 160–2
  as hard lesson for Americans 29
  shift from command and control
    to joint effort and 5
coopetition, definition 116
coordination, definition 161
core ideology, definition 27
core purpose
  Tesco plc experience 113
  three levels 58
  values to vision and **58**
core values, definition 27
corporate governance, codes
    published in relation to 179
corporate scandals, Enron 129
corporate social responsibility,
    Tesco plc 115, 125, 128,
    177
corporatism 63
corruption, power and 16
Cotterell, A. 5
country club style of leadership 13
courage, ancient leadership and 5
Covey, S. R. 55–6, 69
creative leadership, Selznick on 26
creativity, and problem solving 29

Crime and Disorder Act (1997) 47
Crime and Disorder Act (1998)
    155–6
*Crime Numbers Game
    Management by Manipulation*
    (Eterno/Silverman) 152
crisis in leadership *see* leadership
    crisis
critical realism
  definition 40
  gist of the argument 40
  ontological perspective 44
  rejection of the experimental
    approach to research 40
  role of in describing social
    complexity 42
crowdsourcing 32, 167
Crumley, C. L. xxiii
Cs, three *see* three Cs of the public
cultural identity, social value and
    34
Cunliffe, A. L. 195
cybercrime, and information
    sharing 156
cybernetics
  etymological perspective 82
  OED definition 83
  proponents of 84
  relationship between synergetics
    and 84–97
  relevance to the development of
    collective leadership 96–8
Cyborg (Caidin) 83

Damascus moments xiv, 76
dark side of leadership xviii, 7, 16,
    18, 26, 104, 142
data manipulation, by boards
    179
Dawkins, R. xiv
decentralization, advantages and
    disadvantages 160–1
decision-making
  distinction between problem
    solving and 164
  integrated problem solving
    and decision-making model
    165
Dees, J. G. 34
definitions
  administration 208
  altruism xiv
  artificial intelligence 168
  behaviourism 190
  capacity 194
  collective 109
  collective intelligence 168, 177
  collective vision 109–12
  coopetition 116
  coordination 161
  core ideology 27

definitions – *Continued*
  core values   27
  critical realism   40
  cybernetics   83
  definitional aspects of
    leadership   7
  distributed leadership   16
  epistemology   39
  equality of resources   226
  existentialism   190
  frameworks   51
  heterarchy   xxiii
  innovation   182
  knowledge   40
  legitimacy   186
  models   51
  ontology   39
  outcome   72
  patterns   73
  pedagogy   xxiii
  power   62
  practice   71, 181, 206–7
  precessional effect   180
  problemitization   72
  product   74
  professional   204, 206
  programmes   73
  real world   101
  realism   42
  reflexivity   41
  shared leadership   16
  sharing economy   166
  social dilemmas   147
  stakeholder legitimacy   185
  stakeholders   185
  strategy   72
  synergetics   81, 84, 86
  tactics   72
  trustworthiness   148
  wicked problems   162
  see also etymological perspectives
delegation, vs devolution   160
delegative style of leadership   12
delivery, from vision to   120–1
Dess, G. G.   32
destructive consent, Grint's
    argument   192
devolved tasking, coordination and
    cooperation   160–2
Dickens, C.   116
distributed leadership
  axial rotation as representation
    of   89
  behavioural dimensions   139
  definition   16
  normal location   138
  vs shared leadership   16, 111, 136
  Tesco example   139
double-loop learning   85
Dow Chemicals   126

Economic and Social Research
    Council (ESRC)   48, 215
economic crisis *see* global financial
    crisis
Edmondson, A. C.   85, 87
education, and the professionalization
    of practice   203, 210
effectiveness of organizations *see*
    organizational effectiveness
efficiency
  the interpersonal leader's
    contribution   24
  management of   30
  Selznick on the preoccupation
    with administrative efficiency
    25, 30
Einstein, A.   104
elite autonomy, and value
    maintenance   28
Emerson, J.   34
empowerment model of leadership,
    Terry Leahy's preference
    138
engaging with the public *see* public
    engagement
the enlightenment, values brought
    by   23
Enron   xviii, 16, 22, 102
  and the dark side of goal setting
    142
  involvement in political
    funding   129
epistemology, definition   39
equality of resources   119–20
  definition   226
espoused theories   47
Eterno, J.   152
ethical engagement, focusing on
    118
ethics, Aristotle's view   6, 21
etymological perspectives
  administration   208
  capacity   194
  collective public leadership
    framework   53
  context   xxi, 54
  cybernetics   82
  leadership   7
  phronesis   64
  place   64
  policy   71
  quality   75
  synergetics   81
  see also definitions
evidence-based activity
  applied leadership as means of
    aligning   211
  tetrahedron of   **210**
evidence-based decision-making
  levels of adherence   130

  public interest outcomes and
    129–30
  Tesco accounting error example
    129–30
evidence-based leadership, and
  clinical approach to problem
    drug use   137
evidence-based practice, and the
  role of methodology   39
existentialism, definition   190
expansion/contraction   90

facing the real world, as leadership
    challenge   102
fairness   147, 186
feedback, CPD, reflexivity and
    feedback   **209**
Fernie, J.   116, 119
Fielder, F.   14
Finley, M.   5, 170
First Nations, importance of
    partnership to   145
Fixing Broken Windows (Kelling/
    Coles)   169
food and drink analogies of
    leadership   4–5
For Want of a Nail (nursery rhyme)
    98
founding fathers of the USA
  leadership principles   23
  reasons for success   23–4
  and the 'Silverback' analogy
    170
framework for collective leadership
    see collective leadership
frameworks
  definition   51
  vs models   51–3
franchises, comparison of evolution
    of public services with
    160–1
Francis, R.   129, 142–3
Franklin, Benjamin   23
freedom, twelve degrees of *see*
    twelve degrees of freedom
French, J. R. P.   63
Fuller, R. Buckminster 'Bucky'
    (*see also* twelve degrees of
    freedom)   43, 52, 76, 81–2,
    85, 87, 89–91, 97, 104, 111

generalized principles, Fuller's
    hierarchy   85, 87, 178
geometry
  Fuller's design for the geodesic
    dome   53
  geometric foundation for the
    concept of synergy   76, 93–6
global financial crisis
  driving values   22–3

and evidence-based decision-making 129
and leadership 'on trial' xviii, 104
Morris's reflection 197
as outcome of single-minded thinking 85
and short-term thinking 140
global governance, partnership networks as new form of 186
Global World Leaders (GWLs) 4–5, 18
goal-directed action
biological origins 140
Talcott Parsons' reference 59
goals
distinction between objectives and 59
'hard' vs 'soft' 140
setting clear *see* setting of clear goals
good governance, published codes 179
governance
behavioural dimensions 182
and Grint's constitutive approach 180
the role of 179
standards for public services 179
tetrahedron of 181
twelve degrees of freedom as useful portfolio for 180
Great Men theory of leadership 8
Grint, K. xv, xviii, 8–9, 62, 180, 192–3, 195, 212

Handy, C. B. 63
health
challenges of keeping pace with advances in professional knowledge 74
drivers of inequality 124
early emphasis on the development of professional practice in 203
reducing inequalities as public interest outcome 124–5
health inequalities case study
collective leadership inventory 224–8
collective leadership perceptions in tackling inequalities **226**
pattern recognition 177–8
respondents at the second level 226
respondents at the third level 227
Heclo, H. 25

Heifetz, R. A. xix, 28, 30, 65, 160, 169–71
Henry V 5
heterarchy, definition xxiii
hierarchy
Crumley's argument xxiii
influence on theory building xxii
hierarchy of generalized principles, Fuller's 85, 87, 178
Higden, R. 54
history of leadership 5–6
Hobbes, T. 6, 22
Hofstede, G. xxi, 63
holding environment, Heifetz's conception 65
honest serving men (fellows) xxii, 7–8, 41, 45, 241
Honey, P. 190
Hopper, K. & W. J. xviii, 24, 207
horse-meat scandal 117
human behaviour, roles of agency and structure 62
human resources, benefits of shared systems 166
Hyde, D. 175
hypercube, representing internal and external contexts **95**

icosahedron
Beer's preference 96
representation of the twelve degrees of freedom 96
individual leaders
Carlyle's studies 8
Grint's argument 8
mitigating the flaws of 17
individual leadership, traditional focus 136
inequalities in health, drivers of 124
informal insurance, mutual benefit as 153
information sharing
barriers to 155
behavioural dimensions 156
and the Crime and Disorder Act (1998) 155–6
cybercrime and 156
importance to collective leadership 155
and the interpretation of data protection 155
London Olympics 2012 example 156
partnership working and 155–6
'silo' thinking and 155
Wal-Mart and Procter & Gamble example 177

innovation
behavioural dimensions 184
climate change adaptation example 185
conditions for fostering 183–4
connection between problem solving, decision-making, risk and 164
in the context of public leadership 183
crisis and 105
criticality of knowledge-acquisition 183–4
definition 182
electric light bulb example 182
encouraging 182–4
and growth in science xix
link between stakeholder legitimacy and 185
need to allow for flourishing of 24
relationship with risk 182–4
representation on the collective leadership values tree 104
role of in governance 180
and the 'Silverback' analogy 170
spaces where creativity and innovation can flourish 118
inside-outing 90, 99, 127, 179–80
institutional accountability, vs personal 152
institutional leadership 24–6, 30–1, 150
and the 'dark side of leadership' 26
institutionalization, and personal interaction 29–30
The Instruction of Ptahhotep (2300 BC) 8
integrated problem solving
action focus 162–5
behavioural dimensions 165
integrated problem solving and decision-making model **165**
intelligent leadership
alignment of practice and pedagogy and xxiii
development opportunity 244
importance of the process to collective leadership 161
as key to shared and distributed leadership 16
and the need for openness and transparency 237
place of problem solving in the concept of xvii
practical wisdom (phronesis) and 5–6, 64
and 'wicked' problem solving 162–3

Kaplan, R. S.   128
Kellerman, B.   9
Kelling, G. L.   150–1
Kipling, R.   xxii, 8, 41
    see also honest serving men
       (fellows)
knowledge
    academic articles focused on
       183
    criticality of knowledge-acquisition
       to innovation   183–4
    definition   40
    example of knowledge patterns
       177
    interest in the topic of
       knowledge-based approaches
       and leadership   183–4
    qualitative   43
Kolb, D. A.   198
Kotter, J. P.   18
Kramer, M. R.   32, 126
Kuglin, F. A.   149
Kuhn, T.   xix–xx, 92

Labour government, law and order
    mantra   151
Lakatos, I.   xx
language of leadership   53, 207
Lank, E.   98
Latham, G. P.   141
leadership
    the aim of for Heifetz   28
    conceptual context (see also
       context of leadership)   53–65
    etymological perspective   7
    history of   5–6
    key dimensions   139
    key skills and challenges   3
    see also applied leadership;
       collective leadership;
       distributed leadership;
       intelligent leadership; multi-
       level leadership; shared
       leadership; transformational
       leadership
leadership behaviours, types of
    (see also behavioural
       dimensions)   14
leadership crisis
    and the degeneration of values
       105
    focus on shared value as a
       solution to   32
    Porter and Kramer's solution
       32
Leadership in Administration
    (Selznick)   24
leadership literature
    Amazon search results   7
    historical perspective   xx
leadership skills, examples of   17

leadership styles
    measuring   14
    selection process   4
    typology   12–13
leadership theories
    the born leader   8
    contingency vs situational
       theories   13–15
    cumulative nature   7
    evolution   7
    the how question   16–17
    the what question   10–13
    the when question   13–15
    the where question   15–16
    the who question   8–10
    the why question   17–18
leadership theory, trait approach
    8–10
leadership values, measuring   105
Leading without Easy Answers
    (Heifetz)   169
Leahy, T.   113–14
    see also Tesco plc
learning, double-loop vs single-loop
    85
Least Preferred Coworker (LPC)
    style of leadership   14
legitimacy
    association of trust and
       confidence with   147
    commercial definition   186
    as instrumental form of trust   148
    value of to stakeholders   186
Lewin, K.   xxiii
LINKS360®
    collective leadership inventory
       (see also collective leadership
       inventory)   216
    community safety partnership
       and local authority descriptive
       statistics   221
    context of collective leadership
       practice   215–16
    correlation table for collective
       leadership values   220
    exploring collective leadership
       through research   217
    the importance of
       transformational leadership
       (see also transformational
       leadership)   216
    measuring behaviours as
       determinants of collective
       leadership   222–4
    measuring the values of collective
       leadership   217–19
    transformational leadership
       behaviours (see also
       transformational leadership
       behaviours)   228–41
    validity of the research   219–21

Linsky, M.   171
Little Britain (BBC)   175
Locke, E. A.   140–1
Logan, D. C.   87
London Olympics 2012
    'bidding manual' creation   156
    as example of multi dimensional
       leadership   131–2
    information sharing example
       156
    long-term focus   140
L'Oreal   136
lucidly relevant set, Fuller's
    description   92

'Macdonaldization'   203
Machiavelli, N.   9, 64, 147
maintaining momentum
    goal setting and   232
    and individual leadership
       behaviours   239
    key behaviours   234
    performance monitoring as a
       means of   232
    public value outcomes and   240
management
    distinction between leadership
       and   3
    by objectives   141
Marmot, M.   124–5, 178
Matofska, B.   166
Mayors, devolution and   160
measuring leadership   105
mechanisms of collective leadership
    the four Ps   **73**
    pedagogy   72
    policy   71
    from policy to practice   69–72
    practice   71–2
    problemitization   72
    understanding mechanisms
       69–71
medieval rhetoric, 'seven
    circumstances'   7n8
Metatron's cube   93–4
    and collective leadership   **95**
methodology, the role of   39
Methodology of Scientific Research
    Proposals (MSRP)   xx
Microsoft   146
Mid Staffordshire Foundation
    Trust   16, 129
Mid Staffordshire General Hospital
    NHS Trust   142
middle of the road style of
    leadership   13
Milgram experiment   192
Mintzberg, H.   63
mission setting process, Selznick's
    advice   27
mission statement, components   59

models
  definition   51
  vs frameworks   51–3
Moore, M. H.   34, 75
moral responsibility, of corporations
    28
Morecambe, Eric   241
morphogenesis   41, 82
  see also social morphogenesis
Morris, W.   177, 197
motivation, questions about leaders'
    42
Mouton, J. S. J. A.   14
multiagency community safety
    partnership, comparison with
    transformational leadership
    behaviours   230–2
multi-level leadership
  behavioural responses   137
  benefits   103
  distributed leadership (*see also*
    distributed leadership)
    138–9
  as leadership challenge   103
  long-term focus   140
  and openness and
    transparency   238
  Selznick's term   28
  setting of clear goals   140–3
  shared leadership (*see also* shared
    leadership)   136–7
  troubled/dysfunctional families
    example   138–9
Muth, J. J.   154
mutual benefit
  behavioural dimensions   154
  London Olympics 2012 example
    156
  the meaning of   153
  partnership working and   153–4
  Stone Soup Story example   154

National Health Service
  business model suggestion   137
  and the dark side of goal setting
    142–3
national intelligence model (NIM)
    161
negotiated order
  dynamic process   **107**
  theoretical perspective   106–7
network advantage, achieving
    146
New Economy, Greater
    Manchester   118
New Public Management (NPM)
    xviii, 22, 25, 141, 150
New York City Police Department,
    accountability process
    149–52
Newcomer, M.   203

Newton, K.   147
Ning, S.   166
Nokia   146
North West of England project
  evidence of barriers to shared
    leadership   137
  evidence-based decision-making
    130
  performance measurement   127
  research focus   48
  troubled/dysfunctional families
    research   138–9
  use of shared information and
    collective intelligence as key
    challenge for partnerships   168
Northouse, P. G.   14
Norton, D. P.   128
not-for-profit sector
  benefits of pattern recognition
    177
  and evidence-based decision-
    making   129
  and leadership styles   111
  non-profit organizations and
    social value   34
  and the notion of public value
    124
  and partnership working
    117–18
  and shared leadership   137

objectives, distinction between
    goals and   59
Old World Leaders (OWLs)   5, 8, 18
Olympic Games, London 2012 *see*
    London Olympics 2012
ontology, definition   39
openness and transparency
  multi-level leadership and   *238*
  outcome and action focus
    associated with   *238*
  professionalization and   213
  public value outcomes and   *239*
  as transformational leadership
    behaviour   228
orbital rotation   89–90
organizational climate, as driver of
    performance   189
organizational effectiveness
  characteristics   153
  Quinn, Rohrbaugh and
    Cameron's observation   153
organizational legitimacy, as
    important component of
    trust   185
outcome, definition   72
outcome focus, as leadership
    challenge   102
outcome patterns, Pawson on   44
outcomes, in the public interest *see*
    public interest outcomes

outcomes of effective public
    leadership   72–5
  patterns   73–4
  personal impact   74
  product   74–5
  programmes   73
  public value   75

Panorama (BBC)   136
Parsons, T.   59
participative style of leadership   12
partners
  engaging in collective vision
    116–18
  suppliers as   116
partnership
  the concept of   63
  in the context of leadership
    63–4
  importance to First Nations   145
partnership networks, as new form
    of global governance   186
partnership working
  bridging gaps through   146
  building collaborative advantage
    through   146
  the concept of   145–6
  historical perspective   145
  importance of trust   63, 147
  as leadership challenge   103
  mutual benefit and   153–4
  Nokia and Microsoft example
    146
  principles   146
  shared accountability   149–52
  shared information (*see also*
    information sharing)   155–6
  and shared values   118
  trust networks   147–9
patterns
  definition   73
  different forms of   177
  health inequalities example of
    pattern recognition   177–8
  and the lucidly relevant set   92
  pattern recognition as innovative
    approach to identifying risk
    177
  relevance of to leadership   73–4
  value of pattern recognition
    176–7
Pawson, R.   xx, 42–6, 81, 87
Pearce, C. L.   17
Pease, Ken   xiv
pedagogy
  defining   xxiii
  intelligent alignment of practice
    and   xxiii
  as mechanism of collective
    leadership   72
  practice and   72, 197, 210

people, in the context of leadership 62

performance
individual domain vs collective 74
joint monitoring and review 130–2
organizational climate as driver of in public services 189
tailoring monitoring and review 130

performance monitoring and assessment 232, 234
behavioural dimensions 132

personal accountability, vs institutional 152

personal impact, as outcome of effective public leadership 74

personal reflection, behavioural dimensions 198

pessimism, the value of 191

Pfitzer, M. 126

Pharaohs, qualities attributed to 8

Phillips, D. T. 186

phronesis (practical wisdom)
Aristotle's use 5, 95
the concept of 5
etymological perspective 64
geometric perspective 95
Grint's argument 195
place in the collective leadership framework 64
usefulness for action focus and adaptivity 103

place
in the context of leadership 65
etymological perspective 64

Plato 21

policing
broken windows approach 150, 169
professional practice development emphasis 203

policy
etymological perspective 71
as mechanism of collective leadership 71
vs strategy 71

political perspectives
Enron's involvement in political funding 129
law and order mantra of the Labour government 151
political element of public value 35
short-term focus of politicians 139

Porras, J. I. 27–30

Porter, M. E. 32, 126

positional leadership, association with power, legitimacy and authenticity 15

Potter, N. N. 21

Povey, Keith 47

power
abuses of 23, 116
in the context of leadership 62–3
Formal vs Informal 63
French and Raven's classifications 63
Handy's descriptive preferences 63
Hofstede's multidimensional notion 63
literal definition 62
Lord Acton on the dangers of 15
Mintzberg's bases 63
the misuse of 15
partnership and the 'battle for' 63
the traditional notion 63

practice
definition 71, 181
as mechanism of collective leadership 71–2

practice of leadership, the concept of 203

precession 90–1

precessional effect (PE)
challenge for governance 180
the concept of 42–3, 56
Fuller's definition 180
meaning of 91
potential of realism to find and explain 45
in the social world 45
twelve degrees of freedom and the 180
as unintended side-effects of man's fight for survival 91

primates 18, 170

The Prince (Machiavelli) 9, 147

principles, and the link between values and virtues 54

priority alignment
and the collective vision 114–16
shared values and 234
Tesco's strategy 114–16

proactive approach, Covey's description 55

problem drug use, evidence-based leadership and the clinical approach to 137

problem profiles 62, 94

problem solving
distinction between decision-making and 164

integrated (*see also* integrated problem solving) 162–5
Kelling's view 150–1
Selznick's preference 28–9

problemitization
definition 72
as mechanism of collective leadership 72

problems, 'wicked' vs 'tame' (*see also* wicked problems) 72

processes, in the context of leadership 59

Procter & Gamble 177

procurement
and shared leadership models 137
and social value legislation 32

product, definition 74

professional knowledge, challenges of keeping pace with advances in 74

professionalization, professionalizing to **207**

professionalization and practice of leadership
CPD, reflexivity and feedback **209**
defining practice 207
defining 'professional' 204, 206
growing interest 203–4
role of continuous professional development 209
tetrahedron of evidence-based activity **210**
transactional vs transformational 207–10

professionalization of practice, education and the 203, 210

programmes, definition 73

public engagement
in a collective vision 112–14
policy level vs field study level 112
and the three Cs (*see also* three Cs of the public) 112

public health
impact of the industrial revolution 85
as responsibility of society as a whole 124

public interest
importance of focusing on short-term/long-term balance 140
and investigations into Tesco's behaviour 137
personal impact and 74
the three Cs become critical 115

public interest outcomes 106–7,
124–7, 244
balanced scorecard approach
128
behavioural dimensions 127
Dow Chemical example 126
and evidence-based decision-
making 129–30
London Olympics example
131–2
the meaning of being outcome-
focused 123
National Health Service example
124
performance assessment 130–2
reducing inequalities in health
124–5
refocusing performance
assessment 127–8
requirements 124
social care example 127
Tesco plc examples 125, 132
traditional focus on ease of
measurement 127
public leadership, external contexts
55
public service organizations,
'silo-based' performance
targets 137
public services
cross sector partnerships 117
devolution 160
governance code 179
organizational climate as driver of
performance 189
short-term focus 139
trust and public relations 147
Public Services (Social Value) Act
(2012) 32
public value
economic element 34
elements 33, 34, **35**
framework **33**
government's role 137
issues addressed by 34
key elements 33
as outcome of effective public
leadership 75
political element 35
principles and 54–6
rediscovering lost values 35–6
social element 34
public value outcomes
and maintaining momentum
240
and openness and transparency
239
public/private partnerships 63
purpose, in the context of
leadership 58–9
puzzles, as 'tame' problems 62

quality, etymological perspective
75
Quella, J. T. 177
Quinn, R. E. 153

Ramesses II 5
random disturbances 83
randomized control trials 42
reactive approach, vs a proactive
approach 56
real world
definition 101
as leadership challenge 102
realism
definition 42
starting premise 44
understanding the different
approaches to 42
realist inquiry, appropriateness to
leadership research 46
realistic evaluation (RE)
aim and benefits of the approach
xx–xxi
CLI as visible manifestation of
framework 52
the concept of 46
consideration of in terms of a 3-D
model 96
description of mechanisms
70–1
hallmarks 43
relevance to this research 52
synergetics and 87, 96
reflection
behavioural dimensions 178
and organizational and network
improvement 197
the value of 176–8
reflexive thinking, and the
consideration of the 'whom' of
leadership 45
reflexivity
Archer's definition 41
CPD, reflexivity and feedback
209
definition 40
relational leadership 17, 119
relinquishing control and
empowering 228, 232
research
exploring collective leadership
through 217
framework background and
development 46–9
validity of this research
219–21
resources
equality of 119–20
sharing *see* sharing resources
retailers
abuse of power by 116

increasing dependence of
suppliers on 116
see also supplier-retailer
relationships
Revans, R. W. 211
risk
relationship with
innovation 182–4
value of pattern recognition in
identifying 176–7
Rohrbaugh, J. 153
Rossi, S. 110
Rumsfeld, Donald 86

sacred geometry 93
SARA (scanning, analysis, response,
assessment) 164
scale, Tesco's use of as a social value
126
Schumpeter, J. 31
scientific evaluation, Pawson's
proposal of a realist manifesto
for 43–4
scientific management 11, 24–5,
30
The Selfish Gene (Dawkins) xiv
selfless leadership, key challenge xvi
selflessness
altruism and xiv
and crises of leadership xv
enabling xv
Seligman, A. 148
Selznick, P. 24–31, 36, 57, 150
setting of clear goals
behavioural dimensions 143
the dark side 142–3
and development of a collective
vision *235*
Enron example 142
NHS example 142–3
role of 140–3
shared 231
Tesco example 142
testing 230–1
and TLI behaviours 232–4
Shakespeare, William 216
shared accountability, behavioural
dimensions 153
shared leadership
definition 16
vs distributed leadership 16,
111, 136
and drugs policy 137
evidence of barriers to 137
Pearce and Conger's work in
relation to 17
Tesco example 136
shared value
exploring 22–3
focus on as a solution to the
leadership crisis 32

shared value – *Continued*
  implementation difficulties
    127, 146
  increasing importance   124
shared values
  and behaviour of organizations
    23
  behaviours as a high level
    outcome of   xix
  critical nature   xix
  and cross-sector
    partnerships   118
  and the market defining potential
    of societal needs   32
  priority alignment and   234
  role of listening and
    collaborating   105
  skills and behaviour alignment
    and   197
shareholders   xvii, 22, 55, 102,
    152, 179, 182, 185
sharing economy, definition   166
sharing information *see* information
  sharing
sharing resources
  behavioural dimensions   167
  risky nature   119–20
  as social capital   120
silo-based training, and application
    of learning   197
silverback gorilla analogy
  Finney's argument   5, 171
  Heifetz's argument   170
  technical vs adaptive abilities   170
Silverman, E.   152
single-loop learning   85
al-Siqilli, Muhammad ibn Zafar   9
situational leadership theory, vs
    contingency theory   13–15
six honest serving fellows, Kipling's
    xxii, 7–8, 41, 45, 241
Six Million Dollar Man (TV series)
    83
skills and behaviours
  alignment of   189–91
  capability and impact   195–7
  capacity and improvement
    194–5
  consent and dissent/constructive
    and destructive   **193**
  constructive dissent and
    challenge   191–3
  impact through capability,
    capacity and competence   **196**
  personal reflection   197–8
  Selznick's observations on the
    skills gap   30
skills and behaviours alignment
  behavioural dimensions   191
  as leadership challenge   104
'skin in the game'   119

SMART (Specific, Measurable,
    Achievable, Realistic and Time-
    based)   124
Smith, D.   117, 125, 142
Sober, E.   xiv
social capital   34, 119–20, 166
social dilemmas, defining   147
social entrepreneurship, role of   32
social media   32, 185
social morphogenesis, Wright's
    observations   83
social structures
  role of in negotiated order   106
  Selznick's argument   29–30
social value
  capturing the collective spirit of
    31
  the concept of   31
  examples of the creation of   34
  historical perspective   31
  J. Gregory Dees' view   34
  legislation   32
  mutual dependence of
    competitiveness and
    community health   126
  primary focus   34
  public and third sectors' role   32
  scale as a   126
  Selznick's 'moral responsibility' of
    corporations argument   28
Sparks, L.   117, 125
stakeholder legitimacy
  behavioural dimensions   186
  definition   185
  link between innovation and
    185
stakeholders
  definition   185
  'principle of fairness' approach
    186
Stanford prison experiment   102,
    192
statesmanship
  the concept of   24–5
  Selznick's argument   26, 31
Stockdale, Jim   191
Stogdill, R. M.   7
Stone Soup Story, as example of
    mutual benefit   154
strategic alliances
  aims and meaning of   147
  compared with partnerships
    146
  coopetition example   117
  definition   116
  difficulties for   156
  as important element of
    commercial enterprise   63
  tasking and coordination
    equivalent   161
  trust and   149

strategic leadership, Selznick's
    concept (*see also* institutional
    leadership)   150
strategic planning process, as example
    of collective action   118
strategy
  definition   72
  vs policy   71
  practice and   71
Strauss, A. L.   106–7
structural functionalism   63
structure, agency vs   62
sub-prime investments   129
Sun Tzu   145
supplier-retailer relationships
  market position and   116
  Tesco plc   116–17, 136, 139,
    150, 166
supply chain management,
    application of information
    sharing   155
synergetics
  and the benefits of distinguishing
    between the whole and its parts
    87
  the benefits of securing
    collaborative advantage   98
  Bushev's description   82
  and catastrophe theory   83
  definitions   81, 84, 86
  etymological perspective   81
  geometric foundation for the
    concept of synergy   76, 93–6
  relationship between cybernetics
    and   84–97
  relevance to the development of
    collective leadership   84–7
  triangular energy events   **88**
  see also twelve degrees of freedom
systemic behaviours, synergy and
    86
systems, in Selznick's work   29
systems and structures
  development of as leadership
    challenge   103
  distinctive characteristics   176
  encouraging innovation   182–4
  fallibility   175–6
  good governance   178–81
  pattern recognition   176–7
  stakeholder legitimacy   185–6
  tetrahedron of governance   181
  the value of reflection   176–8

tactics, definition   72
tame problems, vs wicked   72
tasking, the concept of   161
tasking and coordination
  the approach   138
  behavioural dimensions   162
  the concept of   161

for-profit sector equivalent 161
overall aim 161
and partnership networks 138
Taylor, F. W. 30
'telling it how it is' 228, 232
Tesco plc
  accounting error 115, 129
  bad press 115
  balanced scorecard approach 128
  business model 113
  buyers' role 139
  CEO's vision for recovery 126
  changes in corporate vision and
    purpose 113
  changes in priority 115
  collective leadership assessment
    114
  corporate social responsibility
    115, 125, 128, 177
  examples of public interest
    outcomes 125, 132
  goal setting and 142
  importance given to its customers
    113
  logistics approach 117
  performance management 132
  priority alignment 114–15
  retailer-supplier relations
    116–17, 136, 139, 150, 166
  revised purpose 119
  Terry Leahy's preference for a
    model of leadership 138
  transformation of the supply
    chain 117
  use of scale as a social value 126
tetrahedron
  of evidence-based
    leadership **210**
  Fuller's preference 52, 92
  of governance 181
  triangular energy events 88
  within Metatron's cube **94**
theories in use 47
third sector 63, 117, 125
three Cs of the public
  and capacity, capability and
    competence 196
  and competitive advantage 118
  and engagement with the public
    112
  illustration of 196
  importance for leading in the
    public interest 115
  importance of understanding the
    perception of 123
Tilley, N. xx–xxi, 3n4, 44, 46, 110
time
  as a currency of leadership 238
  as key dimension of leadership
    139
torque/twist 90

'tragedy of the commons' 166
trait approach to leadership theory
  8–10
transactional leadership 10
  Burns' work 13
  and self-interest 13
  vs transformational leadership
    17, 207–10
transformational leadership
  Burns' description 17
  importance of 216
  Shakespearean perspective 216
  sources of energy for 171–2
transformational leadership
  behaviours
  from actions to outcomes 237
  active participation as a collective
    leadership behaviour 234–6
  association between developing a
    collective vision and the setting
    of clear goals 235
  building capacity and capability
    239–40
  collective leadership values and
    behaviours and 232
  collective vision and trust 237
  community safety partnership
    231, 233
  comparison with multiagency
    community safety
    partnership 230–2
  identifying behaviours 228
  inventory development 217
  local authority **230**, 233
  mnemonic 228
  multi level leadership and openness
    and transparency 238
  outcome and action focus
    associated with openness and
    transparency 238
  private sector organization **230**
  public value outcomes and
    maintaining momentum 240
  public value outcomes and
    openness and transparency
    239
  time as a currency of
    leadership 238
  tipping point 240–1
  transform leadership inventory
    229
  trust **236**
triangular energy events **88**
trust
  alignment with accountability
    sharing 149
  association of transformative
    behaviour with 234
  collective vision and 237
  as enabler for building capacity
    194–5

  importance of in partnership
    working 63, 147
  importance of in relationship
    management 75, 117
  Kenneth Newton on the concept
    of 147
  organizational legitimacy as
    important component of
    185
  role in tackling problems focused
    on agreed outcomes 237
  'thin' vs 'thick' 147
  as transformational leadership
    behaviour **236**
  vs trustworthiness 147
trust cycle **148**
  dimensions 148
trust networks, behavioural
  dimensions 149
trustworthiness
  and confidence 22
  definition 148
Turing, A. M. 82
Turing machine, development 84
twelve degrees of freedom
  alignment to human behaviour
    and leadership 91–2
  basic rules 89–91
  icosahedron representation **96**
  and the precession effect 180
  as useful governance portfolio
    180

United States of America,
  underpinning principles 23
'unknown unknowns,' Rumsfeld's
  phrase 86–7

value maintenance, elite autonomy
  and 28
values
  and behaviours 105
  collective (*see also* collective
    values) 31–6
  the difference between value and
    virtue 21–2
  economic value 34
  elements of public value 33,
    34, **35**
  enlightenment period 23
  historical perspective 21, 23–6
  identifying the values that
    Selznick admired 26–31
  the meaning of 22
  political value 35
  rediscovering lost public values
    35–6
  Selznick's work on the
    importance of 24
  shared value 22–3
  social value 34

values to vision   *60*
  and core purpose   **58**
  with everything in-between
    70
  questions   **60**
virtue, value vs   22
virtues, Aristotle's   6
vision
  from values to *see* values to
    vision
  from vision to delivery
    120–1

Wal-Mart   177
weaving together   xxi, 64
Weir, Tommy   244n1

Weisburd, D.   150
whole systems approaches
  benefits of distinguishing between
    the whole and its parts   87
  relevance to the study and
    practice of leadership   84
  whole systems thinking   81
wicked problems
  characteristics   *163*
  defining   162
  and the integrated approach
    162
  and integrated problem solving
    approaches   165
  vs tame   72
Wiener, N.   82

WIFM (what's in it for me?)   xv, 17
Wilson, D. S.   xiv
Wilson, J. Q.   150
Wilson, T.   7n8
wisdom, forms of   5
Wittgenstein, L.   53
World Health Organization (WHO)
    177
world.com   xviii, 16
Wright, S.   83

Yukl, G. A.   xix, 141

zero tolerance policing   150–1
Zimbardo, P. G.   10, 19, 102, 176,
    192